The Turf Problem Solver

The Turf Problem Solver

The Turf Problem Solver

Case Studies and Solutions for Environmental, Cultural, and Pest Problems

A. J. Turgeon
J. M. Vargas, Jr.

WILEY

John Wiley & Sons, Inc.

Published by John Wiley & Sons, Inc., Hoboken, New Jersey
Published simultaneously in Canada

For general information on our other products and services or for technical support, please contact our Customer Care Department within the United States at (800) 762-2974, outside the United States at (317) 572-3993 or fax (317) 572-4002.

Wiley also publishes its books in a variety of electronic formats. Some content that appears in print may not be available in electronic books. For more information about Wiley products, please visit our Web site at: www.wiley.com.

Library of Congress Cataloging-in-Publication Data:

Turgeon, A. J. (Alfred J.), 1943–
    The turf problem solver: case studies and solutions for environmental, cultural, and pest problems / by A.J. Turgeon and J.M. Vargas, Jr.
        p. cm.
    Includes bibliographical references and index.
    ISBN-13: 978-0-471-73619-6 (cloth)
    ISBN-10: 0-471-73619-8 (cloth)
    1. Turfgrasses—Diseases and pests. 2. Turfgrasses—Ecology. 3. Turf management.
I. Vargas, J. M., Jr. II. Title.
    SB608.T87T88 2005
    635.9′6429—dc22

                                                                    2005008654

Printed in the United States of America

10 9 8 7 6 5 4 3 2 1

Acknowledgments

Reviewers:
Bevard, Darin
Gaussoin, Roch
McCarty, Bert
Meyer, William
Sartain, Jerry
Snow, James

Roch Gaussoin of the University of Nebraska, Bert McCarty of Clemson University, William Meyer of Rutgers University, and James Snow and Darin Bevard of the USGA Green Section.

Artist:
Gretchen Rebarchak

Editor:
Jean Turgeon

Contents

CHAPTER

1

Introduction

Turfgrass science is often studied using standard, discipline-oriented textbooks. Learning from these sources is mostly limited to factual, conceptual, and applied knowledge. *Factual* knowledge is basic information about a particular subject. *Conceptual* knowledge deals with an understanding of how specific facts fit together in meaningful ways to form concepts. *Application* knowledge deals with the performance of specific tasks. Turfgrass management requires the ability to draw from one's knowledge of turfgrass science in order to analyze and solve problems encountered in the field. The higher cognitive levels of analysis, synthesis, and evaluation are required for this purpose (Figure 1.1). *Analysis* is the process by which knowledge of a particular subject is used to explain a situation by responding to such questions as: what does this mean, and how does this work? An analysis is therefore an insightful amplification of a problematic situation that explains why the situation is problematic; while the description deals with *what,* the analysis deals with *why.* The next cognitive level, called *synthesis,* deals with how a particular problem might be resolved. It typically proposes a variety of alternatives for solving the problem but doesn't attempt to determine which is most

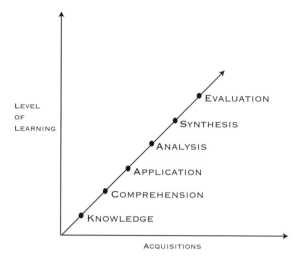

BLOOM'S TAXONOMY

Figure 1.1 The levels of learning: knowledge, comprehension, application, analysis, synthesis, and evaluation in Bloom's taxonomy (Bloom, 1956).

practical or best fits the situation. That is the issue addressed at the highest cognitive level, called *evaluation*.

To conduct the functions of analysis, synthesis, and evaluation in a problem-solving process, one can begin with a *scenario* in which a problematic situation is briefly described:

> The soil profile of a creeping bentgrass (*Agrostis stolonifera* L.) turf is texturally layered, with the top 2 in. (5 cm) composed of a silt loam soil and the underlying medium of a deep layer of coarse sand.

This description could be amplified considerably through an *analysis* in which some relevant knowledge of soil physics is employed. It might begin with the following explanation:

> Water moving through a relatively fine-textured medium—in this case, silt loam—percolates slowly, reflecting the hydraulic

2

conductivity of this medium. The specific percolation rate would be influenced by the soil's structure; it would be faster through a well-structured soil and slower through a compacted soil. When the wetting front reaches the underlying coarser-textured medium—in this case, coarse sand—further downward movement stops and a perched water table is formed. This is due to the adhesion of water to the collective surface area of all of the soil particles comprising the silt loam and the attraction between water molecules (cohesion) due to hydrogen bonding. As a consequence, water retention by this medium is so strong that, despite the pull of gravity, there is essentially no movement of water into the underlying sand. This turf would be poorly drained, as water infiltrating the silt loam soil layer cannot enter the underlying sand and therefore accumulates in and above the silt loam layer, forming a perched water table. The retained water eventually leaves primarily as water vapor produced by evaporation from the soil and transpiration through the turfgrass plants growing in the soil.

In addition to explaining the problem scenario, the analysis provides a foundation upon which to *synthesize* various options for resolving the drainage problem:

One option might be to remove the 2-in. (5-cm) layer of soil with the sod and replant. Another might be to hollow-tine cultivate the turf, removing the soil cores and backfilling the holes with sand matching the underlying sand layer to provide bypass drainage channels through the silt loam layer.

An *evaluation* of these and other options would then be conducted to determine which is best:

Perhaps the decision would be based on comparative costs. In this case, cultivation and topdressing would most likely be cheaper than removing the sod and reestablishing the turf. However, since the residual silt loam layer would probably continue to restrict internal drainage for many years or until successive cultivations and topdressings substantially reduced its presence, the alternative solution might be much more effective. If this evaluation were

3

conducted during the middle of the playing season, cultivation and topdressing might be selected as a temporary solution, while sod removal and reestablishment might be employed later as a more permanent solution.

Thus, evaluation is often context-specific, requiring judgment—and perhaps consultation with stakeholders and coordination of related activities—for satisfactory implementation.

This textbook has been designed to help the student not only learn some important aspects of turfgrass science, but also become proficient in turfgrass management. It is also designed to help current turfgrass managers improve their problem-solving skills. Case studies are employed for this purpose.

CASE STUDIES

Cases are narratives of problematic situations drawn from real-world experiences. Studying cases helps students move from the classroom to professional practice by merging, adapting, and applying knowledge to complex situations. Cases provide information essential to an analysis of a specific situation and for framing alternative action programs, recognizing the complexity and ambiguity of the practical world. Some cases are relatively simple, dealing only with technical problems, while others involve economic, social, and ethical issues.

There are two types of case studies: decision and historical. Decision cases are incomplete narratives of problematic situations that take the reader—in the role of decision maker—to the point at which a decision must be made. Historical cases are complete narratives that provide not only descriptions of the problematic situations, but also their analysis and attempted resolution by the actual decision maker, as well as the results obtained from the actions taken.

In this book, decision cases are presented as brief scenarios. Analyses and solutions are also provided, following the process described in the next section.

CYCLES OF INQUIRY

Descriptions of problematic situations come from a variety of sources. Broad overviews of the turfgrass landscape can reveal the severity of surface drainage problems and the intensity and longevity of shading patterns throughout the day. The close proximity of landscape features—including trees, sand bunkers, and water bodies—can indicate where severe turfgrass wear and soil compaction from intense traffic are most likely. Specific symptoms and signs in a turf can reveal the activity of various pests, including insects and disease-inciting organisms. And data from soil-test and water-quality reports can suggest an array of causal factors, including nutrient toxicity or deficiency and excessive soil salinity and/or sodicity. The accumulation of relevant information obtained from these and other sources and used for describing a problematic situation is called *divergence;* it is the first and most important step in the systematic problem-solving process illustrated in the Cycle of Inquiry (adapted from Kolb's Learning Cycle Model) shown in Figure 1.2. The next step, called *assimilation,* involves an analysis of the problematic situation. The transition from divergence to assimilation moves the process from the real world, where the problem exists, to the conceptual world. During the course of an analysis, it is sometimes necessary to return to the real world of divergence in order to gather additional information or to reexamine the available facts. Successive iterations of this process can lead to what can be described as a *rich picture* of the problematic situation. In some situations, this picture may have big holes, as vital information may be missing. It may be necessary, therefore, to make certain assumptions where critical information is lacking in order to proceed. The next step in the process is the *convergence* phase. Also situated in the conceptual world, convergence involves identifying issues and proposing and evaluating various solution strategies. The first part—identifying the issues that must be addressed—may seem so obvious as to be unnecessary; however, its importance derives from the fact that measures taken to solve the wrong problem are not likely to be very effective or to yield a satisfactory resolution. Proposing and evaluating strategies are synonymous with synthesis and evaluation, as described earlier. The final

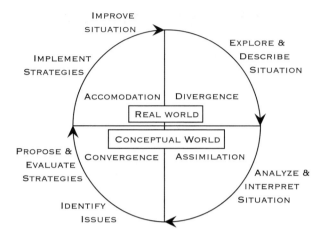

CYCLE OF INQUIRY

Figure 1.2 The four phases of inquiry: divergence, assimilation, convergence, and accommodation in the Cycle of Inquiry adapted from Kolb's Learning Cycle Model (Kolb et al., 1979).

step in the problem-solving process is called *accommodation*. This involves implementation of the strategy or strategies selected and observation of the results obtained. The transition from convergence to accommodation moves the process from the conceptual world back to the real world, as this is where the problem actually exists and where the proposed solution must be implemented. Once the intervention has taken place, the situation originally described will likely change, hopefully for the better. This moves the cycle to the next iteration, when the situation is again described and analyzed, with the possibility of considering additional amelioration strategies.

Many problematic situations involve more than just technical issues. Often there are economic issues that must be addressed, as the best solution might be too expensive. Sometimes there are social issues that frustrate—perhaps even prohibit—the implementation of a technically feasible and affordable solution. And occasionally, there may be ethical issues that pose a significant challenge to the

ETHICAL

SOCIAL

ECONOMIC

TECHNICAL

DISCUSSION ISSUES

Figure 1.3   The management spiral through which decision options at various levels—technical, economic, social, and ethical—should be filtered in the decision-making process.

decision maker's integrity as a human being. For example, the decision to remove several tall trees to reduce a severe shading problem on a particular green or tee might seem to be a straightforward solution at the technical level and a very affordable one at the economic level. But at the social level, one might encounter enormous resistance from players who place great value on retaining these trees, regardless of their effects on the turf. Some might propose that the trees should be removed despite these objections, as "forgiveness is easier to obtain than permission." In this case, an ethical issue is raised: Is it ethical to remove the trees and claim afterward that you were not aware of these objections? More specifically, what is your integrity worth? If it has no value, you can simply give it away. If it does have value, you can sell it. But if you are a person of integrity, your integrity is not for sale at any price under any circumstances. In decision making, one systematically works through the management spiral (Figure 1.3) by filtering options through technical, economic, social, and ethical screens in order to find the best solution.

CHAPTER

2

Turfgrass Problems

Turfgrass problems are those specifically related to the identification, cultural requirements, adaptation, and use of turfgrass species and cultivars. Since climate dramatically influences the adaptation of turfgrasses to specific locations, a climatic classification system adapted from Trewartha (1968) with data from 1971 to 2000 has been included for reference in Plate 1(*a*) (see color insert) for the Western Hemisphere and Plate 1(*b*) (see color insert) for the Eastern Hemisphere. The scenarios are grouped under either cool-season or warm-season turfgrasses; however, some of the scenarios under warm-season turfgrasses involve overseeding with cool-season turfgrasses for winter color and play. Representative examples of both cool-season and warm-season turfgrasses are provided in Figure 2.1a–h.

COOL-SEASON TURFGRASSES

▶ CASE STUDY 2.1

Scenario: On a golf course in central New Jersey, hard fescue (*Festuca trachyphylla* [Hackel] Krajina) was used to establish the rough immediately

(Continued)

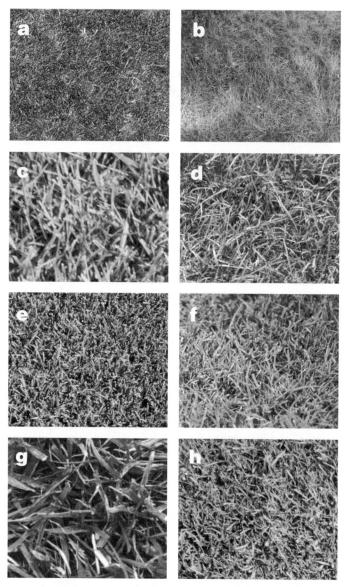

Figure 2.1a hard fescue; 2.1b, red fescue; 2.1c, tall fescue; 2.1d, rough blue-grass; 2.1e, Kentucky bluegrass; 2.1f, Canada bluegrass; 2.1g, annual ryegrass; and 2.1h, annual bluegrass.

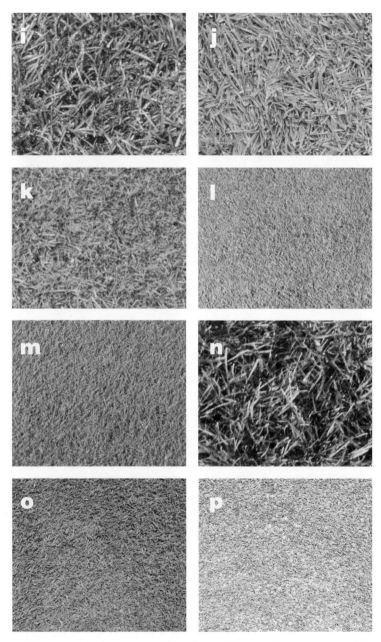

Figure 2.1i perennial ryegrass; 2.1j, redtop; 2.1k, creeping bentgrass; 2.1l, colonial bentgrass; 2.1m, velvet bentgrass; 2.1n, buffalograss; 2.1o, bermudagrass; and 2.1p, hybrid bermudagrass.

Figure 2.1q Japanese lawngrass; 2.1r, hybrid zoysiagrass; 2.1s, St. Augustine-grass; 2.1t, centipedegrass; 2.1u, bahiagrass; 2.1v, seashore paspalum; 2.1w, kikuyugrass; and 2.1x, tropical carpetgrass.

adjacent to a series of sand bunkers. Initially, the turf was excellent; however, by the end of the summer, it was severely worn by traffic and riddled with summer patch disease. What can be done to improve the quality and persistence of this turf?

Analysis: The climate of New Jersey is warm temperate-continental (Dca). Average monthly temperatures increase from north to south, and rainfall is fairly uniform throughout the year. Hard fescue is a fairly heat-tolerant turfgrass. This is an important attribute for a turfgrass selected for use around sand bunkers, as the sand absorbs heat during the day and warms adjacent turf areas (i.e., a *heat-island* effect). It is resistant to red thread, dollar spot, and leaf spot diseases but highly susceptible to summer patch. Compared with other fine fescue species, it has poor traffic tolerance due to the elevated position of its crowns relative to the soil surface; thus, it is best adapted to nontrafficked sites sustained under a low intensity of culture.

Solution: A better alternative for this site would have been strong creeping red fescue (*Festuca rubra* L. ssp. *rubra* Gaud.), as it is more traffic tolerant due to the relatively low position of its crowns relative to the soil surface. It has good resistance to summer patch and dollar spot diseases and moderate resistance to red thread. Strong creeping red fescue forms a more open turf and is especially well suited for use in mixtures with other turfgrass species, such as Kentucky bluegrass (*Poa pratensis* L.). Other alternatives among the fine fescues include Chewings fescue (*F. rubra* L. ssp. *comutata* [Thuill.] Nyman) and slender creeping red fescue (*F. rubra* L. ssp. *litoralis* [Meyer] Auquier), which are also more traffic tolerant due to low crown positioning. Chewings fescue may also be resistant to summer patch disease, depending on the cultivar, and has good recuperative capacity. Slender creeping red fescue is intermediate in density. It has poor heat tolerance and may be susceptible to summer patch, but it is more tolerant to saline soil conditions. Because of the different strengths and weaknesses of these fine fescues, combinations of several species or subspecies are often used to capitalize on their strengths while compensating for their respective weaknesses. Another alternative would be tall fescue (*F. arundinaceae* Schreb.), a relatively coarse-textured species with good heat and drought tolerance. Tall fescue cultivars occur in one of four types: the *forage* types, including Kentucky-31 and Alta, which are very coarse-textured; the *turf* types, such as Rebel, Falcon, and Olympic, which form darker, denser, finer-textured turfs; the *dwarf* types, such as Trailblazer, Bonsai, and Matador, which are even finer-textured but also more susceptible to brown patch disease and less tolerant of heat and drought stresses; and the *intermediate* or *semidwarf* types, such as Millennium, Plantation, and Rembrandt, which are between the turf types and the dwarf types in density and texture, but which are less susceptible to disease and heat and drought stresses than the dwarf types. The inclusion of the *Neotyphodium coenophialum* endophyte in the fescues has been shown to improve drought and insect tolerance and resistance to some diseases. ■

▶ CASE STUDY 2.2

Scenario: In upstate New York, lawn turf consisting of a blend of Kentucky bluegrasses (*Poa pratensis* L.) was established around residences where sunlight intensity ranges from high to low due to differential shading from buildings, trees, and other obstructions in the landscape. The turf in the sunny sites has performed well, but the turf in the moderately to severely shady sites has not. What should have been done to achieve better results in the shady sites?

Analysis: New York has a temperate-continental climate (Dc) that ranges from cool (Dcb) in the upstate portions to warm (Dca) in the vicinity of New York City. While Kentucky bluegrass is well adapted to this climate, it is not very shade tolerant. Selected cultivars exhibit more tolerance of relatively light shade than others, but where moderate shade conditions exist, a more shade-tolerant turfgrass is usually required.

Solution: Selected fine fescue species can be mixed with Kentucky bluegrasses to extend the range of adaptation of the turfgrass community to include shady sites. Among the fine fescues, strong creeping red fescue (*Festuca rubra* L. ssp. *rubra* Gaud.) is especially well suited for use in mixtures with Kentucky bluegrass, as it forms a more open turf than other fine fescues and thus is somewhat better able to coexist with other species in mixed stands. Like all fine fescues, however, strong creeping red fescue must be maintained at relatively low rates of nitrogen fertilization regardless of sunlight intensity, while Kentucky bluegrass usually responds better to higher nitrogen fertilization levels. Therefore, for best turf quality and persistence of these two species, sunny sites should receive higher rates of nitrogen fertilization (3 to 5 lb N per 1000 ft^2, 1.5 to 2.5 kg N per 100 m^2), while shady sites should receive less (1 to 2 lb N per 1000 ft^2, 0.5 to 1.0 kg N per 100 m^2). This should eventually result in the Kentucky bluegrass becoming dominant in the sunny sites and the red fescue becoming dominant in the shady sites, and a mixture of the two species will persist in the margins of these sites. Alternate turfgrasses that may be suitable for shaded sites are rough bluegrass (*Poa trivialis* L.) and supina bluegrass (*P. supina* Schard.). These species work well on moist, fertile, fine-textured soils. As rough bluegrass is not very traffic tolerant and can burn out in response to short periods of intense sunlight, it is best adapted to low-traffic sites that are shaded throughout the day. Because of its stoloniferous growth habit, it does not mix well with other turfgrass species; thus, it should be planted as a single species where other turfgrasses have failed to persist. Supina bluegrass is more traffic tolerant than rough bluegrass; it is widely used in Europe for athletic fields because its strong stoloniferous growth provides considerable recuperative capacity.   ■

▶ CASE STUDY 2.3

Scenario: In central Ohio, a football field originally established with Kentucky bluegrass (*Poa pratensis* L.) has deteriorated from intensive traffic and inadequate maintenance. Is there a better turfgrass for use on this site, and if so, how should it be maintained?

Analysis: Ohio has a temperate-continental climate (Dc) that ranges from cool (Dcb) in the northeastern portion of the state to warm (Dca) to the south and west. Kentucky bluegrass is well adapted for use on football fields in temperate-continental climates, provided that it receives proper care before, during, and after the football season; however, there may be better cultivars of Kentucky bluegrass that are more tolerant of this type of traffic or that recover more quickly from traffic-induced injury than the one(s) used on this site. Properly selected cultivars should provide a strong rhizome base that both enhances the resilience of the turf and promotes rapid recuperative growth following

15

injury from play. An alternative would be a turf-type or intermediate-type tall fescue (*Festuca arundinacea* Schreb.) in a 90:10 mixture (by weight) with Kentucky bluegrass. Since tall fescue is a bunch-type grass, the inclusion of a small percentage of rhizomatous Kentucky bluegrass helps to bind the tall fescue into an interconnected turfgrass community.

Solution: Ensure that well-adapted cultivars have been established on the site and that adequate drainage—both surface and internal—has been provided to support and encourage root growth. Minimize unnecessary traffic on the field prior to and during the playing season. The field should be relatively dry and firm during a game; this may require covering the field with canvas tarps in the days immediately preceding a game. As turf damaged from football cleats is highly susceptible to subsequent desiccation of exposed tissues, light rolling and irrigation immediately following a game can be helpful in reducing this type of injury. Light applications of soluble fertilizer during the playing season can be helpful in promoting rapid recuperative growth. If wear from play is so severe that the Kentucky bluegrass cannot recover sufficiently to sustain acceptable quality, bare areas can be seeded with turf-type ryegrasses (*Lolium* spp.) immediately following a game to accelerate recovery. In tall fescue–Kentucky bluegrass fields, bare areas should be overseeded with tall fescue instead. In midspring, the field should be renovated to alleviate soil compaction, control thatch, and promote deep rooting and dense shoot growth. Stress from traffic, heat, and drought should be minimized during the summer months so that the turf is in excellent condition at the beginning of the playing season. ■

▶ CASE STUDY 2.4

Scenario: In central Indiana, extended sections of a new roadside turf seeding along a bypass constructed around Indianapolis were severely eroded following heavy spring rains. In late May, the affected sites were regraded and made ready for planting. What turfgrass species should be used for planting, and how should the turf be maintained?

Analysis: Indiana has a warm temperate-continental climate (Dca). Erosion from rains or strong winds can severely threaten the successful establishment of a new turf from seed. Appropriate measures should have been employed to minimize the potential for erosion. These include the application of fiber mulches to the site after seeding to stabilize the soil and seed and to provide favorable conditions for germination and seedling development.

Solution: Tall fescue (*Festuca arundinacea* Schreb.) and hard fescue (*F. trachyphylla* [Hackel] Krajina) are species that are well adapted for this purpose. A starter fertilizer containing nitrogen, phosphorus, and potassium should be used at planting to promote aggressive growth for successful establishment. Some sites can be mowed several times during the growing season, while other sites, especially those on steep banks, can be left unmowed. Selected postemergence herbicides should be used on an as-needed basis to control broadleaf weeds. ■

▶ CASE STUDY 2.5

Scenario: On the Oregon coast, a new golf course is scheduled for grow-in, beginning in late summer. While decisions have been made regarding the turfgrass species to be used for establishing greens, tee boxes, and roughs, a suitable fairway species has not been selected. What species could be used for this purpose, and how should the fairways be maintained?

Analysis: Western Oregon (i.e., the western side of the Cascade Mountains) has the same climate as that found throughout northwestern Europe. The climate is cool temperate-oceanic (Dob); the winters are rainy, with moderate temperatures (i.e., the average temperature for the coldest month is greater than 32°F or 0°C), and the summers are warm and relatively dry. Turfgrasses that may not do well in the harsher temperate-continental (Dc) climate, such as colonial bentgrass (*Agrostis capillaris* L.), often form excellent turfs here.

Solution: Colonial bentgrass would be a good choice, provided that it is maintained at a moderate intensity of culture. This would include mowing at 0.3 to 0.8 in. (0.8–2.0 cm), fertilization with 1 to 2 lb N per 1000 ft^2 (0.5 to 1.0 kg N per 100 m^2) per year, and frequent irrigation during drought periods. Creeping bentgrass (*Agrostis stolonifera* L.), perennial ryegrass, or annual bluegrass (*Poa annua* L.) could also be used, but at higher intensities of culture. ■

▶ CASE STUDY 2.6

Scenario: Because of increasing shade intensity from tall trees, the creeping bentgrass (*Agrostis stolonifera* L.) on a push-up practice green constructed on loamy sand in Rhode Island was deteriorating and being invaded by annual bluegrass (*Poa annua* L.). A green committee member asked if a different bentgrass species might perform better on this site. Also, if this turfgrass species were successfully established in place of the current turfgrass community, in what ways would its cultural requirements differ?

Analysis: Rhode Island has a temperate-continental climate (Dc) that ranges from cool (Dcb) in the northwestern portion of the state to warm (Dca) in the southeastern coastal region. Considerable work has been done at the University of Rhode Island on the development of velvet bentgrass (*Agrostis canina* L.) for use on greens and lawns. For many years, superintendents were reluctant to use this species because of the difficulties associated with managing it. Velvet bentgrass forms an exceptionally dense, very fine-textured turf that is highly thatch prone. It is more shade tolerant than other bentgrass species and has relatively low fertility and irrigation requirements, but it must be topdressed very frequently to control thatch.

Solution: Reestablishing the green with velvet bentgrass is one alternative that might be tried; however, as its cultural requirements are quite different from those of most creeping bentgrasses, one must be willing to implement a cultural program specifically adapted to this species. This would include mowing at 0.125 to 0.4 in. (3.2–10 mm), fertilization with 1 to 2 lb N per 1000 ft^2 (0.5–1.0 kg N per 100 m^2) per year, and irrigation as needed to sustain growth and color; however, due to the relatively slow shoot growth of this species, severe cultivations should be avoided to minimize the amount of recovery needed. Hollow-tine cultivations should be performed with small-diameter tines (0.5 in. [1.25 cm] or less), vertical mowing should be done to very shallow depths, and topdressing should be performed frequently to dilute developing thatch while enhancing its biodecomposition.

Alternatives would be to either accept the eventual domination of annual bluegrass on this green or to reduce the shade intensity through selective removal and pruning of adjacent trees to ensure that sufficient sunlight is received to sustain creeping bentgrass. ■

▶ CASE STUDY 2.7

Scenario: After converting greens from Penncross to Penn A-4 creeping bentgrasses (*Agrostis stolonifera* L.), superintendents frequently observe that root systems are shorter, especially during the summer months. What can be done to promote deeper rooting?

Analysis: Rooting depth is a reflection of many environmental and cultural factors. Environmental factors include those specific to the soil, such as pH, aeration, moisture, salinity, and fertility. Wherever any of these factors is substantially above or below optimum levels, rooting can be adversely affected. The development of excessive thatch above the soil surface is also associated with shallow rooting, as roots tend to grow preferentially within the thatch layer. Atmospheric environmental factors such as light can adversely affect root growth where it is insufficient to produce the photoassimilates needed to sustain the plants' growth and energy requirements. Root growth is also adversely affected where atmospheric temperature is substantially above or below optimum levels. In cool-season turfgrasses, optimum temperatures for root growth are between 50°F and 65°F (10°C and 18°C). The biotic component of the environment includes organisms that can destroy roots, such as disease-inciting fungi and bacteria, parasitic nematodes, and root-feeding insects. Cultural factors that adversely affect root growth include close mowing, inadequate or excessive fertilizer nutrient levels, and excessive rolling.

Penn A-4 is one of the ultra-high-density bentgrass cultivars released from Penn State University in the 1990s. Under close mowing (0.125 in. [3.2 mm] or less), these A- and G-series cultivars produce large numbers of tiny shoots, forming very dense, very fine-textured turfs. Root lengths tend to be shallower than those associated with other creeping bentgrass cultivars.

Solution: Generally, root growth can be improved by effective measures for optimizing soil pH, aeration, moisture, and fertility, reducing salinity where it tends to be excessive, controlling thatch, improving light levels where shading from trees or other obstructions reduce photosynthetic activity, controlling root-feeding parasites, applying selected biostimulants on a regular basis to alleviate the effects of heat and drought stresses, and avoiding excessive rolling as well as mowing heights that are below the tolerance level of the particular turfgrass. The ultra-high-density creeping bentgrasses, including Penn A-4, were selected because of their close-mowing tolerance. With these turfgrasses, some cultural practices should be altered to compensate for their high shoot density and shallow rooting. For example, because of their severe thatching tendency, topdressing should be performed as often as needed to dilute the buildup of the organic residues comprising thatch with soil (principally sand) particles so that the uniformity of the turf profile is maintained over time. This may require lightly topdressing every week. Less frequent topdressing schedules may result in the development of alternating layers of soil and organic residues in the turf profile. Where layering is allowed to develop, soil water and air movement can be interrupted and root growth reduced. Hollow-tine cultivation, followed by core removal and backfilling of the holes with sand, can be useful in alleviating soil compaction and creating bypass drainage where layers have developed in the turf profile. More grooming, including light vertical mowing and the use of grooved rollers, is helpful in controlling thatch accumulations. Finally, with a shallower-rooted turf, irrigation should generally be more frequent and of shorter duration, and fertilizers should be foliar applied frequently and in quantities sufficient to sustain healthy growth. ■

▶ CASE STUDY 2.8

Scenario: With seed head emergence from annual bluegrass (*Poa annua* L.) in midspring, golf club members in northern Ohio complained that the greens did not putt true and that the quality of fairway lies was substantially reduced. What can be done to address their complaints?

Analysis: Seed head emergence is a natural occurrence in annual bluegrass turfs. In perennial biotypes of annual bluegrass, this phenomenon is largely restricted to a 3- to 4-week period in midspring, while with annual biotypes it can occur throughout the growing season. The intensive seed head "pulse" that occurs in midspring is often associated with reduced root growth due to the partitioning of photoassimilates to support seed head development, often at the expense of other aspects of plant growth, including rooting. On greens, the massive occurrence of seed heads substantially reduces putting quality. On fairways, the seed heads rise above the leaves, interfering with contact between the club head and the ball and thus reducing the quality of the shot.

Solution: Selected plant-growth regulators (PGRs), including mefluidide (Embark) and ethephon (Proxy), inhibit seed head development; however, effective control requires careful timing. For mefluidide (Figure 2.2), a single application should be made when between 25 and 50 degree days (DD) have accumulated in the spring. Using the Fahrenheit scale, DD begin accumulating whenever the average daily temperature (i.e., [daily maximum temperature + daily minimum temperature]/2) is greater than 50. Cumulative DD can be calculated by subtracting 50 from the average daily temperature each day and accumulating these

Figure 2.2 Comparison of mefuidide-treated (left) and untreated (right) annual bluegrass fairway turf showing the impact of seed head suppression on turf quality.

numbers over time. While some temporary discoloration may occur from this application, seed head development should be inhibited. Also, because photoassimilates that would have supported seed head development are conserved, root growth is sustained, resulting in a more extensive root system in treated turfs.

Ethephon can also be used to inhibit seed head development. Because applications of ethephon often result in an apple green coloration of the turf, it is sometimes tank mixed with trinexapac-ethyl (Primo)—a PGR that reduces vertical shoot growth by inhibiting gibberellic acid biosynthesis and imparts a dark green color to treated turf—to counteract this effect. At present, no good timing model is available for ethephon. Some superintendents have had good success with early applications of ethephon, while others have had success applying ethephon after the seeds heads were first observed. The recommended treatment is one application at 0.08 lb per 1000 ft^2 (39 g per 100 m^2), which is equivalent to 5 fl oz per 1000 ft^2 (160 ml per 100 m^2) from a 2 lb a.i. per gallon of formulation of Proxy. Some superintendents have had success splitting the application, applying 0.05 lb per 1000 ft (23 g per 100 m^2)—equivalent to 3 fl oz per 1000 ft^2 (96 ml per 100 m^2)—followed by a second application 3 weeks later. ■

WARM-SEASON TURFGRASSES

▶ CASE STUDY 2.9

Scenario: Despite severe competition from annual bluegrass (*Poa annua* L.) (Figure 2.1h), the hybrid bermudagrass (*Cynodon dactylon* [L.] Pers. var. *dactylon* × *C. transvaalensis* Burtt-Davy) on greens at a golf course in San Diego emerged from winter dormancy in the warm spring weather during the first few years following establishment and formed turfs of acceptable quality. With the cooler weather of subsequent springs, however, the annual bluegrass was more persistent and eventually crowded out the bermudagrass. Because of the lack of an adequate preventive fungicide application program, summer diseases took their toll and severely reduced the quality of the annual bluegrass turf. What can be done to restore these greens to acceptable quality?

Analysis: Successful spring transition from temporary winter turfs of cool-season turfgrasses to warm-season turfgrass communities is favored by conditions that reduce the persistence of—and competition from—cool-season turfgrasses while stimulating the emergence of warm-season turfgrasses from dormancy. Generally, warm weather and bright sunlight are effective in simultaneously stressing the cool-season turfgrasses and stimulating the bermudagrass. Light vertical mowing and moderate fertilization with nitrogen can often accelerate this transition by enhancing both stress and stimulation. Where abnormally cool weather and overcast skies persist during this period, cool-season turfgrasses may be considerably more persistent and competitive, while the emergence of the bermudagrass from dormancy is suppressed. Eventually, the survival of the bermudagrass may be seriously threatened where these conditions persist for an extended period.

Temporary winter turfs may occur as a result of an overseeding program implemented in the fall or from natural infestations of winter annual species such as annual bluegrass. In subtropical-humid climates, fall overseeding with perennial ryegrass, rough bluegrass, or combinations of various cool-season turfgrasses is typically conducted on bermudagrass greens, tees, and possibly fairways. Often, elaborate measures are employed for controlling annual bluegrass infestations. These may include the following: (1) an application of pronamide (Kerb) preemergence herbicide at least 60 days prior to overseeding (or less than 60 days prior to overseeding with an application of activated charcoal at least 7 days prior to overseeding to adsorb the pronamide residue); or (2) an application of dithiopyr (Dimension) preemergence herbicide at least 8 weeks prior to overseeding (but not on Tifgreen bermudagrass, which is highly susceptible to injury from this herbicide) along with a second application in early winter for extended control; or (3) an application of bensulide (Bensumec, Pre-San) preemergence herbicide at least 4 months prior to overseeding ryegrass (because of its narrow tolerance range for this herbicide); or (4) two or three applications of fenarimol (Rubigan) systemic fungicide 10 to 14 days apart, with the last application made 14 days prior to overseeding ryegrass, with perhaps an early winter application where annual bluegrass seedlings are evident, as this material also provides preemergence and some early postemergence control of the annual biotype of annual bluegrass.

In some subtropical-dry summer climates (Cs), such as that occurring in San Diego, the annual bluegrass pressure during the rainy winter months can be so severe that effective control is nearly impossible. Furthermore, annual bluegrass can often survive the summers, provided that it is irrigated properly and diseases are controlled with an effective preventive fungicide program. With its survival from year to year comes the evolutionary development of perennial biotypes that are even more persistent and less susceptible to the chemical controls commonly employed on annual biotypes.

Solution: Restoring these greens to acceptable quality requires either establishing creeping bentgrasses that are adapted to the summer conditions and sufficiently competitive with annual bluegrass during the winter months or implementing an effective preventive fungicide program to sustain the annual bluegrass throughout the growing season. With either choice, greens should be well drained and irrigation adequate during the dry summer months. To significantly improve the adaptability and quality of the annual bluegrass, one should look for high-quality annual bluegrass greens in the area that have persisted for many years. If these appear to be a better type of annual bluegrass than the one occurring locally, they could be used as a source of cores (from hollow-tine cultivation) with which to establish a nursery green. Cores from the nursery green could then be used to systematically reestablish the playing greens. ■

▶ CASE STUDY 2.10

Scenario: In northern Florida, you have been given the responsibility for establishing new fairways on a golf course catering to "snow birds" visiting from the north. While play occurs all year, it is especially heavy during the winter months. Which turfgrass species are adapted for this purpose? What are their cultural requirements?

Analysis: Florida has climates that range from warm subtropical-humid (Cfa) in the northern and central portions of the state to tropical-wet (Ar) in the southernmost portion. While bermudagrasses (*Cynodon* spp.) thrive in the warm subtropical-humid climate of northern Florida during the summer half of the year, their growth slows down dramatically during the winter months and they become semidormant.

As a consequence, their traffic tolerance is considerably reduced unless temporary winter turfs are established through overseeding with ryegrass (*Lolium* spp.) or other cool-season turfgrasses in the fall. If heavy play is anticipated during the winter months, bermudagrass greens and tees in this area should be overseeded to ensure acceptable playability, as well as the survival of the bermudagrass. The desirability of fairway overseeding varies, depending on climatic conditions. In the cool subtropical-humid (Cfb) climate of the Carolinas, bermudagrasses become completely dormant during the winter months, while some winter growth and color retention are usually evident in these turfgrasses in the warm subtropical-humid climate of northern Florida. Furthermore, as the intensity of traffic is usually sufficiently diluted on fairways, unacceptable damage from traffic is less likely.

Solution: Hybrid bermudagrass (*Cynodon dactylon* [L.] Pers. var. *dactylon* × *C. transvaalensis* Burtt-Davy) should be the permanent turfgrass for the fairways, as it will persist and form an excellent turf during the hot, humid summer months. The decision to establish temporary turfs for winter play should be based on the traffic intensity anticipated. With light to moderate traffic, overseeding may not be necessary. As heavy traffic could severely damage the semidormant bermudagrass, however, the establishment of temporary turfs on these fairways through overseeding ryegrass in the fall would be warranted.

The fall overseeding process usually begins with close mowing and removal of debris to open the turf and allow seed to reach the soil surface. Where thatch occurs, hollow-tine cultivation—with soil cores reincorporated—should be performed 3 to 4 weeks prior to overseeding. Some vertical mowing may be needed as well where the thatch layer is too thick to be completely modified by the reincorporation of soil cores; this is done to remove a portion of the thatch and open up the remainder to facilitate soil core incorporation from subsequent hollow-tine cultivation. The ryegrass (perennial, annual, intermediate) seeding rate is usually 6–10 lb per 1000 ft^2 (3–5 kg per 100 m^2). ■

▶ CASE STUDY 2.11

Scenario: In western Nebraska, the utility turf along roadsides was established from tall fescue (*Festuca arundinaceae* Schreb.). Because of the lack of adequate rainfall, this species never provided acceptable cover for soil stabilization. Which turfgrass species would be better adapted for this use? What are their cultural requirements?

Analysis: The climate of western Nebraska is at or near the interface between warm temperate-continental (Dca) to the east and cold semi-arid dry-winter (BSkw) to the west; thus, it has cold winters and warm summers and receives around 20 in. (50 cm) of annual rainfall, mostly during the summer half of the year. Successfully establishing and maintaining tall fescue without irrigation is difficult in this climate. More drought-tolerant species should be selected, especially for utility turfs that will be maintained under a low intensity of culture.

Solution: Buffalograss (*Buchloë dactyloides* [Nutt.] Engelm.) and crested wheatgrass (*Agropyron cristatum* [L.] Gaertn. × *A. desertorum* [Fisch. ex Link] Schult.) would be good choices for this climate. Buffalograss is a hardy warm-season grass that has excellent tolerance to drought and extreme temperatures; thus, it is well suited for use in unirrigated turfs in semiarid climates. Crested wheatgrass is a cool-season grass with excellent drought and cold hardiness, and is also well suited for use as a utility turf in this climate. Both species can be established from seed and maintained under a low intensity of culture. ∎

▶ CASE STUDY 2.12

Scenario: In east-central Missouri, the bermudagrass (*Cynodon dactylon* [L.] Pers. var. *dactylon*) fairways at a high-end golf course were heavily damaged during an especially severe winter. When this happened twice before, the fairways were simply replanted with bermudagrass. This time, the membership is demanding an alternative species that is less susceptible to winter kill. Which turfgrass species might be employed in place of bermudagrass, and in what significant ways would its cultural requirements differ?

Analysis: The climate throughout most of Missouri is warm temperate-continental (Dca), with the southernmost portion of the state reaching into a cool subtropical-humid climate (Cfb). East-central Missouri is within a geographic belt—measuring approximately 200 miles wide—known as the *transition zone,* where some cool-season and warm-season turfgrasses reach the traditional limits of their climatic adaptation. Within this zone, Kentucky bluegrasses (*Poa pratensis* L.) typically suffer from severe heat and drought stress during the summer months, while bermudagrasses are subjected to severe cold stress during the winter months. As a consequence, some bermudagrasses that have persisted and formed excellent turfs for several years can occasionally suffer severe damage during especially cold winters. This has resulted in the quest for turfgrasses that are better adapted to the unique characteristics of the transition zone, extending from Washington, D.C., through Louisville, St. Louis, and Kansas City. The two species that have emerged as being well adapted to the transition zone are tall fescue (*Festuca arundinacea* Schreb.) and Japanese lawngrass (*Zoysia japonica* Steud.).

Solution: Japanese lawngrass, commonly known simply as *zoysiagrass,* would be a good choice. It is a warm-season turfgrass that is highly tolerant of drought, heat, and cold stresses and thus is well adapted to the transition zone. It is relatively slow to establish from plugs, but zoysiagrass stolons can be harvested from established turfs through vertical mowing and used to propagate new fairways within a single growing season. While this species greens up late in the spring and becomes dormant relatively early in the fall, its characteristic straw color during the winter half of the year is not unattractive, especially if it is managed properly to keep it dense, uniform, and weed-free. Once established, zoysiagrass should be mowed at 0.5 to 1.0 in. (1.3–2.5 cm), fertilized with 1.5 to 3.0 lb N per 1000 ft^2 (0.75–1.5 kg N per 100 m^2) per year, and irrigated as needed to sustain adequate growth during dry seasons.

While tall fescue is also adapted to the transition zone, it has not been widely used for fairways because of its coarse texture and inability to persist under fairway mowing heights. With the continuing development of new dwarf-type cultivars, however, there is the growing possibility that tall fescue may find its way onto fairways in the future, especially if more brown patch–resistant cultivars can be developed. Furthermore, as the inclusion of the *Neotyphodium coenophialum* endophyte in tall fescue cultivars has been shown to improve drought tolerance, as well as resistance to some insects and diseases, the use of this turfgrass on golf courses is likely to become more widespread.

A third alternative would be to try a more cold-tolerant bermudagrass such as Riviera, Yukon, Vamont, Midiron, or Patriot; however, another failure with bermudagrass during an especially severe winter could have serious consequences under the circumstances described in this scenario. ■

► CASE STUDY 2.13

Scenario: In a community near Richmond, Virginia, a college football field seeded earlier in the year to common bermudagrass (*Cynodon dactylon* [L.] Pers. var. *dactylon*) declined dramatically in quality due to the combination of intense traffic and cold temperatures during the fall playing season. Which turfgrass species should be used in place of the seeded bermudagrass, and how should it be maintained?

Analysis: The climate of Virginia ranges from warm temperate-continental (Dca) in the ridge-and-valley region of the northwest to cool subtropical-humid (Cfb) to the east and south. Richmond lies in the east central portion of the state. As average minimum monthly temperatures are 46.4°F, 37.8°F, and 30.0°F (8.0°C, 3.2°C, and −1.1°C) for October, November, and December, respectively, bermudagrass growth slows dramatically in the early fall and it becomes completely dormant before the end of the football season. Under optimum temperatures for growth (i.e., 75°F to 90°F [24°C to 32°C]), bermudagrass is the ideal turfgrass for football; it has exceptional wear tolerance and, to the extent that injury occurs, its recuperative capacity is excellent. In less than optimal temperatures, however, its growth slows and its recuperative capacity is correspondingly reduced. When it is completely dormant, wear tolerance is reduced as well, and there is no recuperative growth. Furthermore, intensive culture and severe traffic can seriously threaten the winter survival of many bermudagrasses.

Solution: To increase the winter survival of bermudagrass, only cold-tolerant cultivars should be used in cool subtropical-humid climates. Vamont is an especially cold-tolerant bermudagrass that has enjoyed wide usage in Virginia, but there are many other cultivars available or under development that could be used as well. To provide satisfactory playing conditions for football, a bermudagrass turf should be overseeded with ryegrasses (*Lolium* spp.), prior to the beginning of the football season in late August or early September, and after each game wherever damage from play is evident. Depending on the persistence of the ryegrass, it may be necessary to remove it chemically to facilitate the transition to bermudagrass the following summer. ■

▶ CASE STUDY 2.14

Scenario: The greens at a golf course near Charleston, South Carolina, were originally planted during the mid-1960s to Tifgreen bermudagrass (*Cynodon dactylon* [L.] Pers. var. *dactylon* × *C. transvaalensis* Burtt-Davy 'Tifgreen'), the first improved hybrid bermudagrass. Over the years, many mutations occurred in the Tifgreen that resulted in a very nonuniform surface. Additionally, a significant thatch problem developed that contributed to a puffy surface, resulting in scalping and poor green speed during the summer months. Putting quality was better during the fall, winter, and spring, when the Tifgreen was overseeded with rough bluegrass (*Poa trivialis* L.). How might the putting quality of these greens be improved?

Analysis: The climate of South Carolina ranges from cool subtropical-humid (Cfb) in the mountainous northwestern part of the state to warm subtropical-humid (Cfa) to the south and east. As Charleston is located along the Atlantic Coast, it is warmer—especially during the winter months—than inland locations at the same latitude; thus, bermudagrass has a relatively long growing season at this location. Old bermudagrass greens that have not been cultivated and topdressed adequately over the years can develop a serious thatch problem and become quite puffy and scalping-prone, especially during the summer months. With genetic mutations occurring as well, they can also become quite variable in both visual appearance and playability. For all of these reasons, replacing old Tifgreen greens with one of the newer improved cultivars may be desirable.

Solution: The greens should be renovated by removing the old bermudagrass sod, tilling the soil and reshaping surface contours, adding 1 to 2 in. (2.5–5.0 cm) of topdressing soil to compensate for the soil removed with the sod, fumigating to kill weed seeds and pathogens, and sprigging at 20 bushels per 1000 ft^2 (760 L per 100 m^2) with an improved ultradwarf-type bermudagrass such as Champion, Classic, MS Supreme, MiniVerde, or TifEagle. ■

▶ CASE STUDY 2.15

Scenario: Small bermudagrass (*Cynodon dactylon* [L.] Pers. var. *dactylon*) tees on a golf course on Maryland's eastern shore performed poorly during the fall months due to slow recuperative growth. In the winter months, when there was no recuperative growth at all, much of the bermudagrass was lost due to traffic stress. Each spring, the tees were replanted with seeded cultivars of bermudagrass to reestablish cover. What might be done to improve the quality of these tees?

Analysis: The climate of Maryland ranges from cool temperate-continental (Dcb) in the west to warm temperate-continental (Dca) in the northcentral part to cool subtropical-humid (Cfb) in the east; thus, the eastern shore is cool subtropical-humid. While cold-hardy bermudagrasses grow well in the summer months and recover quickly from injury in this climate, growth—and, therefore, recuperative capacity—slows dramatically in the fall. In winter, bermudagrasses become completely dormant, with no recuperative capacity and substantially reduced traffic tolerance. As a consequence, the tees are severely damaged from fall and winter play, requiring replanting each spring.

Solution: One alternative would be to build additional tees, planting them to creeping bentgrass (*Agrostis stolonifera* L.). The bermudagrass tees should be replanted with cold-tolerant bermudagrass cultivars such as Yukon, Riviera, Vamont, Midiron, or Patriot. These tees should be used only during the warmer summer months, when the bermudagrass is growing vigorously and recovering well from play. An alternative to bermudagrass would be Meyer zoysiagrass (*Zoysia japonica* Steud. 'Meyer'). While this species does not have the recuperative capacity of bermudagrass, it is more shade tolerant and would perform better on shaded tees. The bentgrass tees should be used only during the cooler spring and fall months, when they are growing optimally. Measures that can be employed to enhance the survival of these turfgrasses during stressful periods include covering the bermudagrass tees with straw mulch during the winter months and raising the mowing height of the bentgrass tees during summer. ■

▶ CASE STUDY 2.16

Scenario: Champion bermudagrass (*Cynodon dactylon* [L.] Pers. var. *dactylon* × *C. transvaalensis* Burtt-Davy 'Champion') greens at a golf course in Baton Rouge, Louisiana, had limited play during the winter months but were heavily used during the favorable weather of spring and fall. Unfortunately, these periods coincided with the fall overseeding and spring transition, resulting in sloppy playing conditions in the fall, when the overseeding must be frequently irrigated to enhance germination, and poor-quality greens in the spring, when the greens are transitioning from the overseeded species to bermudagrass. What can be done to improve the quality of these greens?

Analysis: The climate of Louisiana is warm subtropical-humid (Cfa). Baton Rouge is located in the southern portion of the state, near the Gulf Coast; its average annual temperature is 67.6°F, and the average temperature for January—the coldest month—is 49.6°F. Champion bermudagrass has a very long growing season at this location, provides excellent quality not only during the summer months but in spring and fall as well, and endures the short winter in a semidormant condition, exhibiting its characteristic purplish color.

Solution: Because of the limited play during the winter months when the bermudagrass is semidormant, with reduced traffic tolerance and recuperative capacity, an appropriate alternative would be to eliminate the annual overseeding operation and rely entirely on the bermudagrass turf to support play during the spring and fall, when play is heaviest. For winter color, the greens could be painted with specialized paints specifically developed for this purpose. Where annual bluegrass invasion is a concern, TranXit (rimsulfuron) or Revolver (foramsulfuron) can be used for control. ■

▶ CASE STUDY 2.17

Scenario: Greens converted to an ultradwarf bermudagrass (*Cynodon dactylon* [L.] Pers. var. *dactylon* × *C. transvaalensis* Burtt-Davy) did not produce the same rooting depth as the old Tifdwarf greens during the summer months. What can be done to promote deeper rooting?

Analysis: Like the ultra-high-density creeping bentgrasses (see scenario 2.7), the ultradwarf bermudagrasses produce large numbers of tillers, often at the expense of the root system. Generally speaking, rooting depth is a reflection of many environmental and cultural factors. Environmental factors include those specific to the soil, such as pH, aeration, moisture, salinity, and fertility. Wherever any of these factors is substantially above or below optimum levels, rooting can be adversely affected. The development of excessive thatch above the soil surface is also associated with shallow rooting, as roots tend to grow preferentially within the thatch layer. Atmospheric environmental factors such as light can adversely affect root growth where it is insufficient to produce the photoassimilates needed to sustain the plants' growth and energy requirements. Root growth is also adversely affected where atmospheric temperatures are substantially above or below optimum levels. In warm-season turfgrasses, optimum temperatures for root growth are between 70°F and 85°F (21°C and 29°C). The biotic component of the environment includes organisms that can destroy roots, such as disease-inciting fungi, parasitic nematodes, and root-feeding insects. Cultural factors that adversely affect root growth include close mowing, inadequate or excessive fertilizer nutrient levels, and excessive rolling.

The ultradwarf bermudagrasses produce large numbers of tiny shoots, forming very dense and very fine-textured turfs under close mowing heights of 0.125 in. (3.2 mm) or less. Roots tend to be miniaturized as well, often shallower than those associated with older turf-type cultivars.

Solution: Generally, root growth can be improved by effective measures for optimizing soil pH, aeration, moisture, and fertility, reducing salinity where it tends to be excessive, controlling thatch, improving light levels where shading from trees or other obstructions reduces photosynthetic activity, controlling root-feeding parasites, applying selected biostimulants on a regular basis to alleviate the effects of heat and drought stresses, and avoiding excessive rolling as well as mowing heights that are below the tolerance level of the particular turfgrass. The ultradwarf bermudagrasses were selected because of their close-mowing tolerance. With these turfgrasses, some cultural practices should be altered to compensate for their high shoot density and shallow rooting. For example, because of their severe thatching tendency, topdressing should be performed as often as needed to dilute the buildup of the organic residues comprising thatch with soil (principally sand) particles, so that the uniformity of the turf profile is maintained over time. This may require light topdressing every week. Less frequent topdressing schedules may result in the development of alternating layers of soil and organic residues in the turf profile. Where this condition is allowed to develop, soil water and air movement can be interrupted and root growth reduced. Finally, with a shallower-rooted turf, irrigations should generally be more frequent and of shorter duration, and fertilizers should be foliar applied frequently and in quantities sufficient to sustain healthy growth. ∎

▶ CASE STUDY 2.18

Scenario: A lawn near Austin, Texas, has many bare areas where the shade from trees and other landscape features has limited the growth of bermudagrass (*Cynodon dactylon* [L.] Pers. var. *dactylon*). The soil is moderately alkaline. Which turfgrass species could be used to establish turf in these areas?

Analysis: The climates of Texas range from mostly semiarid (BS) in the west to warm subtropical-humid (Cfa) in the east. While Austin is within the warm subtropical-humid climatic zone, it is located near the interface of these two climates; therefore, it is dryer and has greater annual and diurnal temperature fluctuations than locations that are closer to the Gulf Coast (e.g., Houston). While bermudagrasses are adapted to this location, their lack of shade tolerance limits their use to sites receiving sufficient light intensity. Where trees or other landscape features substantially reduce sunlight, however, a more shade-tolerant species would be needed. Appropriate choices include most cultivars of St. Augustinegrass (*Stenotaphrum secundatum* [Walt.] Kuntze.) and any of the zoysiagrasses, including Japanese lawngrass (*Zoysia japonica* Steud.) and manilagrass (*Z. matrella* [L.] Merr.), as well as hybrids between these species and mascarenegrass (*Z. pacifica* [Gaud.] Hotta & Kuroti).

Solution: Shade-tolerant St. Augustinegrasses are typically planted in shaded locations in the landscape where bermudagrass fails to persist; however, any of the zoysiagrass species could be substituted. ■

▶ CASE STUDY 2.19

Scenario: In Columbia, South Carolina, construction of an amusement park is nearing completion. Because of the desire to have an extensive lawn area ready for traffic as soon as possible, the decision has been made to sod the area. The soil is moderately acidic. As the main pedestrian walkways are paved, this turf is expected to receive only light to moderate traffic and will be maintained at a relatively low intensity of culture. Which turfgrass species are adapted for this lawn, and how should it be maintained?

Analysis: The climate of Columbia, South Carolina, is warm subtropical-humid (Cfa). Many warm-season turfgrass species are adapted to this location, including bermudagrasses (*Cynodon* spp.), zoysiagrasses (*Zoysia* spp.), St. Augustinegrass (*Stenotaphrum secundatum* [Walt.] Kuntze.), and centipedegrass (*Eremochloa ophiuroides* [Munro] Hack.).

Solution: Given the acidic soil conditions and the intention to maintain this turf at a low cultural intensity, centipedegrass should be given serious consideration. It can be maintained at mowing heights of 1 to 2 in. (2.5–5.0 cm), fertilized with 1 to 2 lb N per 1000 ft^2 (0.5–1.0 kg N per 100 m^2) per year, and irrigated during droughty periods to sustain color and growth. ■

▶ CASE STUDY 2.20

Scenario: In central Florida, extended sections of a new roadside turf seeding along a bypass constructed around Orlando were severely eroded following heavy summer rains. In late August, the affected sites were regraded and made ready for planting sod. What turfgrass species should be used for planting, and how should the turf be maintained?

Analysis: The climate of central Florida is warm subtropical-humid (Cfa); however, with nearly 51 in. of rainfall, an average annual temperature of 72.5°F (22.5°C), and an average temperature for the coldest month (January) of 61.2°F (16.2°C), the climate at this location is very close to being tropical (Ar). Soils are predominantly loamy sands with very low cation-exchange capacities. Thus, the turfgrasses selected for use as utility turfs along roadsides must be tolerant of low fertility and hot humid conditions.

Solution: Bahiagrass is the clear choice for this site. In this environment, it requires very little fertility and no irrigation, and mowing can be relatively infrequent at high heights of cut. ■

▶ CASE STUDY 2.21

Scenario: On a golf course along the Florida Gulf Coast, the bermudagrass (*Cynodon dactylon* [L.] Pers. var. *dactylon* × *C. transvaalensis* Burtt-Davy) greens have deteriorated due to a combination of salt spray and saltwater intrusion into the groundwater used for irrigation. Water quality tests revealed that the salinity of the irrigation water is very high (EC$_w$ > 2.25 dS/m). Which turfgrass species would be better adapted to these conditions, and how should it be maintained?

Analysis: While bermudagrass is considered to be moderately tolerant of salinity, water with an EC$_w$ in excess of 2.25 dS/m is considered generally unsuitable for irrigation. As the salt concentration of the soil solution is inversely related to its osmotic potential (Ψ_o), and since osmotic potential is a component of soil water potential (Ψ_{sw}), excessive soil salinity can dramatically reduce a plant's ability to absorb water from the soil by reducing the water potential gradient between the soil and the plant. This can cause a condition called *physiological drought,* resulting in the desiccation of plants growing in the soil.

Solution: A turfgrass species that has been shown to tolerate high soil salinity is seashore paspalum (*Paspalum vaginatum* Swartz.). Where the quality of hybrid bermudagrass greens has declined from excessive soil salinity, seashore paspalum can often persist and form high-quality greens in its place. Selected cultivars can be sustained at mowing heights as low as ⅛th in. (3 mm), nitrogen fertilization levels of 2 to 4 lb per 1000 ft^2 (1–2 kg per 100 m^2) per year, and irrigation intensities that are generally less than those required by many other warm-season turfgrasses. Because of its thatching tendency and associated puffiness, especially during the summer months, seashore paspalum requires frequent vertical mowing and topdressing. ■

▶ CASE STUDY 2.22

Scenario: The fairways at the Royal Hong Kong Golf Course are entirely composed of a stoloniferous, coarse-textured, bright green grass. Close examination of this grass revealed that the vernation is folded, the ligule is a fringe of hairs (1 mm long) fused at the base, there are no auricles, the collar is narrow and continuous, and the leaf blades are 4 to 8 mm wide, with short hairs at the margins near the tip. The native soil is fine-textured and fertile. What is this turfgrass species, and what are its cultural requirements?

Analysis: The climate of Hong Kong is warm subtropical-humid, with annual rainfall averaging 87.3 in. (221.7 cm), most of which (85%) falls in the summer half of the year. Therefore, any turfgrass that performs well at this location must be tolerant of hot weather and persistently wet soils.

Solution: The particular turfgrass described is tropical carpetgrass (*Axonopus compressus* [Swartz.] Beauv.). It is similar to common carpetgrass (*A. affinis* Chase) in appearance and environmental adaptation but is less cold hardy. It should be mowed at 1 to 2 in. (2.5–5.0 cm), fertilized at 1 to 2 lb N per 1000 ft² (0.5–1.0 kg N per 100 m²) per year, and irrigated as needed during dry seasons. ■

▶ CASE STUDY 2.23

Scenario: On a golf course in Johannesburg, South Africa, the fairways are composed entirely of a medium-textured light green grass with tough stolons and rhizomes. Close examination of this grass revealed that the vernation is folded, the ligule is a fringe of hairs (2 mm long), there are no auricles, the collar is broad and continuous, and the leaf blades are flat, keeled, and sparsely hairy on both surfaces. What is this turfgrass species, and what are its cultural requirements?

Analysis: The climates of South Africa range from cool subtropical-humid (Cfb) in the north, to warm subtropical-humid (Cfa) to the southeast, to cool subtropical-dry summer (Csb) in the southwest. As Johannesburg is in the north and at an elevation of 5750 ft (1753 m), it has a cool subtropical-humid climate, with an annual average temperature of 61.3°F (16.3°C) and 33.3 in. (84.6 cm) of rainfall. Under these mild conditions, with warm winters and cool summers, many cool-season and some warm-season turfgrasses thrive.

Solution: The particular turfgrass described is kikuyugrass (*Pennisetum clandestinum* Hochst ex Chiov.). It is adapted to moist, medium-textured soils of high fertility. It is well adapted to high elevations in the moist tropics; however, in the warm, damp tropical lowlands, it becomes severely diseased and does not persist. While active growth occurs between 60°F (15.5°C) and 90°F (32°C), it retains more color and maintains more growth below this range than most other warm-season turfgrasses. It requires a moderate intensity of culture, including mowing at 0.5 to 2.0 in. (1.3 to 5.0 cm), fertilization with 1 to 3 lb N per 1000 ft^2 (0.5–1.5 kg N per 100 m^2) per year, irrigation to maintain growth and color, and intensive hollow-tine cultivation, including reincorporation of soil cores, to control thatch and scalping tendency. Also, Primo Maxx (trinexapac-ethyl) could be applied every 3 weeks during periods of active growth to reduce the mowing requirement. ■

SUMMARY OF TURFGRASS PROBLEMS

Fescues (*Festuca* L.)

The fescues are cool-season grasses that include both fine-textured and coarse-textured subgeneric groups. The fine fescues include members of two complexes: red fescue and sheep fescue. The red fescue complex includes strong creeping red fescue (*Festuca rubra* L. ssp. *rubra* Gaud.), slender creeping red fescue (*Festuca rubra* L. ssp. *litoralis* [Meyer] Auquier), and chewings fescue (*F. rubra* L. ssp. *comutata* [Thuill.] Nyman). The sheep fescue complex includes hard fescue

(*F. trachyphylla* [Hackel] Krajina) and sheep fescue (*F. ovina* L. ssp. *hirtula* [Hackel ex Travis] Wilkinson). Fine fescues appear needle-like when subjected to drought stress due to the folding of their narrow leaves. They typically exhibit good drought and shade tolerance, as well as an intolerance of wet, fertile soil conditions.

- Hard fescue is a noncreeping bunch-type hexaploid grass that forms turfs of high shoot density. It is heat tolerant but relatively intolerant of traffic because of its elevated crowns. While good resistance to several diseases has been achieved with this species, including dollar spot, leaf spot, and red thread, hard fescue is highly susceptible to summer patch disease.
- Strong creeping red fescue, an octaploid species, develops long rhizomes, forming a relatively open turf; thus, it works well in mixtures with Kentucky bluegrass (*Poa pratensis* L.) and other turfgrass species. It is heat and traffic tolerant. Good resistance to summer patch and dollar spot diseases, and moderate resistance to red thread, have been achieved with this species.
- Slender creeping red fescue, a hexaploid species, develops short, slender rhizomes, forming a turf of intermediate shoot density. It is traffic tolerant but relatively intolerant of heat stress. It has also exhibited good salinity tolerance. This species is susceptible to summer patch disease.
- Chewings fescue is a noncreeping bunch-type hexaploid grass that forms turfs of high shoot density. It is heat and traffic tolerant and exhibits excellent recuperative capacity. Depending upon the cultivar, resistance to summer patch disease may be obtainable with this species.

The coarse fescues include tall fescue (*F. arundinaceae* Schreb.) and meadow fescue (*F. elatior* L.). These have been regarded as relatively coarse-textured, bunch-type grasses; however, with the development of improved turf-type, intermediate-type and dwarf-type cultivars of tall fescue, this species has undergone some dramatic changes in texture and density.

- Tall fescue, a hexaploid species, is the predominant lawn grass in many warm-temperate and cool-subtropical climates (collectively referred to as the *transition zone* in the United States) because of its excellent heat and drought tolerance but relatively poor cold tolerance. It is also widely used for utility turfs along roadsides and airport runways.
- Meadow fescue, a diploid species, is similar to tall fescue in appearance and environmental adaptation; however, it is less persistent under heat or drought stresses but may be somewhat more tolerant of cold stress.

The insect and drought tolerance of fescue species are enhanced with the inclusion of the *Neotyphodium coenophialum* endophyte.

Bluegrasses (*Poa* L.)

The bluegrasses are cool-season grasses that include several important turfgrass species: Kentucky bluegrass (*Poa pratensis* L.), Texas bluegrass (*P. arachnifera* Torr.), rough bluegrass (*P. trivialis* L.), Canada bluegrass (*P. compressa* L.), supina bluegrass (*P. supina* Schard.), and annual bluegrass (*P. annua* L.).

- Kentucky bluegrass is a highly variable, rhizomatous polyploid species with cultivars that differ widely in color, texture, density, close-mowing tolerance, disease resistance, and other characteristics. While some cultivars are advertised as being relatively shade tolerant, this species does not generally persist in the shade; it is often mixed with one of the fine fescues—especially strong creeping red fescue (*Festuca rubra* L. ssp. *rubra* Gaud.)—to extend the range of adaptation of the turfgrass community to moderately shaded environments. It is widely used for lawns and sports fields, often in mixtures with other turfgrasses.
- Texas bluegrass is a perennial octaploid species with long, slender rhizomes. Interspecific hybridization with Kentucky bluegrass has yielded offspring that have exhibited greater heat and drought tolerance than their Kentucky bluegrass

parent; thus, it may serve as an alternative to tall fescue for lawns and utility turfs in warm-temperate and cool-subtropical climates.

- Rough bluegrass is a fine-textured, stoloniferous diploid species adapted to moist, shaded environments with fertile, fine-textured soils. It is also used for overseeding bermudagrasses (*Cynodon* spp.) and other warm-season turfgrasses to form temporary winter turfs.

- Canada bluegrass is a weakly rhizomatous grass that forms an open, stemmy turf of low quality. It is best adapted for use as a utility turf in cool-temperate and subarctic climates.

- Supina bluegrass is an aggressive stoloniferous diploid species adapted to cool-temperate climates. Its shade and wear tolerance have accounted for its growing popularity in Northern Europe for use in establishing sports fields; however, its poor heat and drought tolerance have limited its use elsewhere.

- Annual bluegrass is a tetraploid species and a widely occurring winter-annual weed in intensively cultured turfs in subarctic, temperate, and subtropical climates throughout the world; however, highly evolved perennial biotypes of annual bluegrass (*Poa annua* L. f. *reptans* [Hauskins] T. Koyama) form some of the finest golf greens in the world. The relatively poor heat, drought, cold, disease, and insect tolerance of annual bluegrass necessitates careful irrigation throughout the summer, winter protection where ice formation is likely to occur, and effective pest management throughout the year to sustain it. Seed heads emerging from annual bluegrass turfs disrupt putting on greens and reduce the quality of fairway shots. Selected plant-growth regulators, including mefluidide (Embark) and ethephon (Proxy), can be used to inhibit seed head emergence, making this feature of annual bluegrass less objectionable.

Ryegrasses (*Lolium* L.)

The ryegrasses are cool-season grasses that include two diploid species: perennial (English) ryegrass (*Lolium perenne* L.) and annual (Italian) ryegrass (*L. multiflorum* Lam.), as well as intermediate ryegrass

(*L.* ×*hybridum* Hausskn.), which is an interspecific hybrid derived from crossing perennial and annual ryegrasses. Initially, these were used primarily as nursegrasses in seed mixtures because of their rapid establishment and vigorous seedling growth; however, with the development of improved turf types of perennial ryegrass, their role has evolved and expanded dramatically. While all of these species are not especially tolerant of heat, cold, and drought stresses, they do vary considerably in these and other characteristics.

- Where annual ryegrass is used as a nursegrass, it is often so aggressive in its germination and seedling growth that it may threaten the establishment of other turfgrasses in the seed mixture.
- Since many turf-type perennial ryegrasses are less aggressive than annual ryegrass and more aesthetically acceptable as permanent components of a turfgrass community, they have largely replaced annual ryegrass in seed mixtures. When used for overseeding bermudagrasses (*Cynodon* spp.) and other warm-season turfgrasses for establishing temporary winter turfs, however, they may persist longer than desired, threatening the transition back to bermudagrass as temperatures increase in spring.
- The intermediate ryegrasses were developed to combine the superior turf quality of perennial ryegrass with the quick spring transition characteristics of annual ryegrass.

Bentgrasses (*Agrostis* L.)

The bentgrasses are cool-season grasses that include several species used as turfgrasses: creeping bentgrass (*Agrostis stolonifera* L.), colonial bentgrass (*A. capillaris* L.), dryland bentgrass (*A. castellana* Boiss, and Reut.), velvet bentgrass (*A. canina* L.), Idaho bentgrass (*A. idahoensis* Nash), and redtop (*A. gigantea* Roth.). With the exception of Idaho bentgrass and redtop, the bentgrasses have been used extensively for greens and other intensively cultured turfs.

- Creeping bentgrass is a fine-textured tetraploid species with a strongly stoloniferous growth habit. As it is adapted to subarctic, temperate, and cool-subtropical climates, it is the most widely used cool-season turfgrass for golf greens. It has good heat and cold tolerance. Because of its high disease susceptibility, fungicides may be required to sustain healthy growth of this species.

- Colonial bentgrass is a fine-textured tetraploid species with a bunch-type to weakly rhizomatous growth habit. Its relatively poor heat and drought tolerance has limited its use primarily to locations with temperate-oceanic climates. It is especially susceptible to brown patch disease.
- Dryland bentgrass is a hexaploid species but similar in appearance to colonial bentgrass; however, it has better drought tolerance.
- Idaho bentgrass, a tetraploid species, is similar in appearance to colonial and dryland bentgrasses, but it is coarser-textured and lacks rhizomes. It is best adapted for use in lawns and fairways sustained at relatively low intensities of culture.
- Velvet bentgrass is a very fine-textured diploid species with a weakly stoloniferous growth habit. It has good heat and cold tolerance. Compared with other bentgrasses, velvet bentgrass is more tolerant of shade, drought, and soil acidity. Because of its aggressive thatch-forming properties, it should be top-dressed frequently, but severe cultivations should be avoided because of its slow recuperative growth.
- Redtop is a coarse-textured hexaploid species with a rhizomatous growth habit. It was used extensively as a nursegrass in seed mixtures; however, because of its highly competitive seedling growth, its unsightly appearance, and its persistence in new turfs, its use as a nursegrass should be discouraged.

Bermudagrass (*Cynodon* [L.] Rich)

The bermudagrasses are warm-season grasses that include two turfgrass species: bermudagrass (*Cynodon dactylon* [L.] Pers. var. *dactylon*) and African bermudagrass (*C. transvaalensis* Burtt-Davy), as well as hybrid bermudagrass (*C. dactylon* [L.] Pers. var. *dactylon* × *C. transvaalensis* Burt-Davy), which is a man-made interspecific hybrid between bermudagrass and African bermudagrass. Magennis bermudagrass (*C. ×magennisii* Holcombe) is actually a natural hybrid between bermudagrass and African bermudagrass. None of the bermudagrasses is very shade tolerant; thus, other warm-season or cool-season grasses must be used on sites where trees and other obstructions restrict sunlight penetration.

- Bermudagrass, often referred to as *common* or *common-type* bermudagrass, is a species with considerable variation in morphological features and environmental adaptation. It is a tetraploid whose leaf texture ranges from medium to very fine, and its growth habit is both rhizomatous and stoloniferous. There are three recognized races within this species: a *tropical* race that is short in stature and forms a loose turf, a *temperate* race that is similar in appearance to the tropical race but is more winter hardy and forms a denser turf, and a *seleucidus* race that is very cold tolerant and forms a very coarse-textured turf with thick stolons and rhizomes. It is used for lawns and sports fields and along roadsides.
- African bermudagrass is a very fine-textured diploid with soft leaves and thread-like stolons. While rarely used as a turfgrass, it is one of the parents of hybrid bermudagrass.
- Hybrid bermudagrass is a sterile triploid that must be propagated vegetatively. Its cultivars vary widely in cold tolerance. Some cultivars are used for establishing greens, while others are used for other golf turfs, sports fields, and lawns.

Zoysiagrass (*Zoysia* Willd.)

The zoysiagrasses are warm-season grasses that include three primary turfgrass species: Japanese lawngrass (*Zoysia japonica* Steud.), manilagrass (*Z. matrella* [L.] Merr.), and mascarenegrass (*Z. pacifica* [Gaud.] Hotta & Kuroti). The species, all tetraploids, are differentiated in terms of aggressiveness, leaf texture, and cold hardiness. While most are propagated vegetatively, some seeded cultivars of *Z. japonica* are commercially available.

- Japanese lawngrass is a medium-textured grass that spreads by stolons and rhizomes. It is used in temperate, subtropical,

and tropical climates. Because of its outstanding cold tolerance, it will persist in subarctic climates, but its growing season there is very short. Because of its slow growth rate, it is
slow to establish. It is popularly used as a fairway and lawn
grass in warm-temperate and cool-subtropical climates.

- Manilagrass is intermediate in texture and cold tolerance
  between the other two *Zoysia* species. It is suitable for use in
  warm subtropical and tropical climates.
- Mascarenegrass is a fine-textured, very slow-growing species.
  Where it occurs, principally in tropical climates, it is usually
  maintained as an unmowed ground cover. It is the least cold
  tolerant of the three *Zoysia* species.

Buffalograss (*Buchloë dactyloides* [Nutt.] Engelm.)

Buffalograss is a fine-textured warm-season grass that is found as
diploid, tetraploid, and hexaploid clones. It is also dioecious, as male
and female floral parts occur on separate plants. Because of its excellent hardiness to drought and temperature extremes, buffalograss
is especially well adapted for use in unirrigated turfs in semiarid
climates.

(*Paspalum* L.)

The paspalums are warm-season grasses that include two primary
turfgrass species: Bahiagrass (*Paspalum notatum* Flugge) and seashore
paspalum (*P. vaginatum* Swartz.). Both are adapted to tropical and
warm subtropical climates.

- Bahiagrass is a coarse-textured rhimomatous species that
  forms a relatively open turf with erect leaves and low shoot
  density. Bahiagrass includes two subspecific types: *P. notatum*
  L. var. *saurae* Parodi, a small-seeded, sexually reproducing
  diploid, and *P. notatum* L. var. *latiflorum* Doell, a large-seeded,
  apomictically reproducing tetraploid. Bahiagrass is used for
  utility turfs and for low-maintenance lawns.
- Seashore paspalum is a fine-textured diploid species that forms
  turfs of very high shoot density. Both stolons and rhizomes
  may be present. Its outstanding feature is its very high soil salt

tolerance. It is used for greens and other golf turfs, as well as for lawns.

Carpetgrass (*Axonopus* Beauv.)

The carpetgrasses are warm-season grasses that include two turf-grass species: common carpetgrass (*Axonopus affinis* Chase) and tropical carpetgrass (*A. compressus* [Swartz.] Beauv.). Both are adapted to tropical and warm subtropical humid climates.

- Common carpetgrass is a coarse-textured octoploid species that spreads by stolons and seed. It is used as a utility turf and for some lawns.
- Tropical carpetgrass is a coarse-textured tetraploid that is used for fairways and lawns in areas of high rainfall.

Kikuyugrass (*Pennisetum clandestinum* Hochst ex Chiov.)

Kikuyugrass is a medium-textured warm-season tetraploid species that spreads by vigorous rhizomes and stolons. It is well adapted to the high-altitude tropical and subtropical dry-summer climates. It is widely used for golf course tees and fairways and for lawns.

St. Augustinegrass (*Stenotaphrum secundatum* [Walt.] Kuntze.)

St. Augustinegrass is a highly variable medium- to coarse-textured warm-season grass. It is a diploid (or polyploid) grass that spreads by branching stolons, forming a spongy canopy. It is well adapted to tropical and warm subtropical climates, but the more cold-tolerant types can be used in some cool-temperate climates as well. It is mostly used for lawns.

Centipedegrass (*Eremochloa ophiuroides* [Munro] Hack.)

Centipedegrass is a medium-textured warm-season diploid grass. It is adapted to tropical and warm-subtropical climates. Because of its slow growth and minimal cultural requirements, it is used for some minimum-maintenance lawns and utility turfs.

CHAPTER

3

Environmental Problems

A turfgrass community exists in intimate association with its environment. All components of this environment influence turfgrass growth and, ultimately, turf quality. The turfgrass environment is made up of three distinct but interacting components: the atmosphere above and adjacent to the above-ground portion of the turfgrass community; the edaphic (thatch-soil) environment below and adjacent to the below-ground portion of the turfgrass community; and the biotic environment, which is the entire community of above- and below-ground organisms, including people, that have a significant direct or indirect association with the turfgrass community. Since weeds, disease-inciting organisms, insects, and large-animal pests are covered in Chapter 5 (Pest and Pesticide Problems), the organisms covered in this chapter will be confined to people and the influence of various aspects of traffic on turf quality.

ATMOSPHERIC ENVIRONMENT

▶ CASE STUDY 3.1

Scenario: On a new golf course, two of the creeping bentgrass greens began to thin and die in July and August. The distinguishing feature of these greens was that they were severely shaded during the morning hours but received full sunlight for the rest of the day (Figure 3.1). Is there anything that can be done to improve the health of these greens?

Analysis: Tree shade has both qualitative and quantitative effects on turfgrass growth and development. The qualitative effects are due to selective absorption of red light resulting in a reduction in the ratio of red to far-red light and, as a consequence, the conversion of a pigment in plant cells called *phytochrome* (P) from the active to the inactive form. As active phytochrome absorbs far-red light, it is represented by the symbol P_{fr}, while inactive phytochrome, represented by P_r, absorbs red light. P_{fr} inhibits leaf and stem elongation, resulting in smaller plants, and promotes tillering, increasing shoot density. P_r promotes leaf and stem elongation, resulting in larger plants; it also inhibits tillering, reducing shoot density. Therefore, shaded turfgrasses tend to form more delicate, less stress-tolerant turfs with long, upright leaves and

Figure 3.1 Green severely shaded during morning hours but receiving full sunlight for the rest of the day.

low shoot density, while turfgrasses growing in full sun tend to form dense stands of relatively small plants.

   The quantitative effects of shading on turfgrass growth and development are due to the reduction in photosynthetically active radiation (PAR), which is the portion of visible sunlight containing the photosynthetically active wavelengths of red and blue light. Sufficient PAR is needed by plants to support healthy growth by driving photosynthetic activity (Figure 3.2). As PAR increases above 0, a threshold is eventually reached at which the amount of atmospheric carbon dioxide (CO_2) fixed through photosynthesis exactly equals the amount released through respiration. At this threshold, net photosynthesis—total photosynthesis minus total respiration—is 0, and PAR is said to be at the *light compensation point.* This level of photosynthetic activity in not sufficient to sustain plants, however, as photosynthesis ceases during the evening hours, when there is no sunlight, while respiration continues. At the very least, a level of net photosynthetic activity would be needed to "get through the night" by producing and storing a quantity of photoassimilates sufficient to cover nighttime respiration. Actually, considerably more net photosynthetic activity is needed to sustain healthy turfgrass plants. For example, additional photoassimilates are required to provide the carbon building blocks for plant growth, along with the energy to support

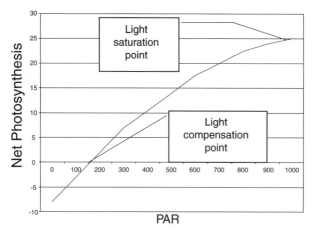

Figure 3.2   The relationship between net photosynthesis in plants and the intensity of photosynthetically active radiation (PAR).

it. In established turfgrass communities, sufficient growth is necessary to compensate for losses due to natural senescence, as well as disease, traffic-induced injury, and other causes. Furthermore, when establishing new turfs, considerably more growth is needed to provide complete ground cover and a sustainable plant population density. Over a fairly broad range, there is a more or less linear relationship between PAR and net photosynthesis. Above this range, however, increasing PAR results in progressively smaller increases in net photosynthesis until a point is reached at which net photosynthesis levels off, despite further increases in PAR. This is called the *light saturation point*. As shaded turfs may be at substantially less than the light saturation point, net photosynthetic activity may be less than that needed to sustain sufficient turfgrass growth and, thus, acceptable turf quality.

The relationship between turfgrass growth and turf quality is critical. A turfgrass plant is dynamic, in that older leaves naturally senesce and are replaced by new leaves, thus maintaining a constant number of leaves per shoot. The same is true for roots and stems. The longevity of leaves varies with the intensity of culture; in greens, it is about 2 to 3 weeks under favorable growing conditions and less in plants under stress. The longevity of individual shoots is usually measured in months; that of their associated roots would be the same or less, depending on the favorability of the soil environment. Therefore, there must be a level of turfgrass growth sufficient to offset losses from natural senescence, as well as disease, damage from insects and other pests, and traffic; otherwise, turf quality will inevitably decline.

Larger trees impose greater restrictions on the amount of sunlight, including the PAR reaching the underlying turfgrass community. PAR is the red and blue wavelengths within the visible light spectrum that energize the photosynthetic process by which plants fix atmospheric CO_2, initially forming phosphoglyceric acid (PGA), then phosphoglyceraldehyde (PGAL), and finally the hexose sugars (glucose, fructose) from which all of the complex molecules comprising the turfgrass plant—structural carbohydrates, lipids, proteins, and nucleic acids—are made. Given the inverse relationship between shade and PAR, as trees become larger turfgrass growth declines, eventually reaching the point at which growth is insufficient to sustain acceptable turf quality.

The timing of tree shading can significantly affect turfgrass health. With full morning sun, the stomata of nonstressed turfgrass plants open widely to allow for rapid absorption of atmospheric CO_2 and release of oxygen (O_2), signaling vigorous photosynthetic activity. As the day progresses, the plants may be under increasing stress during the summer months as temperatures, transpirational water loss, and photorespiration increase, causing concurrent reductions in net photosynthetic activity. If these greens were subjected to afternoon shade from trees situated on the south and west sides, temperature, transpiration, and photorespiration would likely be reduced, while net photosynthesis might increase or decrease, depending on shade intensity. With light shading, net photosynthesis might actually increase and the overall effect could be beneficial, as there would be some relief from atmospheric stress. As shade intensity increased, however, the effect would be increasingly detrimental due to proportionate reductions in PAR and the conversion of phytochrome from the active (P_{fr}) to the inactive (P_r) form.

If the trees were located on the east side of the greens, causing the shading to occur in the morning instead of the afternoon, a very different situation would exist. In the morning hours, the stomata would not be fully open and photosynthetic activity would be constrained by the lack of sufficient light. As the day progressed and sunlight intensity increased, along with temperature, transpiration, and photorespiration, atmospheric stress during the summer months would increase as well, also constraining net photosynthetic activity. Depending on shade intensity, the overall effect would range from suboptimal to disastrous. Furthermore, as the trees grew and became larger, the associated shading would increase proportionately, so that the morning shade problem would become progressively worse over time.

Solution: As the quality of the greens receiving morning shade suffers in direct proportion to shade intensity, the severity of this problem can be lessened by effective measures directed at providing more sunlight. This usually involves removing some of the trees and pruning some or all of the remaining trees. As trees may compete with turfgrasses for water and nutrients—as well as light—some root pruning should also be included. An experienced superintendent knows that the prospect of removing large, stately trees from a golf course, regardless of the justification, is likely to be met with at least some opposition. Therefore, in addition to obtaining the approval of a Green Committee or Board of Directors for a tree-removal program, one should also seek broad support from the membership to avoid serious repercussions afterward. ■

▶ CASE STUDY 3.2

Scenario: At a golf course near Houston, Texas, the quality of one of the tees was extremely poor. This was directly attributed to the shade caused by the surrounding trees. As a consequence, overseeded species persisted much longer into the summer, resulting in severe competition with the bermudagrass (*Cynodon dactylon* [L.] Pers. var. *dactylon* × C. *transvaalensis* Burtt-Davy). As temperatures increased, the overseeded species eventually declined, leaving a sparse bermudagrass population and requiring resodding every summer.

Analysis: Depending on shade intensity, differences in the adaptation of various turfgrasses to reduced-light environments may be expressed through their comparative persistence. As bermudagrasses are very shade intolerant, any problems encountered in the transition from temporary winter turfs composed of overseeded cool-season species to bermudagrass in spring are exacerbated by shade. Also, as trees become larger and shade intensity increases, the persistence and competitive ability of bermudagrass decline even further.

Solution: There are three choices: reduce shade intensity through a program of tree removal and pruning, switch to more shade-tolerant turfgrasses, or move the tee to an unshaded location. Selected zoysiagrasses (*Zoysia* spp.) are sometimes used in place of bermudagrass because of their similar appearance and superior shade tolerance. Given the relatively slow growth and recuperative capacity of zoysiagrass, this may or may not be a satisfactory solution, depending on the size of the tee, the amount of play to which it is subjected, and the shading level imposed by the trees. If zoysiagrass were substituted for bermudagrass under moderate to severe shading, some reduction in shade intensity would still be needed to ensure that sufficient light was available to sustain healthy growth of the zoysiagrass. ■

▶ CASE STUDY 3.3

Scenario: Portions of several greens composed of creeping bent-grass (*Agrostis stolonifera* L.) and annual bluegrass (*Poa annua* L.) on a golf course in central Illinois typically exhibit wilting symptoms and subsequent thinning of the turf during the summer months. These affected areas occur almost entirely on slopes that generally face south. Can anything be done to eliminate this problem?

Analysis: Compared with level sites, less water is likely to infiltrate turf on sloping sites due to the force of gravity pulling water downslope as runoff. The runoff potential is directly related to the precipitation rate and inversely related to the infiltration capacity of the turf. Thus, heavy rains on slowly permeable sites typically result in substantial amounts of runoff. As a consequence, water is likely to be deficient on sloping sites, while oxygen deficiencies may limit turfgrass growth at downslope locations where water accumulates. Under high summer temperatures, rapid transpiration rates can quickly deplete soil water, especially on sloping sites where less water is available. If the slope also faces south, it receives direct sunlight, increasing the moisture stress even more.

Solution: Since intensively cultured turfs on sloping sites—especially slopes facing south—are more likely to show moisture stress than those on level sites, they should receive additional attention to ensure that their cultural requirements are adequately addressed. This may include attempts to increase infiltration capacity and soil water storage, such as intensive core cultivation and the use of wetting agents. Carefully hand-watering these sites can improve soil water storage, reducing the likelihood of water deficiencies during periods of high-temperature stress. To the extent that water deficiencies do occur, selective syringing can increase turfgrass survival and maintain turf quality. ■

▶ CASE STUDY 3.4

Scenario: Substantial amounts of annual bluegrass (*Poa annua* L.) are lost each year from ice that forms in the depressions where water accumulates, especially on greens that are shaded from adjacent trees. What can be done to eliminate this recurring problem?

Analysis: Most ice damage to greens is believed to occur from the formation and growth of ice crystals within the crowns, where alternate freezing and thawing cycles lead to increased crown hydration levels. This is especially likely on sites where surface water accumulates due to poor surface drainage (Plate 2; see color insert). The potential for ice damage varies with the species: annual bluegrass (*Poa annua* L.) is more susceptible than creeping bentgrass (*Agrostis stolonifera* L). It is more likely to occur on shaded sites; this has been attributed to lower levels of nonstructural carbohydrates in shade plants, the effects of reduced irradiance on plant hardiness, and more prolonged coverage of snow and ice in the shade. Also, annual bluegrass greens subjected to alternating freezing and thawing conditions may lose proteins associated with cold tolerance and die when freezing temperatures return.

Solution: Surface drainage should be improved to reduce the likelihood that ice will develop and persist on greens. Shade should be reduced to increase the production and storage of nonstructural carbohydrates and enhance cold tolerance. During the early fall period when plants are going through a hardening-off process in preparation for winter, fertilization with soluble nitrogen should be avoided, as this can substantially reduce cold hardiness. Greens that are highly susceptible to ice damage should be covered by porous fabrics, which in turn are covered first by straw and then by nonporous fabrics, to minimize temperature fluctuations, provide insulation, and reduce water and ice accumulation on the green. Excelsior mats have also been shown to prevent or reduce ice damage. ■

▶ CASE STUDY 3.5

Scenario: On a golf course in Green Bay, Wisconsin, 4 to 6 in. (10–15 cm) of clear ice completely covered several greens in early December (Figure 3.3). The ice sheet remained intact for over 50 days due to heavy snow cover and cold temperatures. These greens had a

Figure 3.3   Green with snow removed to reveal ice accumulation.

history of winterkill to annual bluegrass when the ice cover persisted for extended periods, despite the use of breathable geotextile turf covers. What could be done to reduce the potential for ice damage to these greens?

Analysis: Damage from extended ice cover is still a mystery. It may reflect low-oxygen (hypoxia) and oxygen-depleted (anoxia) conditions or the accumulation of toxic gases (e.g., CO_2, ethanol) under the ice. Alternatively, it may be due to the death of crowns from the formation and growth of ice crystals, despite the presence of insulating covers.

Solution: Snow should be removed with a rotary bristle sweeper. The exposed underlying ice should then be broken up using a solid-tine cultivator; this can be done in ½-in. (1.25-cm) increments, with the shattered ice removed with the rotary bristle sweeper, until all layers have been removed. This technique is best employed in the early morning hours, when the ice is brittle and more easily shattered. The use of insulating covers on these greens is still beneficial since the ice is prevented from adhering to the turf.   ■

▶ CASE STUDY 3.6

Scenario: On a golf course in York, Pennsylvania, a major hailstorm occurred just 2 days prior to a USGA-sponsored tournament, resulting in significant damage to the greens. Close examination of the turf revealed numerous depressions resembling ball marks on virtually all of the greens. As this would dramatically influence the putting quality of the greens, what measures might be taken to restore these greens to a playable condition?

Analysis: Depressions in a green created by hail are essentially indistinguishable from ball marks, except that they are usually far more numerous; thus, implementing a program for repairing them in a short period of time is a logistical challenge requiring many personnel.

Solution: Local community members can be recruited by announcements made on local TV and radio stations and quickly trained, equipped, and supervised to lift the depressions with ball mark–repair tools. ■

▶ CASE STUDY 3.7

Scenario: A creeping bentgrass green surrounded by high hills and a dense planting of trees has limited air movement. Despite the use of two fans, the turf is of poor quality and routinely suffers from brown patch and other diseases. What can be done to improve the conditions for and the quality of this green?

Analysis: Dense plantings of trees and shrubs in close proximity to a green can restrict air movement across its surface, resulting in a microclimate that can be substantially warmer and more humid than that of other, more open sites. As a turf is warmed by solar radiation, it subsequently radiates energy, warming the air immediately around and above the shoots. Simultaneously, the humidity of this air also increases with the release of water vapor from the leaves through a process called *transpiration*. The water vapor comes from soil water that was absorbed through the roots, translocated through the plant's vascular system up to the leaves, and diffused from veins, coating the mesophyll cells inside the leaves with films of moisture. The evaporation of this water is an endothermic reaction that cools the plant during warm weather, enabling it to maintain itself at physiological temperatures. Normally, the warm, moist air in the immediate vicinity of the turf is mixed by winds with a much larger volume of air above the turf. At sites where air movement is restricted by dense plantings or other structures, this mixing may not occur, resulting in a warmer, more humid microenvironment that, in turn, favors the development of selected diseases.

Solution: Where trees and shrubs obstruct air movement, their selective removal can substantially improve the microenvironment of the turf; however, the removal of other obstructions, such as hills and buildings, may not be feasible. Sometimes, fans can be effective in promoting sufficient air movement, but not always. An alternative or supplementary method is the installation of an air-injection system, which forces air into the green through the drainage pipes. This system has been shown to reduce soil temperatures up to 5°F (2.8°C). Further reductions are possible by refrigerating the air before injection. ■

SOIL ENVIRONMENT

► CASE STUDY 3.8

Scenario: Because of poor internal drainage, a green in southeastern Michigan frequently allowed puddles to form during rainfall events (Figure 3.4) and experienced numerous problems, including crown rotting anthracnose disease in summer and ice damage in winter. Resources are not available for reconstructing the green. Also, because green fees are necessary to cover operating expenses, the course cannot be closed down while corrective measures are implemented. What can be done to address this problem?

Analysis: Oxygen deficiencies associated with poorly drained soils reduce the health and vigor of turfgrass plants growing in those soils

Figure 3.4 Poorly drained green with standing water in depressions.

and increase their susceptibility to various diseases, including crown rotting anthracnose. Poor drainage is also associated with high hydration levels of turfgrass crowns, increasing their susceptibility to ice damage in winter. Improving internal drainage can reduce the incidence or severity of these problems. Effective measures for improving surface drainage would reduce the amount of water that must be moved through the soil profile and thus partially alleviate an internal drainage problem. Most "quick-and-dirty" solutions to drainage problems are directed at improving surface drainage.

Solution: Strips of sod measuring 3 in. (7.5 cm) in width should be removed every 6 ft (1.8 m) across the green. The underlying soil is then removed to a depth of 1 ft (30 cm) using a trenching machine. Drain pipes are placed in the trenches and connected to another drain pipe installed in a similar fashion around the perimeter of the green; an additional drain pipe is installed to connect the perimeter pipe to the existing drainage system. The trenches should be backfilled with sand or amended sand and the sod replaced. Strips of turf immediately above the drain pipes may exhibit wilting symptoms before the rest of the green in summer due to reduced water retention by the sand; however, this is a small price to pay for the benefits obtained and will be less obvious after a few years. ■

▶ CASE STUDY 3.9

Scenario: At a golf course in Sun City, South Africa, greens were constructed in accordance with USGA specifications and seeded to Penncross creeping bentgrass (*Agrostis stolonifera* L. 'Penncross'). While drainage seemed adequate initially, it eventually declined to an unacceptable level. The decision was made to switch to coarser-textured sand for topdressing to improve soil aeration and drainage. With the accumulation of a ½-in. (1.3-cm) layer from the new topdressing sand, internal drainage declined even more. An examination of a plug extracted from one of the greens revealed the presence of black layer near the surface of the finer-textured construction sand (Plate 3; see color insert). How could this problem develop in greens constructed in accordance with USGA specifications, and what can be done to improve drainage?

Analysis: Sometimes the sand delivered to a site is not the same as the sand contained in the sample submitted to a lab for initial testing; consequently, the green may not perform as expected. If the sand actually delivered in bulk to the site contained too many fines, internal drainage will be adversely affected. Initially, this may not be very obvious; with extensive root growth and the accumulation of organic residues in the sand from senescing tissues, however, infiltration and subsequent percolation of water will eventually decline to the point at which drainage becomes a concern. Often, when problems of this nature occur, superintendents will select coarser-textured sand for topdressing in an attempt to improve infiltration. Where a layer of coarser-textured sand is positioned on top of poorly drained, finer-textured sand (Figure 3.5a), a temporary water table develops, leading to the development of black layer (Figure 3.5b). This is a jam-like accumulation of metal sulfides that clog soil pores, exacerbating the drainage problem.

Solution: There are two possible solutions. The first is reconstruction. If this solution is chosen, provisions must be made to ensure that the sand delivered to the site conforms to USGA specifications. Representative samples should be taken at the plant where the sand mixture

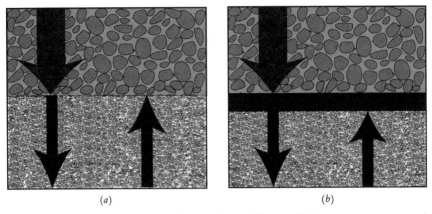

(a) (b)

Figure 3.5 Water movement in a soil profile in which a coarser-textured medium is situated on top of a finer-textured medium (a) and the subsequent formation of black layer at the interface of the two media (b).

is prepared and submitted to an independent lab for testing. With each truckload of sand delivered, additional samples should be taken by the grow-in superintendent or his representative for subsequent testing. A contract should be established with the sand supplier in which consequences are detailed whenever the sand does not conform to USGA specifications. These provisions should include statements to the effect that any truckload of sand not meeting specifications will be removed and replaced with sand that does, and these and all ancillary costs will be borne by the contractor.

The alternative solution is less expensive and is intended to salvage the existing greens. It has three objectives: achieve adequate drainage, develop a suitable medium for supporting turfgrass growth, and eliminate the black layer. The first objective—achieve adequate drainage—can be met through a "drill-and-fill" operation to create bypass drainage channels from the surface to the gravel layer. Specialized equipment with multiple drills is employed to extract sand from the green and replace it with sand conforming to USGA specifications. As the new sand columns created are more permeable than the extracted sand (including the portions with black layer), drainage will be dramatically improved. The second objective—develop a suitable medium for supporting turfgrass growth—is met incrementally through an aggressive program of topdressing with the same sand used in the drill-and-fill operation. Some of the topdressing sand can be applied in conjunction with hollow-tine cultivations for removing some of the black layer—the third objective—to accelerate the buildup of the surface sand layer. Thus, the sand blanket developed at the surface to support turfgrass growth is connected through a series of sand channels to the gravel blanket for drainage, and the original sand medium is reduced to the role of subsurface structural support. If desired, additional drill-and-fill operations can be performed to provide more drainage.   ■

▶ CASE STUDY 3.10

Scenario: Three greens were reconstructed to USGA specifications at a golf course in Richmond, Virginia. Washed sod of Penncross creeping bentgrass (*Agrostis stolonifera* L. 'Penncross') was installed on the greens in an effort to ready them for play as soon as possible. Despite the fact that washed sod was used, a layering problem developed at the sod/soil interface due to the presence of a substantial thatch layer that persisted as a distinct organic layer following sand topdressing. Because of restricted water movement, black layer soon developed near the surface, exacerbating the drainage problem. What can be done to improve this situation?

Analysis: Washed sod is used to avoid layering problems that occur where the soil brought in with sod differs texturally from the soil at the transplant site. Assuming that the washing process removed essentially all soil particles from the sod, problems can still arise if the sod is not handled properly at the transplant site. First, the potential for damage to the sod from sod heating can be minimized by storing it in a cool place or by planting the sod as soon as it is received. Second, because of the absence of soil in the sod, washed sod is highly susceptible to damage from desiccation; therefore, care must be taken to ensure that it does not dry out during and immediately after planting. Establishing new turfs with washed sod is best done during cool weather to promote rapid rooting. To prevent damage from desiccation, newly laid sod should be hand-watered in sections, and subsequent irrigations should be light and frequent until the sod is well rooted. Finally, topdressing should be initiated as soon as possible after the sod has rooted to prevent the development of excessive thatch on sites where sand is the medium supporting turfgrass growth. If the sand topdressing fails to become thoroughly incorporated into the sod, it may be necessary to employ vertical mowing operations to facilitate this process; otherwise, a subsurface organic layer can persist to impede water movement through the profile.

Solution: After a substantial thatch layer has developed, the best choice may be to remove the sod, including all thatch, and replant. Salvaging the existing turf would probably require such intensive vertical mowing, hollow-tine cultivation, and topdressing operations that replanting would be more likely to provide satisfactory turf more quickly. Nevertheless, this is the program that should be followed if, for financial reasons, the greens cannot be taken out of play.   ■

▶ CASE STUDY 3.11

Scenario: The greens at a golf course in Waco, Texas, were originally planted to Tifdwarf bermudagrass (*Cynodon dactylon* [L.] Pers. var. *dactylon* × *C. transvaalensis* Burtt-Davy 'Tifdwarf'). Because of the loss of the greens to low-temperature kill 2 years after construction, the decision was made to seed the greens to creeping bentgrass (*Agrostis stolonifera* L.) in place of the more costly sprigging operation necessary to restore bermudagrass. Although the quality of the greens was occasionally acceptable, especially during cool spring weather, it ranged from fair to very poor most of the time. Examination of the greens' profiles revealed severe layering in the top 4 in. (10 cm) from improper topdressing practices. Infiltration rates were very low, and standing water was evident on the greens and in the cups following irrigation or rainfall. The sand used in the original construction was found to be highly calcareous. Noncapillary porosity was less than 10% both in the original rootzone (likely due to a breakdown in the particle size of the soft sand) and in the layered upper rootzone accumulated from topdressing.

Analysis: There are three issues that should be addressed in this case: bermudagrass versus creeping bentgrass, improper versus proper topdressing practices, and calcareous versus silica sand. With respect to species selection, both species are susceptible to damage from temperature extremes: bermudagrass from cold stress in the winter months and bentgrass from heat stress in the summer months. While both species can be found in the Waco area, bermudagrass is the more popular of the two, reflecting the slightly higher average maximum summer temperature and the slightly lower average minimum winter temperature in Waco compared with other warm subtropical-humid locations where bentgrass use is greater. However, the capacity of both species to survive temperature stress is significantly reduced by poor soil aeration, drainage, and fertility. With respect to topdressing, one of its important purposes is to control thatch by diluting the organic residues generated by the turfgrass community within the turf profile. When the shift to sand-based media and sand topdressing occurred, it became necessary to topdress more frequently and at lighter rates to facilitate the integration of sand particles and organic residues; otherwise, alternating layers of organic matter and sand developed, impeding water and air movement within the turf profile. Finally, calcareous sands are likely to be so alkaline that the availability of many plant nutrients is below that needed to support healthy growth.

Solution: While the best solution might be to rebuild all of the greens using silica sand, perhaps a more affordable one would be to renovate the existing greens by removing the sod and replanting with either bentgrass or bermudagrass. This assumes that the underlying calcareous sand is reasonably stable—with the proper pore-size distribution—and conforms to USGA specifications. The bentgrass or bermudagrass can be propagated by seed or stolons, respectively; however, if sodded, either washed or sand-based sod should be used. If washed sod is selected, be sure to initiate topdressing as soon as possible to blend it in with the underlying sand. If sand-based sod is used, ensure that the sand on which the sod was grown is texturally similar to the sand medium on which it is planted. To ensure that nutrients are sufficiently available to support healthy turfgrass growth, a program of foliar fertilizer application should be initiated so that essential nutrients are directly absorbed by the leaves.   ■

▶ CASE STUDY 3.12

Scenario: A push-up green in eastern Pennsylvania composed of creeping bentgrass (*Agrostis stolonifera* L.) and annual bluegrass (*Poa annua* L.) typically deteriorated during the summer months. The top several inches of the soil profile consisted of alternating layers of sand and organic matter from sand topdressing laid down in conjunction with core cultivation each spring and fall. As this layer was underlain by a native soil with high percentages of silt and clay, internal drainage was poor. The surface contours of the green provided good surface drainage, but this was not sufficient to compensate for poor internal drainage. What can be done to improve the quality of this green?

Analysis: Despite the reduction in hydraulic load provided by favorable surface drainage, internal drainage can still be poor where the composition of the turf-soil profile severely restricts downward water movement. Alternating layers of sand and organic matter in the top several inches, developed in this case because of only two sand topdressings per year, can restrict water movement by creating a series of perched and temporary water tables (Figure 3.6). Water moving through a sand layer is slowed by the finer-textured organic layer, resulting in the formation of a temporary water table in the sand. Water moving into an organic layer is held so tightly by the tiny pores pervading this

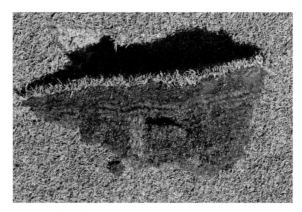

Figure 3.6   A slice of turf extracted from a green showing alternating layers of sand and organic matter from topdressing and thatch, respectively.

medium that it is restricted from moving into an underlying sand layer, resulting in the formation of a perched water table. Light topdressing with sand must be done every few weeks to ensure proper blending of sand and organic constituents and avoid the development of a layered profile. This cannot be accomplished through heavy sand topdressing performed in conjunction with hollow-tine cultivation in spring and fall, as this is a complementary practice, not an alternative. Assuming the removal of extracted soil cores, hollow-tine cultivation makes holes that can be filled with sand, creating bypass drainage channels in the top several inches of the turf profile. Partially alleviating restrictions on soil air and water movement imposed by alternating sand and organic layers is one of the many reasons for including hollow-tine cultivation in the cultural program; however, these bypass drainage channels might not have been necessary if a more frequent sand topdressing program had been followed.

As this is a push-up green, the construction soil would be finer-textured than the topdressing sand; therefore, as water reaches the interface between the sand and the construction soil, its downward movement will slow and accumulate above the interface, forming a temporary water table. Depending on the percolation rate of the construction soil, the amount of water received by the turf, and the rate at which it is applied, this water table could extend up to the surface of the green, compounding the drainage problem.

Solution: Presumably, the basis for initiating a sand topdressing program was to improve the internal drainage of this green; however, a satisfactory solution requires sufficiently rapid percolation of water both in the sand that has accumulated through successive topdressings and through the underlying soil. If alternating sand and organic layers have developed, hollow-tine cultivation, followed by removal of soil cores and backfilling the holes with sand, will be needed to create bypass drainage channels through these layers. Depending on the severity of this problem, it may be desirable to employ this practice more than twice per year. If there is a restriction to water movement imposed by the underlying construction soil due to its low permeability, it may lessen as the depth of the sand increases over time; otherwise, some additional procedures might be considered. For example, a drill-and-fill procedure might be helpful, especially if the deeper bypass drainage channels created through this procedure extend to a more permeable region in the underlying soil. If this problem persists, it may be desirable to install drain pipes, following the procedure outlined in the solution to Case Study 3.8. ■

▶ CASE STUDY 3.13

Scenario: A golf green in Beacon, New York, was reconstructed using a rootzone mix consisting of 17% gravel, 12% very coarse sand, 16% coarse sand, 21% medium sand, 5% fine sand, 4% very fine sand, 11% silt, and 14% clay. Drainage was extremely poor, and the turf was thin and poorly rooted. Changing hole locations was extremely difficult or impossible, as the constituents of the rootzone mix formed a concrete-like medium. Can anything be done to improve the condition of this green?

Analysis: This green's rootzone includes a multicomponent sand in which all of the sand particle sizes (very coarse, coarse, medium, fine, and very fine) are included in significant quantities, as well as gravel, silt, and clay. As a consequence, the large pore spaces—macropores, noncapillary pores, aeration-type pores—from which gravitational water would normally drain are mostly filled by *fines* (i.e., very fine sand, silt, and clay), dramatically reducing percolation and drainage. Additionally, the presence of gravel essentially guarantees that cup cutting will be a difficult and frustrating operation. Obviously, this green was not constructed in accordance with USGA specifications, as this mixture is entirely unsatisfactory.

Solution: The green should be reconstructed in accordance with USGA specifications.   ■

▶ CASE STUDY 3.14

Scenario: During the spring and fall, when rainfall was abundant, the tees at a golf course in central Illinois were often soft and wet. During the summer months, they became hard and dry between irrigations. As the soil on which these tees were constructed contained a high percentage of clay, they did not drain well. Turf cover was thin and recuperative capacity low. What could be done to improve the quality of these tees?

Analysis: The macroporosity of high-clay soils is highly dependent upon the soil's structure. In well-structured soils, most of the constituents are organized into aggregates composed of clay *micelles* (stable associations of clay particles held together electrostatically) intermingled with individual silt and sand particles, as well as organic matter in varying stages of decomposition. Because of the large size of the aggregates, well-structured soils have an abundance of correspondingly large pore spaces from which gravitational water quickly drains following a saturating rain or irrigation. However, as soil aggregates are rather fragile, they are easily destroyed under heavy traffic, dramatically reducing macroporosity and associated drainage. As declines in soil structure are more likely to occur when soil moisture is high, the combination of heavy traffic and abundant rainfall inevitably leads to the conditions described in this scenario.

Solution: There are two alternatives: reconstruction and renovation. Reconstruction involves the use of a sand medium that conforms to USGA specifications for composition (60% medium and coarse sands, not more than 20% fine sand, not more than 5% very fine sand, not more than 10% of a combination of very coarse sand and fine gravel, with the gravel component not exceeding 3%, and 1–5% organic matter), porosity (35–55% total porosity, including 15–30% macroporosity), and infiltration (saturated hydraulic conductivity of 6–12 in. [15–30 cm] per hour). This medium should be installed to a depth of 4 to 6 in. (10–15 cm) atop a base sloping 1% away from the cart path or entrance to the tee and with a drain line placed near the edge of the tee at the base of the sand to collect seepage water.

Renovation primarily involves intensive hollow-tine cultivation and sand topdressing. Cultivation should be conducted as often as possible with large-diameter tines, with soil cores removed. It should be followed with sand topdressing to fill the holes and provide a layer of sand across the entire surface. Additional sand topdressings should be performed as often as possible to build a sand rootzone on top of the clayey soil.

Once a shallow sand layer has developed, root growth may be largely restricted to the sand, with little rooting evident in the underlying soil. Also, temporary water tables are likely to form in the sand layer with heavy rains or irrigations. Both of these conditions may be partially alleviated by installing sand channels through which water can be transported down to more permeable soil regions. This can be accomplished through drill-and-fill operations or by deep hollow-tine cultivation followed by backfilling the holes with sand. However, as the sand layer increases in thickness with successive topdressings, these problems should gradually lessen over time. In the relatively rare instances in which they do not, it may be necessary to install drain pipes, following the procedure outlined in the solution to Case Study 3.8. ■

▶ CASE STUDY 3.15

Scenario: A golf course with fine-textured fairway soils is located in an area of the Pacific northwestern United States that averages 80 in. (200 cm) of rainfall annually. As a consequence, it must be closed many days during the golfing season because the course is too wet to play. What can be done to improve drainage?

Analysis: As explained in the analysis of the previous case, high-clay (fine-textured) soils are susceptible to dramatic declines in soil structure and drainage where they are subjected to heavy traffic when soil moisture is high. With 80 in. (200 cm) of annual rainfall, the soil is likely to be wet for long periods, guaranteeing that compaction will increase with increasing traffic intensity.

Solution: The solution is similar to that provided under "renovation" in the previous case. The fairways should be hollow-tine cultivated at least once annually with large (at least ¾-in. or 1.9-cm) tines followed by removal of the soil cores. This should be followed by a heavy application of sand to fill the holes and provide a layer of sand across the surface. In addition, two or three other applications of sand should be made during the cooler weather. This should be repeated until a cap measuring at least 5 in. (12.5 cm) thick covers the fairways; then cultivations should be continued, with the cores returned to control thatch development. ■

▶ CASE STUDY 3.16

Scenario: Three bunkers were added to a fairway located in a level portion of a golf course in upstate New York. Perforated, corrugated plastic drain pipes (4 in. [10 cm] in diameter) were installed in the base of the bunkers. Because of inadequate elevation change across the fairway, however, the bunkers did not drain well following rainfall. What can be done to improve the drainage of these bunkers?

Analysis: The function of drain pipes is to carry water from higher to lower elevations, where it can be conducted to a highly porous region within the soil profile or deposited into a storm sewer or surface water body (e.g., pond, lake, stream). Without a sufficient elevation change, however, the drain pipes cannot move the water away from the drainage site.

Solution: Under these conditions, water can be transported a short distance away through drain pipes to a catch basin. If this is not adequate to handle the hydraulic load, a septic tank for collecting the water can also be installed, along with a sump pump to push the water to a higher elevation from which it can flow into the drain pipe system.   ■

▶ CASE STUDY 3.17

Scenario: A golf course near Seattle, Washington, has a rocky soil composed of predominantly clay and silt that is poorly drained. Because the rocks made excavation difficult, few drain lines were installed at the time of construction. The golf course was originally seeded in the early 1970s with Kentucky bluegrass (*Poa pratensis* L.); however, because of poor drainage and shade from an abundance of large fir trees, the turf quickly converted to annual bluegrass (*Poa annua* L.). Despite numerous pleas from the superintendent, the membership refused to consider removing any of the trees despite the fact that they provided nearly continuous shade over much of the course. The fairways and roughs were wet most of the year and were difficult to maintain in the summer due to heavy thatch and soil. Fairways and roughs were unmowable during this time.

Analysis: Three factors are contributing to the drainage problems at this golf course: a highly compacted soil through which water moves very slowly, the lack of a drainage system for transporting water away from the turf, and a pervasive shade problem from too many trees that reduce evapotranspirational water loss from the turf and thus exacerbate the drainage problem.

Solution: Because of the slow permeability of the soils, an extensive sand topdressing program should be initiated to eventually provide a 5-in. (12.5-cm) sand cap on top of the native fairway soils. This accumulation of thatch can be controlled and progress in sand cap development accelerated if intensive vertical mowing and hollow-tine cultivation are done in conjunction with sand topdressing. A system of catch basins and drain pipes should be installed in the fairways and roughs to provide conduits through which excess water can be conducted away from the turf. Furthermore, as the membership observes the progress being made in dealing with the drainage problem, their resistance may lessen, allowing selective tree removal to allow more sunlight penetration and faster evapotranspirational water loss from the turf. Regardless of their attitude toward trees, however, they should be kept informed of what is being done to their golf course and the results obtained from these efforts. ∎

▶ CASE STUDY 3.18

Scenario: A sand-based football field in northern Illinois was planted with washed sod composed of a blend of Kentucky bluegrass (*Poa pratensis* L.) cultivars. For a variety of reasons (e.g., high summer temperatures at planting, improper handling techniques), the sod did not root. Based on the advice of a consultant, the washed sod was replaced with 3-in. (7.5-cm)-thick muck sod 3 weeks prior to the first scheduled game. The consultant explained that the weight of the sod would provide stability during the playing season and, as this was only a temporary measure, the sod should be replaced with washed sod the following spring to ensure satisfactory performance afterward. Unfortunately, the sod was not replaced, and the quality of the turf declined over the next three seasons as thatch and an array of pest problems developed. What can be done to improve the quality of this field?

Analysis: Allowing the muck sod to remain in place is an example of a temporary solution becoming a permanent problem. As the muck is a relatively fine-textured medium and the underlying sand is a relatively coarse-textured medium (Plate 4; see color insert), water moving into and through the muck layer will stop its downward movement as soon as it reaches the interface between the muck and sand, forming a perched water table (Figure 3.7). Thus, the muck will be wet and the sand dry immediately after a rain or irrigation. Furthermore, the muck will continue to retain water until it is removed by evapotranspiration. The turf is therefore subjected to alternating extremes of wetness and dryness—conditions that promote disease and weed problems and inhibit healthy turfgrass growth.

The subsequent development of thatch imposes an additional textural layer, as thatch is a relatively coarse-textured medium situated above the finer-textured muck soil. Water moves into and through the thatch layer fairly rapidly but slows when it encounters the muck, forming a temporary water table whenever the rate at which water enters the turf exceeds the percolation rate through the muck. As the thatch layer dries from the combination of water infiltration into the underlying muck and evapotranspiration of water vapor into the atmosphere, there

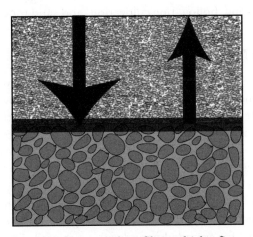

Figure 3.7   Water movement in a soil profile in which a finer-textured medium is situated on top of a coarser-textured medium and the perched water table that forms just above the interface of the two media.

is no replenishment of water from upward capillary flow. This reflects the principle that water will not move from a finer-textured medium to a coarser-textured one until and unless forced to do so by a hydraulic head of sufficient size to overcome the adhesive and cohesive forces by which water is retained in the finer-textured medium. Since no hydraulic head is operating to force water upward from one medium to the other, the thatch can remain dry regardless of the moisture content of the underlying muck soil. If turfgrass rooting is largely restricted to the thatch layer—a common occurrence—the turfgrass may exhibit wilting symptoms despite an abundance of moisture in the underlying muck soil. Therefore, the problems encountered earlier become more severe with the added complication of a thatch layer in the turf profile.

Solution: There is little likelihood that a combination of cultivation and topdressing methods will satisfactorily address the problems in this turf. Therefore, the only satisfactory solution is the removal of the sod, including all thatch and muck soil, and replanting with washed sod. This time, however, the sod should be planted under environmental conditions that favor rapid rooting into the underlying sand. Light vertical mowing and sand topdressing should begin as soon as sufficient rooting has occurred to anchor the sod to the sand medium. Any residual thatch-like layer should be eliminated through a combination of vertical mowing, hollow-tine cultivation, and sand topdressing. ■

▶ CASE STUDY 3.19

Scenario: A football field in central Pennsylvania was constructed by excavating to a depth of 24 in. (60 cm) and removing all material from the site, spreading a layer of pea gravel on top of the exposed subsoil, installing drain pipes in a herringbone pattern on top of the gravel, covering the drain pipes with additional gravel to create a 6-in. (15-cm) gravel blanket, and installing 18 in. (45 cm) of silt-loam topsoil on top of the gravel. After the field was planted to Kentucky bluegrass (*Poa pratensis* L.), it soon became apparent that a serious internal drainage problem existed. Water would stand along the sidelines, and the field would be wet for extended periods after a rainfall. To improve surface drainage, the crown was later raised 2 in. (5 cm) with the placement of additional soil under the sod, and catch basins were installed along the sidelines. Despite careful management, including completely covering the field with canvas tarps whenever possible during rainfalls, the turf gradually deteriorated, requiring sod replacement from time to time. What can be done to improve the quality of this field?

Analysis: The existence of a gravel layer at the base of the silt-loam soil virtually guarantees that internal drainage will be problematic. As water cannot move from the soil to the gravel, it accumulates within the soil, beginning at the base, forming a perched water table (Figure 3.8). Because of the fine texture and compacted condition of this soil, its water retention is so strong that a hydraulic head of sufficient size to force water across the soil–gravel interface is unlikely to develop. In fact, tests conducted at the outlets of the drain pipes emerging from the gravel layer showed that there was no water movement into or through these pipes, indicating that no water had ever moved from the soil to the gravel. While attempts to improve surface drainage had successfully reduced the hydraulic load on the surface, water that actually entered the turf could leave only through evapotranspiration. As a consequence, elaborate measures were required to limit the amount of water entering the turf, including tarping the entire field whenever rainfall appeared likely and very careful irrigation to satisfy

Figure 3.8   Photograph of a 6-in. (15-cm) gravel blanket with drain pipes just prior to the installation of an 18-in. (45-cm) layer of silt loam soil during construction of a football field in central Pennsylvania.

the moisture requirements of the turf while limiting water penetration to the rootzone.

Solution: Ideally, this field should be rebuilt to USGA specifications; a less expensive alternative would be to remove the sod and replace it with either washed or sand-based sod. If the replacement is done during the football season, thick (preferably 3 in. [7.5 cm]) sand-based Kentucky bluegrass sod should be used so that the weight of the sand will stabilize the sod under normal play. This should be followed by a series of drill-and-fill operations to provide sand channels connecting the sand blanket at the surface with the gravel blanket located 18 to 20 in. (46 to 51 cm) below the surface. The field should be top-dressed with sand as often as possible to increase the depth of the sand layer to at least 5 in. (12.5 cm), as this is the actual rootzone of the turf-grass community. ■

▶ CASE STUDY 3.20

Scenario: In a baseball field in northern New Jersey, heavily trafficked portions of the outfield typically decline during the summer, with large populations of crabgrass (*Digitaria* spp) invading the sparse stand of Kentucky bluegrass (*Poa pratensis* L.). Close examination of the affected areas reveals depressions in which water tends to accumulate and persist during and after rainfall. What can be done to improve the quality of the turf in these portions of the field?

Analysis: To ensure adequate surface drainage, the outfield of a baseball field should gradually slope from the skinned area where the bases are located to the perimeter fence where catch basin may be located to conduct the water away. Weed species, including summer annuals such as crabgrass, tend to emerge where competitive turfgrass growth has been reduced by some unfavorable factor. In this scenario, the depressions in the field collect water from rainfall and irrigation, resulting in oxygen deficiencies in the rootzone, where internal drainage is slow, and reduced root and shoot growth. Because of concentrated traffic from the outfielders at these locations, the resulting soil compaction exacerbates oxygen deficiencies, and wear reduces the turfgrass community's resistance to weed invasion.

Solution: While selected herbicides can be used to control crab-grass populations, they cannot address the underlying causes of this problem. The best solution would be to reestablish the field with the proper grading to favor surface drainage; a less expensive alternative would consist of removing the weed-infested sod from depressions, adding topsoil to bring the grade up to the proper level, and replacing the old sod with new sod from a nursery. At the same time, the entire cultural program should be reviewed and corrections made to ensure that the turf is being managed optimally. ■

▶ CASE STUDY 3.21

Scenario: The sand bunkers in front of the 15th green at a golf course in Westchester County, New York, have always been a maintenance nightmare. Their steep walls and loose sand were not only difficult to play, but required considerable labor to repair the washouts that occurred with every heavy rainfall. For some time, players and crew members alike pleaded for something to be done about these bunkers. Now the board wants a plan for reconstructing the bunkers and a time frame for completion.

Analysis: The structural stability of sand on sloping sites is influenced by the shape of the sand particles (Figure 3.9). Highly spherical, well-rounded sands are the least stable, while the most stable sands are those with the lowest sphericity and highest angularity. The movement of water into and through the sand also influences its erosion potential. Where a substantial amount of water is retained in small pore spaces between sand particles, the resulting hydraulic load increases the potential for sand erosion. Conversely, in sands with considerable macroporosity, less water is retained and more percolates through the large pores, reducing the potential for sand erosion. This assumes that there are no major obstructions to downward water movement at lower depths within the soil profile. The provision of a properly functioning drainage system, along with relatively unobstructed movement of water between the sand layer and the drain pipes, will ensure that water moving through the sand will exit the bunker in a timely fashion.

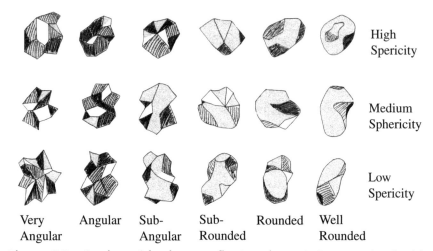

High
Sphericity

Medium
Sphericity

Low
Sphericity

Very   Angular   Sub-   Sub-   Rounded   Well
Angular   Angular   Rounded   Rounded

Figure 3.9   Sand particle shapes reflecting the variation associated with sphericity (top = high; bottom = low) and angularity (left = very angular; right = well rounded).

Solution: While limiting the steepness of slope faces in bunkers can dramatically reduce the potential for sand erosion during heavy rains, other factors may dictate the construction of some bunkers with steep slopes. Therefore, some measures may be required to address this problem. One such measure would be to reduce the hydraulic load on sloping sites by diverting runoff water before it enters the bunker; this can be accomplished by constructing a 1-ft (30-cm) lip around the entire bunker, which will reduce sand erosion from both runoff water and wind. Other measures include improving internal drainage and isolating the sand from adjacent media. Internal drainage is primarily dependent upon the proper selection of sand, with particular emphasis on particle size. Bunker sands should have a hydraulic conductivity of at least 20 in. (50 cm) per hour. And while ensuring adequate internal drainage almost always involves the installation of drain pipes, an innovative method developed at Augusta National Golf Course also included the use of pea gravel. The gravel was placed in trenches cut into the subgrade where the drain pipes were installed and on top of the subgrade. While this is similar to the underdrainage system employed in USGA specifications for green construction, a gravel blanket at a

compacted depth of only 1.5 to 2 in. (3.8–5 cm) was found to be sufficient for this purpose. The presumed advantage of this method is that
water movement from sand to gravel occurs wherever a hydraulic head
sufficient to force water across the sand–gravel interface occurs, thus
facilitating subsequent water movement to the drain pipes and away
from the bunker. Also, by installing a series of cross-slope drain pipes
within the bunker to intercept downslope water movement, the hydraulic
load on the sand slopes can be reduced, lessening the potential for
washouts.

A liner of some type is sometimes used to isolate the sand from the
adjacent media, including the subgrade (or gravel) on which the sand
is placed and the soil associated with the turf surrounding the sand
bunker. Commonly employed liners include geotextiles and other fabrics
that allow water but not soil particles to penetrate, thus preventing
cross-contamination. Care should be exercised in selecting a liner to
ensure that it will continue to conduct water despite inevitable reductions in conductivity over time from congestion due to lodged soil particles, as well as accumulations of chemical and organic residues. ■

BIOTIC ENVIRONMENT

▶ CASE STUDY 3.22

Scenario: A golf course in Reading, Pennsylvania, has several sites
where cart traffic has substantially reduced turf quality. The 18th hole
is a 556-yard par 5 with a slight dogleg to the right. As the fairway
slopes from right to left, most golf shots are played to the right to avoid
having the ball roll into the left rough; consequently, the right rough
receives most of the cart traffic. With the average width of the rough
between the 18th fairway and a line of evergreen trees to its right being
less than 25 ft (7.6 m), the right rough receives especially heavy traffic
(Figure 3.10). The 2nd hole is a 167-yard (153 m) par 3 with a pond
situated about halfway between the tee and the green. Cart traffic usually proceeds along the right side, with the graveled cart path beginning at the edge of the pond and ending at the 3rd tee. Cart traffic
usually halts just to the right of a series of trees separating the cart

path from the green. The affected turf at this location measures approximately 8,100 ft² (753 m²); it is very thin and remains shaded for most of the day (Figure 3.11). Much of the area is essentially bare soil that is dusty when dry and muddy when wet. The 5th hole is a 369-yard (337 m) par 4 with the green situated to the left side of the main axis of the fairway; as a consequence, much of the traffic comes at the green from the right rough. There is a poorly drained depression measuring approximately 16,200 ft² (1505 m²) in which the turfgrass cover is either very thin or nonexistent. Finally, the 14th hole is a 402-yard (368-m) par 4 with a slight dogleg to the left. The average width of this fairway is 80 ft (24 m). A 90-ft (27-m) graveled cart path abruptly terminates in the left rough; the area immediately beyond the path is completely worn down to bare soil, and much of the left rough between the fairway and a row of trees has been severely thinned by cart traffic (Figure 3.12). What can be done to improve the turf quality at these sites?

Analysis: While any established turf can withstand some traffic, there is for each turf a traffic-intensity level that, when exceeded, will result in a measurable decline in turf quality. This is called the *traffic threshold.* In attempting to address traffic-related problems, one should employ one or both of two strategies for ensuring that the traffic intensity does not exceed the traffic threshold. The first is to reduce the

Figure 3.10 Severe wear from cart traffic in narrow rough situated between a line of trees and a fairway.

Figure 3.11   Loss of turf from pedestrian traffic and tree shade.

traffic intensity to a level that is below the traffic threshold; the second is to raise the traffic threshold to a level that is greater than the traffic intensity (Figure 3.13). The first strategy—reducing traffic intensity—can be accomplished by either diluting the traffic across a larger turf area or concentrating it on an inanimate surface, such as concrete, asphalt, stones, or other materials. For the second strategy—increasing the traffic threshold—one can employ various methods, including improving drainage, reducing shade, establishing more traffic-tolerant

Figure 3.12   Loss of turf at the end of a gravel path where cart traffic is concentrated.

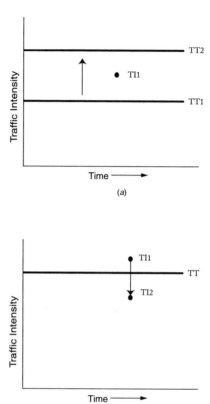

Figure 3.13 Two strategies for traffic management: (*a*) raise the traffic threshold (TT1 –> TT2) to a position that is above the traffic intensity (TI1) and (*b*) reduce the traffic intensity (TI1 –> TI2) to a level that is below the traffic threshold (TT).

species, raising the mowing height, optimizing fertilization and irrigation practices, and, perhaps, topdressing with crumb rubber.

Solution: As the deterioration of the rough along the left side of the 18th fairways was due to concentrated traffic, one possible course of action would be to expand the size of the rough to allow traffic to be spread over a larger area, thus reducing traffic intensity. An alternative would be to simply allow cart traffic on the fairways instead of confining it to the roughs. A careful examination of the cultural program might reveal opportunities for increasing the traffic threshold as well, such as establishing perennial ryegrass, improving drainage, reducing irrigation to maintain a firmer surface, and raising the mowing height.

As tree shade contributed to the problem observed between the 2nd green and the 3rd tee, selective removal of trees would go a long way toward improving the quality of this turf by increasing its traffic threshold. An alternative would be to install a stone or shredded-bark walkway through the trees to minimize traffic on the turf and establish a more shade-tolerant turfgrass (fine fescue or rough blue-grass, depending upon soil fertility and moisture retention) on the surrounding area.

As poor surface and internal drainage reduced the traffic threshold of a large area of turf in the right rough of the 5th hole, installing a catch basin at the lowest point in the depression could be helpful. A slit trench backfilled with gravel or sand could be installed upslope of the depression to intercept surface runoff and reduce the hydraulic load at this site. The possibility of recontouring the site to extend the depression downslope, providing uninterrupted surface drainage to another location, should also be explored.

Finally, because of the abrupt termination of the asphalt cart path in the left rough of the 14th hole, cart traffic at this location is so concentrated that turf cover cannot be sustained. The most obvious solution would be to extend the asphalt cart path to a point near the 14th green. To ensure that the same problem does not develop at that location, the cart path should be flared to direct traffic to an area of sufficient size that traffic intensity is reduced to a level below the traffic threshold.

To the extent to which traffic-induced damage has occurred, various cultivation methods, including hollow-tine and solid-tine cultivation, should be employed to alleviate soil compaction and promote turfgrass recovery. ■

► CASE STUDY 3.23

Scenario: During the summer months when the number of rounds of golf played per month reached its maximum, the centers of the small creeping bentgrass (*Agrostis stolonifera* L.) tees throughout the course deteriorated as the rate at which new divots were created exceeded the rate at which older divots recovered (Figure 3.14). What can be done to prevent this deterioration of the tees?

Figure 3.14   Divot damage on golf course tee.

Analysis: Recuperative capacity can be substantially reduced by cultural and environmental factors that inhibit turfgrass growth, including severely compacted soils, inadequate or excessive fertility and moisture, unfavorable temperatures, insufficient light, toxic soil residues, and disease. The recuperative capacity of a creeping bentgrass tee is also limited by the rate at which lateral shoot growth can fill divots unless worn areas are reseeded, in which case it is also influenced by the rate at which germination and seedling growth can fill the divots.

Solution: First, a comprehensive analysis of the cultural and environmental factors inhibiting turfgrass growth should be conducted and, to the extent possible, appropriate adjustments made. Additionally, the recuperative capacity of a creeping bentgrass tee can be enhanced by providing a soil-and-seed mix for players to use in filling divots. Some increase in the use of nitrogen fertilizer may promote recuperative growth if the current fertilization program is inadequate for this purpose. If possible, some of the smaller tees should be enlarged to better distribute traffic and provide more teeing areas and thus longer periods between use. Finally, eliminate any tree interference that may force golfers to favor one side of the tee, thereby concentrating traffic.   ■

SUMMARY OF ENVIRONMENTAL PROBLEMS

Atmospheric Problems

Atmospheric problems include turfgrass responses to light, temperature, moisture, and wind. With respect to light, shading from trees not only reduces the amount of sunlight (specifically, PAR) reaching the turfgrass community, but also alters its quality by reducing the ratio of red to far-red light transmitted though tree leaves.

Reflecting a direct relationship between PAR and net photosynthesis, substantial reductions in PAR are likely to result in reductions in the carbohydrates (photoassimilates) produced to meet the plants' respiratory requirements and to provide the new growth to offset losses due to natural plant senescence, as well as disease, damage from insects and other organisms, and traffic. Thus, insufficient light can result in reduced carbohydrate reserves, shallow rooting, and reduced shoot growth. With reductions in the red/far-red light ratio resulting from the transmission of sunlight through tree leaves, the phytochrome pigment in plant cells may be transformed from the active form (P_{fr}) to the inactive form (P_r), resulting in more turfgrass leaf and stem elongation and less tillering. Presumably, this reflects the increased production of gibberellic acid and its effects on plant growth. Thus, shade turfs tend to be more upright-growing, with thinner, longer leaves and lower shoot density. The combination of reduced PAR and altered light quality from tree shading produces a more delicate turf that is less tolerant of traffic and other environmental stresses and more susceptible to the activities of various disease-inciting organisms and other pests. Also, bermudagrass may be slower to emerge from dormancy in spring on shaded sites, especially where temporary turfgrass communities were established by overseeding cool-season turfgrasses the previous fall. If the cool-season turfgrasses are allowed to persist through the normal spring-transition period and into the summer months in shaded environments, the survival of the bermudagrass could be seriously threatened. Successful attempts to reduce shade intensity and improve sunlight penetration can eliminate or reduce the severity of these problems. Also, the proper use of plant-growth regulators (PGRs) that inhibit gibberellic-acid biosynthesis, such as trinexapac-ethyl (Primo Maxx), could be helpful by countering the suppressive effect of tree shading on phytochrome activity. Also, while PGRs would have little or no effect on net photosynthesis, they might reduce the consumption of photoassimilates by reducing turfgrass growth.

During the summer months, turfgrass communities established on south-facing slopes in the Northern Hemisphere (and on north-facing slopes in the Southern Hemisphere) receive more direct sunlight than those established on level sites. With more direct sunlight, these turfs are likely to experience more heat stress, with proportionate increases in consumptive water use for transpirational cooling. At the same time, sloping sites, especially those with low infiltration capacities, are likely to lose much of the water received from rainfall and irrigation to runoff. And the combination of less retained water and higher consumptive water use is likely to result in greater drought stress, reducing growth and increasing the potential for losses of turfgrass from desiccation. These effects can be offset by successful attempts to improve water infiltration and reduce runoff on these sites. The use of wetting agents and various cultivation practices can be helpful under these circumstances. Where drought stress is evident as wilting symptoms, timely syringing can be helpful in promoting the survival of the turf.

During the winter months, ice can form on greens and persist for extended periods. Damage is believed to occur from the formation and growth of ice crystals within the crowns, where alternate freezing and thawing cycles lead to increased crown hydration levels. This is least likely on sloping sites, where water quickly runs off, and most likely in depressions, where water accumulates. Shaded greens are more likely to have ice-related damage due to lower levels of non-structural carbohydrates, the effects of reduced irradiance on plant hardiness, more extended ice coverage in the shade, and the loss of proteins associated with cold hardiness. Therefore, providing good surface drainage and reducing shade intensity can substantially reduce the potential for ice-related damage. Covering greens during winter can provide protection from ice-related damage. The most effective cover includes a porous fabric applied directly to the turf, then straw, and finally a top cover of a nonporous fabric. Often, the biggest concern is during late winter or early spring, when the ice melts and refreezes or when a rainfall is followed by a sudden drop in temperature to below freezing. Prolonged ice cover can be damaging to the turf, especially to annual bluegrass populations. Exposed ice can be broken up with solid-tine cultivation in ½-in. (1.3-cm) increments and the shattered ice removed with a rotary bristle sweeper.

Another form of ice-related damage is from hailstorms. Large hail stones cause numerous depressions in a green resembling ball marks. This damage can be repaired with a screwdriver or another device for lifting the depressed turf to reestablish a smooth, level surface.

Dense populations of trees and shrubs planted in close proximity to greens can restrict air movement over the turf, resulting in a microenvironment with higher temperatures and higher relative humidity than in areas without restricted air movement. As the turf is warmed by solar radiation, it reradiates heat, warming the air above the turf. At the same time, the turfgrass community absorbs moisture from the soil and releases it to the atmosphere as water vapor, increasing the humidity of the air above the turf. With a small amount of air movement, these warm, moist parcels of air mix with the larger volume of air above the turf, diluting the accumulated heat and humidity. Without air movement, however, these warm, moist parcels of air remain near the turf, increasing its susceptibility to selected diseases, especially brown patch and *Pythium* blight. Selective removal of trees and shrubs or the installation of fans to promote air movement can effectively address this problem.

Edaphic Problems

Edaphic problems reflect unfavorable physical, chemical, or biological conditions in the soil. Since chemical and biological problems will be addressed in Chapters 4 and 5, respectively, this chapter deals only with the physical problems encountered in soil. Soil physical problems often arise where internal drainage is insufficient to enable a wet soil to quickly dry out, become firm, and provide adequate soil aeration. This often reflects the loss of macroporosity in compacted soils in which the structural integrity of soil aggregates has broken down. Since macropores release water in response to gravitational force, this movement of gravitational water from the macropores is accompanied by the movement of atmospheric air into the macropores, maintaining an aerobic environment for plant roots and the community of organisms inhabiting the soil. Methods for improving the aeration capacity of compacted soils include various types and intensities of cultivation to complete tillage and reestablishment of the turf.

Even structureless sands can be deficient in macroporosity despite their resistance to compaction. A sufficient number of fine and very fine sand particles can fill in the spaces between larger particles, creating a very dense, poorly drained medium. Such *multicomponent* sands can be screened to remove the finer (or, for that matter, coarser) particles, rendering them more suitable for constructing or topdressing greens and other turfs.

Calcareous sands, which are rich in calcium carbonate, may present some unique problems from high pH levels, structural instability, and cementation. The high pH of calcareous sands can limit soil nutrient availability, requiring foliar application of fertilizers to satisfy plant nutrient requirements. Some calcareous sands are easily crushed under traffic, causing changes in particle size and pore size distribution within the medium. During weathering, some calcareous sand particles may become cemented together, forming a rigid medium with reduced water percolation.

Poor internal drainage may also reflect the presence of obstructions to water percolation within the soil matrix. For example, repeated hollow-tine cultivations of a green at the same depth of penetration can lead to the formation of a *cultivation pan* several inches below the surface. Because of their high soil density (and low porosity, especially macropores), cultivation pans slowly absorb water but do not readily release it, obstructing water percolation.

Textural layers in the soil can also obstruct water movement. A relatively fine-textured soil layer situated atop a coarser-textured layer will absorb water at a rate reflective of its hydraulic conductivity and accumulate it as a *perched* water table that will persist until a hydraulic head of sufficient magnitude forces its release to the underlying coarser-textured soil. Conversely, a relatively coarse-textured soil layer situated atop a finer-textured layer will absorb and conduct water relatively rapidly and allow it to continue its movement into the finer-textured layer, but at a slower rate. If the rate at which water is entering the coarser-textured layer is faster than the rate at which the underlying finer-textured soil can absorb it, water will accumulate as a *temporary* water table in the coarser-textured layer. With persistent wetness, anaerobic conditions can develop and various elements, including sulfur and various metals (iron, magnesium), may be reduced and react with each other to form jam-like deposits of metal sulfides (iron sulfide, magnesium sulfide), called *black layer,* which clog soil pores, further restricting internal drainage. Where a sand topdressing program is initiated to develop a coarser-textured medium atop a finer-textured soil, care must be exercised to control the amount of water accumulating as temporary water tables (the installation of slit trenches with drain pipes and backfilled with sand to the surface can be helpful in disposing of this accumulated water). Also, when the coarser-textured medium dries out, capillary water from the underlying finer-textured medium will not move up and into the coarser-textured medium for the same reason perched water tables formed in the previous example: water will not move from a finer-textured to a coarser-textured medium until and unless sufficient force is exerted to release it from the finer-textured medium. Turfgrasses growing in the coarser-textured medium are thus subjected to "feast-or-famine" cycles with respect to water. They must tolerate the presence of temporary water tables immediately following precipitation events, and they must endure temporary droughts when the coarser-textured medium dries from drainage and evapotranspiration (i.e., evaporation of water directly from the coarser-textured medium and transpiration of water by turfgrass plants growing in this medium), as there is no replenishment of water from deeper soil depths through capillary water movement.

Where a thatch layer develops, it often forms a coarser-textured layer atop a relatively fine-textured soil. Temporary water tables may form within the thatch layer and persist until the underlying soil can absorb it. When the thatch dries from drainage and evapotranspiration, there is no capillary water movement from the soil to the thatch, as water does not move from the small pores of the finer-textured soil medium to the larger pores of the coarser-textured thatch medium situated above it. Thus, severely thatched turfs may be subjected to the same feast-or-famine cycles as sand-topdressed turfs; however, effective incorporation of soil from topdressing—or reincorporation of soil cores extracted by hollow-tine cultivation—into a thatch layer can change its pore-size distribution so that it resembles that of the underlying soil, reestablishing upward capillary water movement into the thatch-like derivative. Where the topdressing material (e.g., soil, sand) is not effectively incorporated into a thatch layer, alternating layers of organic material from the thatch and soil from topdressing may form, creating a texturally diverse profile through which water movement may be severely disrupted.

The installation of sod during turf establishment can result in drainage problems where the soil transported with the sod differs substantially from the soil at the transplant site. This is most apparent where a muck-grown sod is planted on a sand medium. Even washed sod can be problematic on sand if the sod is not fully integrated into the medium through aggressive sand topdressing.

Internal drainage problems are exacerbated by poor surface drainage. On sloping sites, some of the water received by a turf during rainfall or irrigation infiltrates and the remainder is carried downslope as runoff, perhaps reaching a stream or pond. But often runoff water accumulates in depressions in the turfgrass landscape and persists until it eventually infiltrates or evaporates, resulting in a soggy, wet turf for extended periods. The installation of catch basins, slit trenches, and other devices for intercepting surface water and transmitting it directly to drain pipes located below the surface can reduce the amount of water that must otherwise infiltrate the turf and percolate through the soil matrix.

Biotic Problems

Biotic problems result from interaction between the turfgrass and an organism with the capacity to cause injury. Many of these organisms will be discussed in Chapter 5 under pest problems. But one organism—man—can cause enormous damage through traffic. While most turfgrasses will withstand moderate amounts of traffic with little or no observable injury, for every turf there is a traffic intensity level that, when exceeded, will result in a measurable deterioration in turf quality; this is called the *traffic threshold*. There are two general courses of action for dealing with a traffic problem: reduce the traffic intensity below the traffic threshold or raise the traffic threshold to a level above the traffic intensity. To reduce traffic intensity, one can employ either a dilution strategy or a concentration strategy. A dilution strategy requires distributing the traffic across a larger area of turf so that the traffic intensity per unit area is reduced. A concentration strategy requires construction of an inanimate surface (e.g., asphalt cart path, brick or stone walkway, gravel or bark mulch) on which the traffic can be concentrated so that it is kept off the turf. To the extent that injury does occur from pedestrian or vehicular traffic or from divoting, these activities should be directed to other areas to allow sufficient time for recovery. Where severe damage has occurred, recovery can be stimulated by cultivation, topdressing, and/or overseeding. The traffic threshold of a turf can be increased by maintaining a firm, dry surface by improving surface and internal drainage and avoiding excessive irrigation; optimizing fertilizer use rates, especially for nitrogen and potassium; raising the mowing height; reducing shade intensity; and establishing more traffic-tolerant turfgrass species and cultivars.

CHAPTER

4

Cultural Problems

Cultural problems are those associated with the nature, frequency, and intensity of turfgrass cultural operations. These include mowing, fertilization, irrigation, cultivation, and topdressing. Often they occur where cultural operations are performed improperly. But sometimes they develop in response to cultural operations performed under specific sets of conditions encountered at particular times during the growing season, posing challenges that must be overcome to restore the turf to an acceptable quality level.

MOWING

▶ CASE STUDY 4.1

Scenario: The fairways at a golf course in the Chicago area exhibited a wavy or washboard-like appearance after mowing. Closer examination revealed that there were distinct ridges and valleys in the turf, reflecting different mowing heights (Figure 4.1). What caused this problem, and how can it be addressed?

Figure 4.1   Improper mowing with a reel mower caused marcelling of the turf; it occurs where CR is substantially longer than MH.

Analysis: Mowing quality is influenced by the relationship between mowing height (MH) and the clip of the reel (CR), which is defined as the forward distance traveled between successive clips. CR is determined by three factors: the number of blades on the reel, the rotational velocity of the reel blades, and the forward operating speed of the mower. While the first two factors are reflections of mower design and selection, the third—forward operating speed—reflects how a particular mower is used. The most uniform cut is achieved when CR equals MH; if CR is appreciably longer than MH, the turf takes on a wavy appearance, called *marcelling*. With clipping, turfgrass shoots are drawn together—by the pulling action of a reel blade and the pushing action of the bedknife—to form an isosceles triangle. After clipping, the shoots return to an upright orientation, resulting in a marcelled surface with measurable peaks and valleys. The height difference between the peaks and valleys is called the *restitution height* (R), which can be calculated using the formula $R = (MH^2 + [CR/2]^2)^{1/2} - MH$. Where CR = MH, the percent variation (%V = R/MH) is approximately 12%—an acceptable level that does not result in a marcelled appearance. Where CR > MH,

92

however, larger RHs and greater shoot height variations occur, resulting in observable marcelling.

Solution: Instruct the mower operator in the proper operation of a riding mower. Typically, riding mowers should be operated at a forward speed of 4 mi (6.4 km) per hour. Assuming that CR = MH at that speed, operating the unit at twice that speed would result in a corresponding increase in CR, substantially increasing %V, with marcelling as the inevitable consequence.   ■

▶ CASE STUDY 4.2

Scenario: On a golf course in Vermont, the quality of the greens progressively deteriorated during the growing season in the outer ring of the greens, known as the *triplex ring* (Figure 4.2). How might this unsightly wear pattern from triplex mowers be eliminated?

Analysis: Measurable damage from mowing the perimeter of a green with triplex mowers is the result of at least three types of stress: tire traffic, wear from rollers and bedknives, and wear from twisting

Figure 4.2   Triplex ring damage from a mower on a narrow portion of a green requiring a small turning radius.

mowing units during turns. As the perimeter of a green is fixed, the tires of a triplex mower usually cover the same curved paths during perimeter mowing. Depending upon the actual pressure imposed by the tires and the composition and moisture content of the soil, some turfgrass wear and soil compaction are likely from repeated mowing at these locations. The weight of the mowing units is distributed to the turf through the bedknives and rollers, with some bruising of the shoot tissues likely, especially where grooved—as opposed to smooth—rollers are used. Turns cause the mowing units to twist, sometimes cutting into the turf along the edges, especially where the turning radius is relatively short. The severity of this damage is directly proportional to the operating speed of the mower; that is, the faster the speed, the greater the damage in tight turns. The effects of these stresses, including shoot thinning and discoloration, are most evident during summer, when turfgrasses must endure additional stress from hot, humid weather.

Solution: Numerous strategies have been effectively employed to prevent triplex ring damage. These include reducing the operating speed of the mower in tight turns, emptying the baskets before making the cleanup pass, skipping perimeter mowing or moving the mowing perimeter 1 ft (30 cm) into the green on alternate days, and mowing the perimeter of the green—or the entire green—with walk-behind mowers. Where soil compaction from tire traffic is the principal concern, specialized triplex mowers with offset or adjustable mowing units could be employed. With offset units, mowing in opposite directions on alternate days adjusts the tire traffic pattern, reducing traffic stress by half. Adjustable units can be moved 12 in. (30 cm) to the left or right of center, with corresponding shifts in the tire traffic pattern. Where triplex ring damage has occurred, the mowing height should be increased slightly and the area hollow-tine or solid-tine cultivated each month— perhaps in combination with overseeding—to alleviate soil compaction and promote recovery. ■

▶ CASE STUDY 4.3

Scenario: While conducting the late-morning tour of his golf course in eastern Maryland, a superintendent observed a grayish cast on the fairways. Close examination of the turf revealed that the leaf tips were

Figure 4.3   Shredded ends of leaves cut with a dull mower.

frayed, with dieback evident on some leaves (Figure 4.3) and breakage on others (Figure 4.4). What caused this problem, and what can be done to solve it?

Analysis: The symptoms indicate poor mowing quality. With reel mowers, mowing quality is, in part, a function of the sharpness of the

Figure 4.4   Broken leaf blades from an improperly adjusted mower.

cutting edges and the adjustment of the bedknife against the reel blades. Dull cutting surfaces or poor adjustment result in tearing and bruising of the leaves. The mutilated leaves turn gray, then brown, at the tip. This appears initially as a grayish cast on the turf; however, the symptoms are gradually obscured by the emergence of new leaves from vertical shoot axils and then reappear following the next mowing.

Solution: The reel blades and bedknives should be sharpened by backlapping the unit until the cutting edges are sharp. If this does not produce satisfactory results, it may be necessary to mill the bedknife on a lathe. After washing the lapping compound from the unit, the bed-knife-to-reel clearance should be adjusted for zero metal-to-metal contact using the *cut one, leave one* method; this involves placing two strips of newspaper between the reel and the bedknife and adjusting the clearance so that the reel cuts one paper and leaves the other. ■

▶ CASE STUDY 4.4

Scenario: Over the years, the putting greens at a golf course in southeastern Pennsylvania became progressively smaller. This was the result of a phenomenon called *green creep* that results when an operator mows inside a green's perimeter to avoid scalping (Figure 4.5), allowing

Figure 4.5   Scalping along the edge of a green.

the outermost edge of the green to become part of the collar. What can be done to deal with green creep?

Analysis: With green creep, less putting surface is available for hole locations and more pressure is placed on the remainder of the green to sustain play. Because of the increased traffic intensity per unit area of green, there is more wear and compaction. An attempt to immediately recover portions of a green that had been lost from green creep would likely result in a serious scalping problem. This is due to the changes that occur in a turfgrass population when the mowing height is raised: shoot density declines and leaf texture becomes coarser, reflecting an increase in shoot size. If the mowing height were to be abruptly lowered to that of the green, most of the leaf tissue would be lost, with a sparse stand of shoot stubble remaining. If this was accompanied by severe heat and drought stress, many—perhaps most—of these shoots would subsequently die. To the extent that this occurs, recovery would depend upon the presence of surviving axillary buds on residual stems and their ability, under prevailing environmental conditions, to form new plants. Substantial tillering and stolon development would then be needed to eventually cover the affected areas and bring shoot density back to that of the rest of the green.

Solution: There are two strategies for dealing with green creep: avoidance and recovery. Implementation of an avoidance strategy requires training personnel to locate and maintain the green's perimeter with each mowing. The location of the perimeter can be determined by measuring its distance from fixed features such as irrigation heads. When there is early evidence that some green creep has occurred, the perimeter should be immediately reestablished; otherwise, significant scalping may occur. A recovery strategy should be implemented after it has become apparent that a substantial amount of green creep has already occurred. One method for doing this is to resod these areas. Another is to remove the sod, add rootzone media, and seed. Still another is to gradually lower the mowing height of the turf using a walk-behind mower specially designated for this purpose. Also, the areas should be hollow-tine cultivated and topdressed several times before lowering the mowing height to accelerate recovery.   ■

▶ CASE STUDY 4.5

Scenario: Creeping bentgrass (*Agrostis stolonifera* L.) greens that responded well to the use of grooved rollers in the cool weather of spring and fall showed excessive wear during the summer months. Should their use in the summer be suspended to reduce wear, and will this increase the potential for grain and thatch development?

Analysis: Wear on the greens during the summer months can be exacerbated by the continued use of grooved rollers. Grooved rollers can be helpful in controlling grain, but they are best used during the spring and fall, when temperatures are cooler and cool-season turfgrasses are under less stress. It is also in the cooler weather that the grooved rollers are most beneficial, as this is when the creeping bentgrass is growing most vigorously and producing an abundance of new stolons.

Solution: During the summer months, grooved rollers should be replaced by smooth rollers to reduce turfgrass wear and associated stress-related injury. With the return of cool weather in late summer and early fall, grooved rollers can be reinstalled.   ■

▶ CASE STUDY 4.6

Scenario: The superintendent at a golf course on Long Island was fit to be tied. Hydraulic leaks had occurred before, but this time the damage was far more severe and widespread than he had ever experienced. Now he would have to face the embarrassment of explaining to the members how such extensive damage could have resulted from a single mower. How should he communicate this problem, and what measures should he undertake to reduce the likelihood of having more problems of this nature?

Analysis: Plant tissue scorching can occur where hot (160–200°F, 71–93°C) hydraulic oil leaks from equipment that has been operating for some time. Damage from relatively cool oil occurs as plant desiccation, where sufficient quantities are absorbed by turfgrasses from direct foliar application or from root absorption of soil residues.

Petroleum-based oils are more persistent in the soil than newer vegetable-based oils, with 30% and 80% degradation, respectively, within 28 days of application. Turfgrasses that have absorbed lesser quantities may be weakened, reducing their resistance to pests and their tolerance of environmental stresses.

Solution: While some hydraulic leaks are inevitable where sophisticated equipment is used, with proper supervision, many—perhaps most—can be prevented, and all can be limited in their effects. To prevent or minimize hydraulic oil damage: (1) perform routine inspections of equipment, with particular attention to worn hoses and seals, wetness on hoses and motors, and puddles under equipment from leaks; (2) identify leaks during operation, concentrating on certain sights (shiny turf, splashing or misting from mowers) and unusual smells and sounds; (3) move equipment to a safe place to limit damage when leaks are evident; (4) follow proper cleanup procedures, such as applying products to absorb oil residues and flushing leaks with water and dishwashing soap; and (5) establish systems and conduct training on equipment operation and preventive maintenance. Finally, in communicating with the membership, one should be honest and take full responsibility for the damage that has occurred.   ■

FERTILIZATION

▶ CASE STUDY 4.7

Scenario: On a golf course in North Carolina with greens of Penncross creeping bentgrass (*Agrostis stolonifera* L. 'Penncross') and annual bluegrass (*Poa annua* L.), there is very little growth of the creeping bentgrass when annual bluegrass is actively growing during the early and late months of the growing season. The creeping bentgrass also takes on a red or purplish coloration (Plate 5; see color insert). Were it not for the annual bluegrass, the greens would not require mowing. What can be done to improve the uniform quality of these greens?

Analysis: In the early and late portions of the growing season, differences in coloration and vertical shoot growth may be evident between creeping bentgrass and annual bluegrass populations in a green. These turfgrass responses are influenced by many factors, including temperature, plant ecotype, and cultural operations; however, their differential occurrence may also reflect differences in the relative nutritional status of the two turfgrass populations. If creeping bentgrass does not have mycorrhizal formations on its roots, phosphorus absorption is impeded when soil temperatures are below 50°F (10°C), and its competitive ability in mixed communities with annual bluegrass may be reduced. Mycorrhizae are fungi that form mutually beneficial associations with plants. Several species of vesicular arbuscular mycorrhizae (VAM) colonize turfgrass roots, including *Glomus intraradices, G. mosseae,* and *G. aggregatum.* Once established on the turfgrass root system, fungal filaments radiate out from the roots and permeate the surrounding soil. VAM function in obtaining nutrients and water from the soil and transporting them to the roots; they are especially important for the uptake of nutrients that are not very soluble or mobile in the soil, including phosphorus.

Solution: Foliar applications of soluble phosphorus formulations—such as $NH_4H_2PO_4$ (monoammonium phosphate) or $(NH_4)HPO_4$ (diammonium phosphate)—can alleviate the phosphorus deficiency and promote the creeping bentgrass population's competitive growth. ■

▶ CASE STUDY 4.8

Scenario: During the first few months following seeding of a new golf course, 5 acres (2 ha) of greens and tees received approximately 13 lb N, 16 lb P, and 5 lb K per 1000 ft² (6.3 kg N, 7.8 kg P, and 2.4 kg K per 100 m²), while 75 acres (30 ha) of fairways and roughs received approximately 16 lb N, 14 lb P, and 15 lb K per 1000 ft² (7.8 kg N, 6.8 kg P, and 7.3 kg K per 100 m²). This amounted to more than 28 tons (25.4 metric tons) of nitrogen and approximately 25 tons (22.7 metric tons) each of phosphorus and potassium applied to the golf course in the first few months following seeding. When asked about the environmental consequences associated with the substantial quantities of fertilizer nutrients applied, the grow-in superintendent responded that "this is what it takes to establish new golf course turf" and "once fully established, much lower rates will be used for maintenance." Afterward, he began to wonder about the potential for pollution of surface and subsurface water bodies from applications of these fertilizer nutrients. If groundwater and surface water sampling and analysis had been done within or immediately adjacent to the golf course, what would these analyses have revealed? If local news reporters or environmentalists were to conduct investigations, what might they discover and how would they use this information? Finally, if he had to do this over again, what might he have done differently?

Analysis: The tendency to employ excessive quantities of nutrients in grow-in fertilization programs is based on the principle that it is better to err on the side of too much than too little, as even modest deficiencies can significantly slow turfgrass establishment rates. The downside of this principle is that excessive application rates are associated with nutrient leaching and runoff losses, which can pollute surface and subsurface water bodies. Also, new turfgrass stands receiving excessive rates of nitrogen fertilizer are more susceptible to seedling diseases that can cause such extensive losses that reseeding may be required.

Solution: Optimizing the use of grow-in fertilizer nutrients requires reasonable estimates of the nutrient-retention capacity of the soil, as well as its current nutrient content. This information is obtainable from a soil-test report in which an estimate of nutrient retention capacity is given as the cation-exchange capacity (CEC) and current nutrient content is given on a per-nutrient basis. As soil pH can influence the availability of nutrients, the specific pH and the amount of lime required to adjust it to an optimal level are usually provided as well. With this information in hand, specific amounts of phosphorus and potassium—as well as lime or other amendments, where needed—can be incorporated into the soil prior to final grading. The amounts of nitrogen and other nutrients required at planting and subsequently are influenced by the nutrient carriers and the application methods employed. For example, quickly available nitrogen carriers are applied at lower rates than slowly available carriers due to the differences in burn potential. Also, as application equipment cannot be operated safely on wet soil, unpredictable rainfalls sometimes require the use of liberal amounts of fertilizer nutrients whenever equipment can be allowed onto the soil. Alternatives include aerial application or application through the irrigation system, called *fertigation,* which can be done at almost any time. With fertigation, very small amounts of fertilizer nutrients can be applied as often as desired. Some superintendents apply 0.125 to 0.25 lb N per 1000 ft^2 (61–122 g N per 100 m^2) per week in small—sometimes daily—increments after seeding and reduce the rates by half after the first mowing. To reduce the potential for leaching phosphates in sand media, some superintendents incorporate 2.5% of an iron humate amendment into the rootzone mix. Periodic tissue testing can be employed to measure the actual concentrations of nutrients in the foliage and determine if sufficient or excessive levels are being reached through the fertilization program. ■

IRRIGATION

▶ **CASE STUDY 4.9**

Scenario: The kikuyugrass (*Pennisetum clandestinum* Hochst ex Chiov.) fairways at a golf course in Athens, Greece, ranged from bright green where the sprinklers provided adequate water to sustain healthy growth to brown where they didn't (Plate 6; see color insert). Growth differences were directly proportional to differences in thatch development and associated scalping tendency (Plate 7; see color insert). What can be done to improve the quality of these fairways?

Analysis: The reason the once popular center-line sprinklers failed to provide uniform coverage of fairways is the wedge-shaped distribution pattern of rotating sprinkler heads. While there was overlapping coverage of the turf between adjacent heads, the turf on either side received decreasing amounts of water from the line of heads outward and some portions of the fairway received little or no water, resulting in the characteristic "rabbit ears" where coverage from adjacent heads did not extend. Replacement of center-line sprinklers by more sophisticated multiple-row sprinklers has largely corrected this problem and provided turfgrass managers with much greater control over the distribution of water—as well as fertilizers and other materials—through the irrigation system. In the warm subtropical dry-summer climate of Athens, the lack of irrigation coverage was responsible for the brown color and dormant turf on portions of the fairways. Because kikuyu-grass is a thatch-forming turfgrass, the lack of seasonal growth results in a corresponding decrease in thatch development. And with less thatch, there was less scalping with mowing.

Solution: As uniform coverage from an irrigation system is essential for sustaining acceptable fairway turf quality, especially in climates with a long summer dry season, the irrigation system should be modified or rebuilt in accordance with contemporary standards. Then, with proper use of this system, uniform growth should be sustainable throughout the growing season. The scalping problem can be addressed through a thatch-management program involving periodic vertical mowing, hollow-tine cultivation, and reincorporation of soil cores to modify the properties of residual thatch over the short term while accelerating its biodecomposition over the long term. ∎

▶ CASE STUDY 4.10

Scenario: Several years of below-average precipitation reduced groundwater resources to levels requiring severe restrictions on future water use by the community. Annual water use by the golf course over the past 5 years averaged 28.3 million gallons, 64% of which occurred in July and August. This year, the golf course will be limited to 19.8 million gallons. What should be done to ensure that water use will not exceed this amount?

Analysis: While the intended use of water in turfgrass management is satisfying the moisture requirements of the turfgrass community, much of the water moving through the irrigation system may not be used for this purpose. For example, water leaking from irrigation system components may not be absorbed by turfgrasses at all because the leak occurs below the rootzone, or it may be available to turfgrasses in such abundance that oxygen becomes limiting, adversely affecting turfgrass growth and turf quality. Also, because of winds and high temperatures, water released by sprinkler heads may be diverted from targeted sites or lost to the atmosphere directly as water vapor. Finally, the amount of water applied to the turf may be excessive relative to that actually required to sustain healthy growth.

Solution: There are many opportunities for achieving significant water-use efficiencies in golf turf management. First, the irrigation system should be checked and appropriate repairs or modifications made to maximize water use efficiency. Next, try to avoid irrigating when there are high winds that seriously disrupt water distribution patterns. During high-temperature periods, water primarily at night to reduce direct evaporative losses. Conduct irrigation practices based on reliable measurements of site-specific consumptive water use to avoid overwatering as much as possible. If the amount of water available is still likely to be less than that required to sustain all turfgrass communities covering the golf course, prioritize water use based on the importance of each turf, giving greens the highest priority and roughs the lowest. Finally, in relatively dry climates, turfgrasses that are adapted to dry conditions, such as buffalograss (*Buchloë dactyloides* [Nutt.] Engelm.) and fairway wheatgrass (*Agropyron cristatum* [L.] Gaertn.), can be used in roughs and fairways to reduce the dependency on irrigation water. ■

▶ CASE STUDY 4.11

Scenario: A water quality report indicated high concentrations of sodium in the water used for irrigating the turf. What effects might this water have on turf quality, and what can be done to prevent these problems from occurring?

Analysis: The sodium hazard posed by irrigation water is reflected by its sodium adsorption ratio (SAR_W), which can be calculated with the formula

$$SAR_W = [Na^+] \div (([Ca^{2+}] + [Mg^{2+}])/2)^{1/2}$$

in which the concentrations of sodium (Na^+), calcium (Ca^{2+}), and magnesium (Mg^{2+}) are in milliequivalents per liter (meq/L). If the water quality report provides these concentrations in parts per million (ppm) or milligrams per liter (mg/L), they can be converted to meq/L by dividing each by their equivalent weights, which are their atomic weights divided by the valence (i.e., number of charges) of the ion. The equivalent weights of Na^+, Ca^{2+}, and Mg^{2+} are 23, 20, and 12 mg/meq, respectively. Therefore, if the Na^+, Ca^{2+}, and Mg^{2+} concentrations were

756, 62, and 29 mg/L, respectively, the conversions would be made as follows:

$$Na^+: 756 \text{ mg/L} \div 23 \text{ mg/meq} = 32.87 \text{ meq/L}$$

$$Ca^{2+}: 62 \text{ mg/L} \div 20 \text{ mg/meq} = 3.10 \text{ meq/L}$$

$$Mg^{2+}: 29 \text{ mg/L} \div 12 \text{ mg/meq} = 2.42 \text{ meq/L}$$

Plugging these values into the formula for calculating SAR_W yields the following:

$$SAR_W = [32.87] \div (([3.10] + [2.42]) \div 2)^{1/2}$$
$$= [32.87] \div [2.76]^{1/2} = [32.87] \div [1.66] = 19.8$$

To determine the significance of this value, one would reference the U.S. Department of Agriculture (USDA) water quality chart (Figure 4.6). In this case, an SAR_W of 19.8 indicates that the sodium hazard is level S3, which is high. Using this water for irrigation would result in sodium replacing other ions on the exchange sites of clay particles. Because of the six water molecules (H_2O) surrounding each sodium ion, clay particles would be forced farther apart, resulting in the breakdown of clay micelles and, thus, soil aggregates. As a consequence, the permeability of sodium-saturated soils would be dramatically reduced. In sands with very low CECs (<5 meq per 100 g), however, the medium is essentially a structureless sand in which there are few exchange sites and no loss of permeability due to sodium. Under these conditions, the addition of gypsum would be counterproductive, as it would increase the salinity of the soil solution, perhaps to excessive levels.

Solution: As the sodium hazard reflects the concentration of sodium in relation to the calcium and magnesium concentrations, the addition of sufficient quantities of calcium or a combination of calcium and magnesium to the irrigation water can reduce the SAR_W to an acceptable level. The principal sources of calcium and magnesium for this purpose are gypsum ($CaSO_4$) and Epsom salts ($MgSO_4$), respectively. Other forms of calcium may be used in place of gypsum; these include calcium hydroxide ($Ca(OH)_2$) and calcium oxide (CaO), which would increase the pH of the water and of the soil to which it was added, and calcium citrate, which eliminates the sulfur where black layer formation is a concern. Once the adverse effects of sodium have

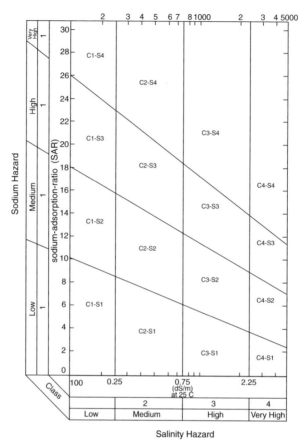

Figure 4.6 USDA water quality chart showing the sodium hazard level along the vertical axis and the salinity hazard along the horizontal axis.

been expressed as reduced soil permeability, these materials should be applied directly to the soil to begin the slow process of replacing sodium on the exchange sites. In pure-sand systems of low CEC, however, soil permeability is not likely to be affected by sodium. ■

▶ CASE STUDY 4.12

Scenario: A water quality report shows high concentrations of bicarbonates in the well water used for irrigating the turf. Could this be problematic and, if so, what can be done about it?

Analysis: Bicarbonate (HCO_3^-) ions, as well as carbonate (CO_3^{2-}) ions, can precipitate calcium ions (Ca^{2+}) and magnesium ions (Mg^{2+}) as calcium and magnesium carbonates ($CaCO_3$, $MgCO_3$), resulting in a change in the relative concentrations of soluble sodium, calcium, and magnesium in the irrigation water. As explained in Case Study 4.11, such a change would be expressed as an increase in the SAR_W and thus in the sodium hazard posed by the use of this water for irrigation. The specific effects of bicarbonate and carbonate ions can be assessed by calculating the residual sodium carbonate (RSC) as follows:

$$RSC = ([HCO_3^-] + [CO_3^{2-}]) - ([Ca^{2+}] + [Mg^{2+}])$$

in which the concentrations of these ions must be expressed as milliequivalents per liter (meq/L). Calculating the equivalent concentrations of calcium and magnesium ions was explained in Case Study 4.11. Where the bicarbonate and carbonate ion concentrations are expressed as parts per million (ppm) or milligrams per liter (mg/L), the molecular weights of these ions are first calculated and then divided by the valence to yield the value for converting these concentrations to meq/L. For example, since the atomic weights of hydrogen, carbon, and oxygen are 1, 12, and 16 mg/mmol, respectively, the molecular weight of the HCO_3^- ion is 61 mg/mmol. Dividing this by the valence (1) of this ion yields an equivalent weight of 61 mg/meq. For the CO_3^{2-} ion, the molecular weight is 60 mg/mmol and the equivalent weight is 30 mg/meq, since the valence in this case is 2. If the HCO_3^- concentration were 488 ppm (488 mg/L), the equivalent concentration would be calculated by dividing this value by 61 mg/meq, yielding 8.0 meq/L. If the equivalent concentrations of the carbonate, calcium, and magnesium ions were 0, 2.3, and 1.5 meq/L, respectively, the RSC would be calculated as follows:

$$RSC = ([8.0] + [0]) - ([2.3] + [1.5]) = 4.2$$

Since there is more HCO_3^- in the water than calcium and magnesium (i.e., RSC is a positive number), all of the calcium and magnesium could be precipitated out of solution, changing the relationship of the sodium, calcium, and magnesium ion concentrations and increasing the SAR_W and thus the sodium hazard posed by using this water for irrigation. As explained in Case Study 4.11, if this results in a high SAR_W level, the expected result from using this water for irrigation would be a decline in soil permeability over time.

Solution: This problem can be addressed by injecting sulfuric acid (H_2SO_4) or gypsum ($CaSO_4$) into the irrigation water. H_2SO_4 is a strong acid that yields hydrogen ions (H^+) that react with bicarbonate to produce carbon dioxide (CO_2) and water (H_2O):

$$H^+ + HCO_3^- \rightarrow CO_2 + H_2O$$

Since CO_2 is a gas that is liberated from the soil, it cannot precipitate calcium and magnesium from the irrigation water. As an alternative, gypsum can be used to precipitate out HCO_3^- from solution:

$$CaSO_4 + HCO_3^- + H_2O \rightarrow CaCO_3 + H_2SO_4$$

The amount of sulfuric acid or gypsum required for these reactions can be determined by the following formulas:

$$RSC \times 133 \text{ lb } H_2SO_4 \text{ per acre-ft of water}$$

$$RSC \times 234 \text{ lb } CaSO_4 \text{ per acre-ft of water}$$

▶ CASE STUDY 4.13

Scenario: An effluent water supply line was provided to a golf course in southern California for irrigation in order to conserve local potable water resources. The greens were constructed with native soil (loam) and no subsurface drain pipes. The club was concerned that the higher salinity of the effluent water (measuring 0.9–1.1 dS/m) would lead to salt accumulation on the greens and contribute to summer turf decline. What could they do to ensure that soil salinity does not become a problem?

Analysis: The salinity of an irrigation water source may be expressed as the soluble salt (SS) concentration in parts per million (ppm) or milligrams per liter (mg/L), or as the electrical conductivity of the water (EC_W) in decisiemens per meter (dS/m). The two expressions of salinity can be converted using the formula $SS/640 = EC_W$. The values of 0.9 to 1.1 dS/m fall within the high range (0.75–2.25 dS/m) on the salinity scale shown in Figure 4.6. High (C3) salinity means that the water should not be used on soils with restricted drainage or for irrigating salt-sensitive species on soils with good drainage. The effect of high soil salinity on water absorption by plants can be explained by water potential (Ψ_w), which is a measure of the energy status of water. Free-standing water has a water potential of 0, while soil water has a potential that is less than 0 because the energy status of water that is being stretched by its adherence to soil particle surfaces is reduced. However, as long as the water potential in the soil (Ψ_{sw}) is greater than the water potential in the plant, the resulting *water potential gradient* causes water to flow into plant roots from the surrounding soil. The reduction in plant water potential is due to transpiration, which removes water from plants, creating a water potential gradient between the plant and the soil. The soil water potential is determined by two components: matric potential (Ψ_m) and osmotic potential (Ψ_o), as shown in the formula $\Psi_{sw} = \Psi_m + \Psi_o$. Matric potential is a measure of soil water content; therefore, as a soil dries, its matric potential is reduced. Osmotic potential is a measure of the effect of salinity on the energy status of soil water; as salinity increases, osmotic potential decreases. Therefore, increasing soil salinity can reduce soil water potential to a point at which the water potential gradient becomes 0, resulting in a phenomenon called *physiological drought* (Plate 8; see color insert), caused by the cessation of water absorption by plant roots.

Solution: A dilution program can be employed to mix effluent and potable water together to reduce salinity to a level below 0.75 dS/m for tees and fairways, but only potable water should be used on greens. In subtropical and tropical climates, seashore paspalum (*Paspalum vaginatum* Swartz.) can be used in saline environments; however, if the Na concentration is also excessive, a soil permeability problem can result.   ■

▶ CASE STUDY 4.14

Scenario: A water quality report indicates that the water used for irrigating the turf at a golf course in central Maryland has a pH of 8.2. Is this likely to increase the pH of the soil? If so, should anything be done to reduce the pH?

Analysis: There is certainly a possibility that alkaline irrigation water will increase the pH of the soil to which it is applied; however, the rate at which this change takes place depends upon the buffering capacity of the soil. Sandy soils of low CEC can change their pH fairly quickly in response to alkaline irrigation water, while clayey soils, which have much higher CECs and thus tend to be highly buffered, change very slowly.

Soil pH influences the availability of soil nutrients. With the exception of calcium and molybdenum, most nutrients are less available at excessively high pHs. At excessively low pHs, soluble aluminum concentrations can be so high that they are phytotoxic and severely limit turfgrass growth or survival. For cool-season turfgrasses, a soil pH in the range of 5.5 to 6.0 favors bentgrasses (*Agrostis* spp.) and fescues (*Festuca* spp.), while the range of 6.0 to 6.5 favors bluegrasses (*Poa* spp.) and ryegrasses (*Lolium* spp.). Most warm-season turfgrasses are adapted to pHs that are slightly acid (6.5–7.0); the exceptions are buffalograss (*Buchloë dactyloides* [Nutt.] Engelm.), which is well adapted to alkaline soils, and centipedegrass (*Eremochloa ophiuroides* [Munro] Hack.) and carpetgrasses (*Axonopus* spp.), which are adapted to acid soils.

Intensively cultured turfs, including greens and possibly fairways, may be less sensitive to excessive alkalinity if they receive frequent foliar applications of essential plant nutrients. Foliar absorption of nutrients can substitute for root absorption, reducing the plant community's dependency on the soil for meeting its nutritional requirements.

Solution: In highly buffered soils, the effect of alkaline irrigation water on soil pH is not likely to be of great concern. In sand-based systems, however, consideration should be given to treating the water with sulfuric acid (H_2SO_4) to reduce its pH. Where this is already being done to liberate bicarbonates as CO_2 (as shown in Case Study 4.12), pH reduction can be an added benefit. Also, foliar application of essential plant nutrients can be employed to compensate for the reduced availability of some nutrients at high soil pHs. ■

▶ CASE STUDY 4.15

Scenario: Because of the fine soil particles suspended in the fast-moving streams (Plate 9; see color insert) feeding the small irrigation pond at a golf course in eastern Iowa, substantial quantities of dispersed clay and silt were added to several nearby sand-based greens with each irrigation. As a consequence, a thick black layer developed in the top 3 in. (7.5 cm) of the soil profiles of these greens, resulting in greatly reduced water infiltration rates and turf quality. A check of the water inlet in the pond revealed that a 12-μm filter that was in place for screening out suspended soil particles from the water had been removed. What can be done to improve the quality of these greens now and in the future?

Analysis: Irrigation water should be relatively free of suspended particles, as they can increase wear on irrigation system components and clog soil pores. Small ponds receiving water from fast-moving streams often have large quantities of suspended solids that, if applied to turf through irrigation, could substantially reduce infiltration and drainage, leading to other problems such as black layer.

Solution: While filters at water inlets can be helpful in screening out suspended particles, it may also be necessary to reduce the load by using measures to encourage settling, including installing dams to capture and slowly release water into the pond and expanding the pond size to reduce turbulence. Once suspended particles have entered the turf and filled a large percentage of the pore spaces in the surface soil, it may be necessary to employ intensive measures—including hollow-tine cultivation, core removal, and backfilling the holes with a suitable medium—to restore infiltration and drainage to an acceptable level. In sand-based greens, this usually means replacing dirty sand with clean sand to regain sufficient macroporosity. ■

▶ CASE STUDY 4.16

Scenario: For many years, the pond between the second and third fairways on a golf course in southeastern New York had served three functions: water hazard, landscape feature, and irrigation water source. Now, because of pond scum—large growths of aquatic algae—that had accumulated on the surface, it was an eyesore (Figure 4.7). And its utility as an important source of irrigation water was reduced because of the persistent clogging of filters at the intake valves. How can this important resource be restored to its former condition?

Analysis: Aquatic algae are free-floating microscopic organisms that form frothy mats on the surface of shallow, warm, stagnant or slowly

Figure 4.7 Large growths of aquatic algae accumulating on the surface of an irrigation pond.

moving water bodies, including irrigation ponds. In addition to fixing atmospheric CO_2 during the day through photosynthesis, some blue-green algae can also fix atmospheric nitrogen at night and thus are not dependent upon runoff nitrogen for their nutritional requirements. Ponds in which large concentrations of nutrients—especially phosphorus—have accumulated are especially susceptible to algal blooms. In addition to blocking filters and fouling pumps, they can discolor the water, produce noxious odors as they decompose, and seriously reduce the pond's aesthetic value. Furthermore, some types of blue-green algae produce microcystins that, if consumed in drinking water, can be fatal.

Solution: Since populations of algae develop in response to the accumulation of nutrients—called *cultural eutrophication*—measures should be taken to ensure that the flow of nutrients into the pond is substantially reduced; these might include avoiding heavy applications of phosphorus to nearby turfs, controlling the direction of nearby sprinkler heads used for fertigation, and preventing clippings from entering the pond. Other measures for controlling algae populations include aeration, precipitating agents, dyes, algaecides, and barley straw.

While oxygen can enter pond water from the atmosphere and as a by-product of photosynthesis by aquatic plants and algae, the dissolved oxygen content may not be sufficient to keep the pond system in balance. Dissolved oxygen is utilized for microbial decomposition of organic residues that accumulate from the turnover of algae and aquatic plants. Simultaneous treatment of the water with commercial formulations of specialized aerobic bacteria may enhance this process. Dissolved oxygen also drives chemical reactions that cause metals to precipitate, accumulating in the bottom sediment, where they form insoluble compounds with phosphorus and other nutrients. Conversely, at low oxygen concentrations, anaerobic bacteria drive reactions that force metals back into solution, where they can stimulate algal blooms. Therefore, installing an aeration system in a pond can provide the additional oxygen needed to maintain a balanced pond system in which algal blooms are less likely to occur.

Applications of aluminum sulfate ($Al_2[SO_4]_3$) may be helpful in precipitating soluble phosphorus out of the water, accumulating as aluminum phosphate ($AlPO_4$) in the bottom sediment.

Aquatic dyes impart a blue or blue-green color to pond water to restrict sunlight penetration and reduce the growth of algae by inhibiting photosynthesis. Reports of control from the use of dyes have been variable, but complete control is rarely achieved by this method alone.

Algaecides such as copper sulfate ($CuSO_4$) and other copper-containing compounds can provide relatively quick kill of algae when used properly; however, the dead algae decompose, releasing nutrients back into the water to encourage more algal growth. With repeated use of copper-containing compounds, toxic residues may accumulate over time, with potentially devastating effects. Chemical control with algaecides must be combined with efforts to reduce the flow of nutrients into the pond so that its nutrient level declines as water is drawn for irrigation.

Finally, the use of barley straw has gained popularity in recent years because of the suppressive effects of chemicals released as it decomposes. As barley straw is largely ineffective once algae have bloomed, fall application is recommended to discourage blooms the following spring. It is most effective when stabilized several feet below the surface in well-aerated water. ■

CULTIVATION AND TOPDRESSING

▶ CASE STUDY 4.17

Scenario: At a golf course near Philadelphia, the native soils have a high percentage of silt and clay. Under heavy traffic, the fairways became severely compacted, requiring intensive core cultivation to sustain healthy turf (Figure 4.8). As the cores dried following extraction, they became hard and difficult to break up, requiring repeated dragging that increased damage to the turf. Without dragging, the cores were not easily reincorporated into the turf, causing damage to the cutting units on the mowers and an unsightly mess on the fairways.

Analysis: While the resistance of soil cores to physical decomposition—especially those extracted from highly compacted, fine-textured soils—can be formidable, it varies considerably with soil moisture. When compressed between the fingers, wet soil cores exhibit high plasticity, behaving like putty. As the cores dry, they eventually reach an optimum moisture level at which they are most friable; with further drying, friability is gradually reduced and the cores become more resistant to crushing, reaching a brick-like condition when completely dry.

Figure 4.8   Soil cores generated from hollow-tine cultivation of a fairway.

Attempts to break up soil cores and reincorporate them into the turf should be timed to occur when they exhibit maximum friability.

Solution: While hollow-tine cultivation should be conducted on relatively moist soils to favor maximum penetration of the tines, subsequent attempts to break up the extracted soil cores through vertical mowing or matting should be delayed until they have had time to dry to the point of maximum friability, but not so long that they become brick-like. If the cores are highly resistant to physical decomposition, allow them to dry completely and then rewet them by irrigating the turf. Rapid absorption of water by dry soil cores will often cause them to shatter, facilitating their reincorporation into the turf. If the intention is to remove the soil cores in order to backfill the holes with a coarser-textured medium, however, they may be more easily removed by sweepers if first allowed to dry to a brick-like condition. ■

▶ CASE STUDY 4.18

Scenario: A golf course superintendent in southern Michigan decided to convert his push-up soil-based greens to sand-based greens via a sand topdressing program. He initiated the conversion with hollow-tine cultivation, then topdressed to fill the holes with calcareous sand. Light sand topdressing was conducted every 3 weeks thereafter. The pH of the sand was found to be 8.5. In an attempt to lower the pH, monthly applications of granular sulfur at the rate of 1 lb per 1000 ft^2 (0.5 kg per 100 m^2) were initiated. After the second month, turf density declined and some turf loss was evident in depressions. An examination of the soil profile revealed the formation of a foul-smelling black layer just below the sand layer (Figure 4.9). What can be done to eliminate the black layer?

Analysis: The initiation of a sand-topdressing program on a soil-based green results in the creation of an expanding sand layer at the surface, setting up the conditions for black layer development. Within the sand layer, water infiltrates relatively quickly, moving through the layer at a rate reflective of its hydraulic conductivity. When the wetting front reaches the soil, however, further percolation slows to a rate reflective of the hydraulic conductivity of the soil. If the rate at which water is applied to the turf is greater than the rate at which water moves

Figure 4.9   Plug of turf showing a substantial black layer within the soil profile.

through the soil, a temporary water table will develop in the sand layer and persist until the underlying soil can fully absorb the water. Because of the persistently wet conditions, anaerobic microorganisms reduce sulfate (SO_4^{2-}) to sulfide (S^{2-}) ions, forming hydrogen sulfide (H_2S) gas that reacts with iron and other metals to form metal sulfides (e.g., iron sulfide, FeS) that accumulate, forming black layer (Figure 4.10). As a consequence of the filling of many of the soil pores by jam-like metal sulfides, the rate at which water moves into the soil is further reduced, exacerbating the internal drainage problem. With persistently wet sand and soil, turfgrass growth is reduced and turf quality declines.

Solution: An intensive hollow-tine cultivation program is needed to break through the black layer to provide opportunities for replacing some of the metal sulfide–infested soil with sand. Subsequent exposure of the remaining soil to atmospheric air would encourage the oxidation of some of the residual metal sulfides, further eroding the black layer. It has been suggested that the use of potassium nitrate (KNO_3) as an NK fertilizer would move additional oxygen to the soil, promoting further oxidation of the black layer. If tests showed that deeper soil regions were substantially more permeable than the surface soil, deep hollow-tine cultivation followed by sand topdressing to fill the holes (or drill-and-fill operations) could be employed to provide bypass drainage, further reducing the hydraulic load on the turf. Deep solid-tine cultivation

Figure 4.10   These two soil cores were treated with granular sulfur and anaerobic sulfur-reducing bacteria prior to submerging them in water for 3 days. Upon removal from the water, black layer was evident where the sulfur was placed, indicating its importance in the formation of black layer.

might be considered as an alternative; however, for this to significantly improve soil macroporosity by uplifting and shattering the soil matrix, the soil would have to dry almost completely before the operation is performed. In wet soil, the tines would simply make holes, further compressing the surrounding the soil. Finally, to compensate for the high pH of the soil and associated concerns over the low availability of some nutrients, fertilizer nutrients should be applied as foliar sprays for direct absorption by the leaves.   ■

SUMMARY OF CULTURAL PROBLEMS

Mowing-Related Problems

Mowing is the most fundamental turfgrass cultural operation. Because of the frequency with which it must be performed and the sophistication of the equipment employed, mowing also consumes the largest percentage of the turf maintenance budget, often more than 50%. It also poses one of the greatest challenges in ensuring that the resources invested in mowing consistently yield the desired outcomes. These include a turf that is sufficiently dense, fine-textured, smooth, upright-growing, and uniform to be aesthetically satisfactory. They may also include a turf that has the playability and safety characteristics demanded for specific sports and recreational activities.

While mowing can be performed with a variety of mower types, including reels, rotaries, and flails, the highest turf quality is produced by reel mowers. These cut turfgrass leaves by the coordinated action of a series of rotating reel blades and a stationary bedknife. As the mower moves forward, turfgrass shoots are pushed forward by the bedknife. At the same time, the rotating reel blades pull shoots back toward the bedknife. At the point of contact between these two cutting edges, an isosceles triangle is formed by the shoots. Once the cutting action has been completed, these shoots spring back to their vertical positions. Depending upon the length of the isosceles triangle's base (called the *clip of the reel* [CR]—the forward distance traveled between successive clips) relative to its height (mowing height, MH), the surface of the turf may have a ribbed appearance, called *marcelling*. As long as CR approximately equals MH, the height variation (called the *restitution height*, R) is small and the percent variation in height ($\%V = R/MH$) is about 12%, which is largely undetectable. However, where CR is appreciable longer than MH, R and %V are proportionately larger, eventually causing observable marcelling. Reel mowers are designed to provide a smooth cut with only modest and undetectable variation in cutting heights, as long as they are operated at the proper speed. Most reel mowers are designed to be operated at 4 mi/hr (6.5 km/hr). Where this forward operating speed is exceeded, CR increases proportionately, increasing the likelihood of a marcelling problem.

Reel blades and bedknives must be sharp to provide a clean cut. They must also be properly adjusted so that they are not quite touching, but are sufficiently close to cut grass leaves. When the cutting edges are dull and improperly adjusted, tearing and bruising of grass leaves during mowing is the likely result. Frayed leaf tips typically desiccate and turn gray, causing a grayish cast over the surface of the turf.

Plate 1 (*a*). An illustration of the climates of the western hemisphere, including: A (tropical), B (dry; includes BS [semiarid] and BW [arid] climatic types), C (subtropical), D (temperate), E (subarctic), and F (polar). Modifiers include: a (warm—average temperature for warmest month > 72°F), b (cool—average temperature for warmest month < 72°F), c (continental; used for temperate climates), f (no dry season), h (hot; used for dry climates) k (cold; used for dry climates), o (oceanic; used for temperate climates), r (rainy; used for tropical climates), s (dry summer; used for subtropical and tropical climates), and w (dry winter; used for subtropical and tropical climates).

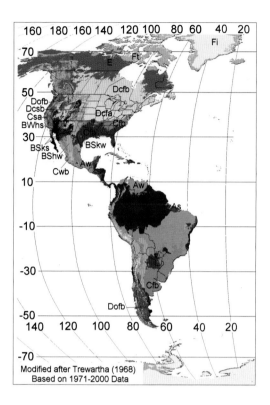

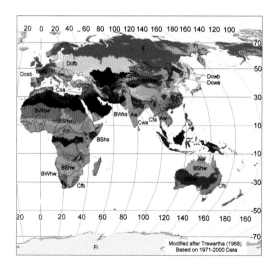

Plate 1 (*b*). An illustration of the climates of the eastern hemisphere (see Figure 2.1a for legend).

Plate 2. Green with portions showing severe ice-related damage in early spring following heavy rainfall and a sudden drop in temperature. (Photo courtesy J.L. Snow, USGA Green Section)

Plate 3. Close-up of plug extracted from a green showing black layer at the interface of coarse- and fine-textured sand layers.

Plate 4. A soil core extracted from a football field showing several inches of muck from muck-grown sod that was planted on a sand base.

Plate 5. Creeping bentgrass showing severe phosphorus deficiency and annual bluegrass during early spring.

Plate 6. Kikuyugrass fairway showing the effects of non-uniform irrigation during an extended drought. (Photo courtesy J.L. Snow, USGA Green Section)

Plate 7. Scalping injury on a kikuyugrass fairway in which a substantial thatch layer has accumulated.

Plate 8. Annual bluegrass green showing "physiological drought" symptoms from salt accumulation in the soil.

Plate 9. A feeder stream with a large concentration of suspended soil particles flowing into a water retention pond used for turfgrass irrigation.

Plate 10. Differential growth and color of creeping bentgrass (center) and annual bluegrass following treatment with paclobutrazol plant-growth regulator.

Plate 11. Creeping bentgrass overgrowing annual bluegrass at fairway mowing height after treatment with paclobutrazol plant-growth regulator.

Plate 12. Dollar spot disease in annual bluegrass turf.

Plate 13. Brown patch disease.

Plate 14. Differential incidence of foliar anthracnose disease on annual bluegrass (susceptible) and creeping bentgrass (resistant).

Plate 15. Crown rotting anthracnose disease on annual bluegrass green.

Plate 16. Frog-eye symptom of take-all patch in newly established creeping bentgrass turf.

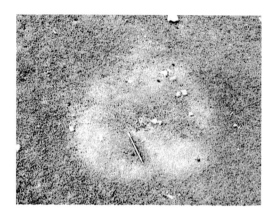

Plate 17. Creeping bentgrass growing where annual bluegrass was destroyed by summer patch disease.

Plate 18. Light-green shoots of annual bluegrass showing symptoms of bacterial wilt disease.

Plate 19. *Pythium* blight disease on a green.

Plate 20. Close-up of mycelium and brown turfgrass leaves from *Pythium* blight.

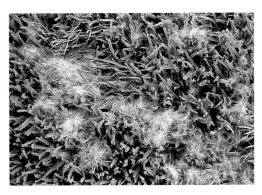

Plate 21. *Microdochium* patch disease on a green.

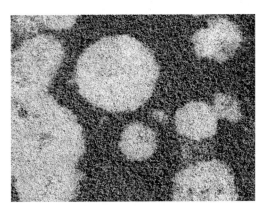

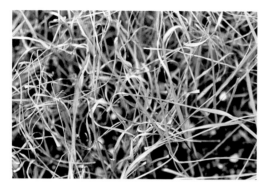

Plate 22. Severely twisted leaf blades from a fairway with gray leaf spot disease. (Photo courtesy W. Uddin, Penn State University)

Plate 23. Gray leaf spot esion with gray center and distinctive yellow halo. (Photo courtesy W. Uddin, Penn State University)

Plate 24. Damage from annual bluegrass weevils.

Plate 25. Damage from black cutworms feeding on turfgrass shoots.

Other types of mower damage include wear from the tires or mowing units. Tire-related damage usually results where the tires cover the same ground with each mowing. There are two dimensions to this type of damage: turfgrass wear and soil compaction. While the obvious solution to this problem would be to alter the mowing pattern to avoid concentrated tire traffic, this has not been feasible in the perimeter of greens where the cleanup pass is made, causing the infamous *triplex ring*. Today, with the introduction of offset or shifting mowing units on triplex mowers, it is now possible to vary tire traffic and reduce this type of mowing stress. Mowing unit-related damage is due to wear from the rollers, bedknives, and other components that come into contact with the turf. While grooved rollers may be helpful in reducing the excess surface biomass that can develop in high-density turfs, they also impose an additional stress that, coupled with summertime heat and drought stresses, can be especially damaging to greens and other closely mowed turfs. Substituting smooth rollers for grooved rollers during the summer months can be helpful in reducing the severity of stress from rollers. Also, substituting segmented rollers for continuous rollers can reduce wear from the twisting action of the rollers during turns. If at all possible, tight turns should be avoided, as centrifugal force accentuates turfgrass wear from mowing; if that is not possible, mowing speed should be reduced.

The fear of scalping along the perimeter of a green during mowing often leads to overcompensation by the mower operator, pulling the green's perimeter slightly inward. The resulting loss of a green's total area over time is called *green creep*. Care must be exercised to minimize green creep, even at the expense of some minor scalping along the outer edge of the green. Where a substantial amount of green creep has occurred, the affected area should be brought back into the green by various means, including reestablishing the area with sod or seed or gradually lowering the mowing height with a walk-behind mower, along with hollow-tine cultivation and top-dressing prior to each mowing height adjustment.

The introduction of triplex mowers required the use of hydraulic systems for raising and lowering the mowing units. An inevitable consequence of this innovation is the occasional spills of hydraulic fluid when a pressurized line breaks or a connection leaks. The extent of the damage resulting from spilled hydraulic fluid depends upon the amount of fluid applied to the turf and its temperature at the time of application. Absorption of relatively cool hydraulic fluid can cause the desiccation of plant tissues. Damage can be minimized by immediately flushing the fluid off the leaves and into the soil, initially with soapy water, followed by a thorough soaking with water alone. After the mower has been operated for some time, however, the temperature of the hydraulic fluid increases to the point at which damage is immediate and severe from the scorching of plant tissues. The best solution to hydraulic fluid leaks is prevention. This can be done by routinely inspecting the equipment before each use, immediate identification of leaks during operation, moving the equipment to a safe place to minimize damage, following proper cleanup procedures, and conducting an effective preventive maintenance program on the equipment.

Fertilization-Related Problems

Fertilizers should be applied to new turfgrass plantings in sufficient quantities to promote vigorous turfgrass growth and development. While the efficiency with which a new turf is established can be strongly influenced by the availability of essential nutrients, excessive fertilizer application during grow-in can result in nutrient runoff and leaching into surface and subsurface water bodies. To minimize the potential for nutrient pollution, accurate estimates of a soil's nutrient-retention capacity (i.e., CEC) and nutrient content should be obtained to determine the amounts of specific nutrients needed prior to planting. Following germination, moderate amounts of nitrogen should be applied to favor vigorous seedling development. Nutrient application through the irrigation system—called *fertigation*—can provide the proper amounts of nitrogen and other nutrients whenever they are needed while eliminating the need to drive application equipment over a planting bed that may be too wet to support vehicular traffic.

In established turfs, foliar coloration and/or restricted growth may indicate that specific nutrients are deficient. For example, the availability of phosphorus can be severely reduced by cold temperatures early in the growing season and by fixation as iron, aluminum, or manganese oxides at soil pHs that are too low (<5.0) or as calcium phosphates at pHs that are too high (>6.5). Despite conventional wisdom to the contrary, phosphorus deficiencies can reduce the competitive ability of creeping bentgrass, resulting in the dominance of annual bluegrass on greens where both species are present. The pH of some highly buffered clayey soils (or, for that matter, calcareous sands) may be so resistant to change from sulfur or other additives that it may be necessary to resort to foliar feeding, bypassing the soil and relying on direct uptake of essential nutrients by the leaves to sustain healthy turfgrass growth.

Irrigation-Related Problems

Contemporary irrigation systems should be designed to provide a uniform distribution of water at precipitation rates that maximize infiltration and minimize runoff. Uniform coverage is provided by overlapping wedge-shaped patterns of distribution from adjacent sprinklers. For example, a section of turf receiving the smallest amount of precipitation near the periphery of the coverage pattern from one sprinkler also receives the largest amount of precipitation near the center of the coverage pattern from an adjacent sprinkler. And where the combined coverage patterns from adjacent sprinklers provide a precipitation rate that is less than the infiltration capacity of the turf, there is no runoff. But if the infiltration capacity of the turf is less than the precipitation rate, perhaps due to severe soil compaction or other restrictions to internal drainage, runoff will occur on sloping sites and standing water will accumulate in depressions.

Where the coverage of water from sprinklers with overlapping distribution patterns is not uniform, portions of the irrigated turf may receive too little water, while other portions may receive too much. With some irrigation systems, especially those installed decades ago, portions of the turf may not receive any water at all, becoming dormant and turning off-color during extended dry periods. Under these conditions, extensive hand watering may be required to maintain color and sustain growth until the irrigation system can be improved or replaced.

Where water restrictions are imposed, steps should be taken to improve water-use efficiency. These could include repairing leaks from the irrigation system, avoiding irrigation when there are high winds that seriously disrupt water distribution patterns, watering at night when there is less evaporative loss due to high atmospheric temperatures, and matching irrigation amounts with consumptive water-use rates as closely as possible. Where these measures are inadequate to meet the imposed restrictions, water use must be prioritized based on the relative importance of each turf, with greens receiving the highest priority and roughs the lowest.

The specific constituents of a particular water source, including ions in solution and particles in suspension, can dramatically affect the quality of greens and other turfs receiving this water for irrigation. High concentrations of sodium [Na^+] ions—relative to calcium [Ca^{2+}] and magnesium [Mg^{2+}] ion concentrations—can displace other ions and eventually saturate the exchange sites on clay particles with sodium. Sodium ions and the six molecules of water surrounding each ion are so large that they cause individual clay particles within micelles to spread apart, causing the micelles—and the soil aggregates in which they occur—to disperse. As a consequence, the soil's structure can be destroyed and its permeability substantially reduced. The sodium hazard associated with a particular source of irrigation water is reflected in its sodium adsorption ratio (SAR_W), which is the sodium ion concentration divided by the square root of the average of the calcium and magnesium ion concentrations ($[Na^+]/([Ca^{2+} + Mg^{2+}]/2)^{1/2}$, with all ion concentrations expressed in milliequivalents per liter (meq/L). Irrigation water with high SAR_W values poses a significant threat to soil permeability. Addition of gypsum ($CaSO_4$) or other sources of free calcium to the irrigation water increases its calcium ion concentration and correspondingly reduces its SAR_W, reducing the sodium hazard.

Where high concentrations of bicarbonate [HCO_3^-] ions occur in irrigation water sources, an additional sodium hazard exists. When in close proximity to calcium and magnesium ions, bicarbonate ions can react with them to form calcium carbonate ($CaCO_3$) and magnesium carbonate ($MgCO_3$), which precipitate out of solution because of their very low solubility, with corresponding increases in the SAR_W, increasing the sodium hazard. Bicarbonates can be neutralized with the addition of gypsum ($HCO_3^- + CaSO_4 = CaCO_3 + HSO_4^-$) to precipitate out the bicarbonate as calcium carbonate, or sulfuric acid ($HCO_3^- + H_2SO_4 = H_2O + CO_2 + HSO_4^-$) to drive off the bicarbonates as CO_2.

High concentrations of soluble salts applied through irrigation water can accumulate in the soil, resulting in increased salinity and decreased osmotic potential (Ψ_o) of the soil solution, since osmotic potential and matric potential (Ψ_m) are the two principal components of soil water potential (Ψ_{sw}), decreases in osmotic potential result in corresponding decreases in soil water potential. And since the absorption of water by plant roots is in response to a water potential gradient created by transpirational water loss from leaves, significant reductions in soil water potential lower the water potential gradient between the plant and the soil, reducing water absorption. With further increases in soil salinity (i.e., reductions in osmotic potential), water absorption by plants ceases altogether, causing a phenomenon called *physiological drought.* The solution to excessive soil salinity is to leach the salts from the soil with large quantities of water. Where water percolation through the soil matrix is high, this can be done with little difficulty, provided that there is an abundant supply of water of acceptable quality. In soils of low permeability, however, leaching salts from the plant rootzone may not be possible.

Alkaline water contains substances that increase its pH above 7.0. When used for irrigating turf, this water may increase the pH of the soil; however, the rate of increase depends upon the soil's composition and CEC. Sandy soils composed primarily of silica sand with low CECs change fairly quickly, while calcareous sands or clayey soil with high CECs change very slowly. If necessary, alkaline irrigation water can be treated with sulfuric acid (H_2SO_4) to reduce its pH to 7.0; however, if the soil underlying the irrigated turf is a calcareous sand or a soil high in clay content and is already at a high pH, acidification of the irrigation water may not produce positive results. Because of the influence of pH on nutrient availability, foliar application of nutrients can be employed to satisfy the nutrient requirements of turfgrasses growing in strongly alkaline soils.

Suspended or floating materials not only reduce the aesthetic appearance of a water resource, but can seriously reduce the quality of the water for turfgrass irrigation. Some suspended soil particles in fast-moving streams pass through intake filters, increase the wear on sprinkler components, and clog soil pores, restricting internal drainage and leading to other problems such as black layer formation. Measures for encouraging settling of suspended particles, including damming portions of streams to capture and slowly release the water into ponds or increasing pond size to reduce turbulence, can substantially reduce the amount of these particles entering the turf. Once suspended particles have entered the turf and filled a large percentage of the soil pore spaces, it may be necessary to hollow-tine cultivate, remove cores, and backfill the holes with sand or another suitable medium to restore acceptable infiltration and drainage. Floating algae and other aquatic vegetation in ponds can clog intake filters and foul pumps, diminishing their utility as irrigation water repositories. Since these populations develop in response to the accumulation of nutrients, heavy applications of phosphorus to nearby turfs should be avoided, the direction of nearby sprinkler heads used for fertigation should be controlled, and clippings should be prevented from entering the pond. Where algae populations have developed, aeration, phosphate-precipitating agents, dyes, algaecides, and barley straw can be used for control.

Cultivation- and Topdressing-Related Problems

Cores extracted from turfs with severely compacted soils can strongly resist attempts to break them up for uniform reincorporation of the soil into the turf. When wet, the cores tend to behave like putty and smear when compressed between the fingers. As the cores dry, they gradually reach an optimum moisture level at which they are most friable; however, with further drying, friability is reduced and the cores become more resistant to crushing, reaching a brick-like condition when completely dry. While hollow-tine cultivation should be conducted when the soil is relatively moist to facilitate maximum tine penetration, subsequent attempts to break up the cores by vertical mowing or matting operations should be delayed until maximum friability is reached, but not so long that they become brick-like. Hard cores should be allowed to dry completely and then irrigated to promote rewetting and shattering as water is rapidly absorbed through all external surfaces. Where the decision is made to remove the cores, this is sometimes best done after they have dried to a brick-like condition. However, if the medium supporting turfgrass growth is predominantly sand, extracted cores should be removed when they are relatively wet and firm, as the sand from dry cores can easily flow back into the turf.

Texturally layered profiles are commonly observed where sand topdressing—composed principally of coarse to medium sands—has been practiced on either pushup greens or sand-based greens in which the construction sand is poorly drained (often because of the presence of too many fine particles clogging the macropores). Because of the relatively slow percolation rate of water through the underlying finer-textured medium, temporary water tables tend to form and persist at the base of the coarser-textured layer formed from topdressing. Under the persistently wet conditions existing at or just below the interface of these two media, sulfate (SO^{2-}) may be reduced to sulfide (S^{2-}) and react with iron (Fe^{2+}), manganese (Mn^{2+}), and other metals, forming a black layer composed of metal sulfides (FeS, MnS). This jam-like material clogs soil pores, further reducing internal drainage. While various methods (coring, KNO_3 treatment) may be employed to physically reduce and/or oxidize the black layer, the problems resulting from poor internal drainage will probably persist until some way is found to remove the excess water from the soil matrix. In pushup greens, this often requires the installation of drain pipes (ultimately joined and connected to the drainage system) in slit trenches that are subsequently backfilled with sand to connect the coarser-textured layer at the surface to the drain pipes, allowing the drainage water to flow unimpeded toward and into the pipes, through which it is conducted away from the green. In USGA greens constructed with a gravel layer beneath the rootzone medium, drill-and-fill operations can provide the connection between the coarser-textured surface sand and the drain pipes previously installed in the gravel.

CHAPTER

5

Pest and Pesticide Problems

Pesticides are valuable tools for controlling weeds, disease-inciting organisms, insects, and other pests. They are also potentially dangerous chemicals that should be used as part of an integrated pest management program and in strict accordance with label directions. As the most important factor in fighting pests is a well-adapted turfgrass that is healthy and vigorously growing, an integrated pest management program should include proper turfgrass selection, establishment, and culture, as well as pesticides.

PESTICIDES

▶ CASE STUDY 5.1

Scenario: A golf course in central Pennsylvania applied an experimental granular formulation of ethofumesate herbicide for annual bluegrass (*Poa annua* L.) control in its Penncross creeping bentgrass (*Agrostis stolonifera* L. 'Penncross') greens. Two applications at ¾ lb a.i. per acre (0.84 kg/ha) were made 4 weeks apart, beginning October 20th.

With the second application, pentachloronitrobenzene (PCNB) was also applied at the rate of 1 lb a.i. per 1000 ft^2 (0.5 kg per 100 m^2). For 2 days prior to this application and immediately afterward, heavy rains occurred, causing some runoff of the chemical formulations. Essentially constant rain occurred well into December. There was no evidence of a harsh reaction to the chemical treatments during the winter months; however, with snow melt the following spring, extensive damage was evident, especially in the swales and depressions in the greens. What caused the damage, and how might it have been prevented?

Analysis: While effective against snow mold diseases, PCNB at the full rate of 1 lb a.i. per 1000 ft^2 can be quite injurious to turf. As the ¾-lb rate of ethofumesate is the maximum permitted on creeping bentgrass, two closely spaced applications would also pose some hazard. The combined application of these materials would be even more dangerous, especially if any runoff occurred that would result in their accumulation in depressions. And, given the conditions described above, the likelihood of runoff is quite high.

Solution: With respect to the fungicide PCNB, combinations at half rate (0.5 lb a.i. per 100 ft^2, 2.4 kg per 100 m^2) with other fungicides (chlorothalonil [Daconil], fludioxonil [Medallion], fosetyl-aluminum [Chipco Signature], iprodione [Chipco 26GT], propoconazol [Banner], triadimefon [Bayleton], trifloxystrobin [Compass]) for snow mold control have been shown to offer the advantages of high efficacy and reduced phytotoxicity. This is especially important where other potentially phytotoxic materials are applied at the same time. Applications of ethofumesate to greens during periods of high rainfall should be delayed or avoided, as runoff is likely, resulting in severe phytotoxicity in depressions where the herbicide may accumulate. ∎

WEEDS

► CASE STUDY 5.2

Scenario: Despite the fact that an emulsifiable-concentrate formulation of ethofumesate (Prograss) was applied experimentally at recommended rates each fall for several years on a creeping bentgrass (*Agrostis stolonifera* L.) green, annual bluegrass (*Poa annua* L.) patches that appeared dead the following spring eventually recovered, indicating unsatisfactory control.

Analysis: With daily mowing at ³⁄₁₆th in. (4.8 mm) or less, individual creeping bentgrass plants are very small; thus, their capacity to fill voids through tillering and stolon growth is very limited. As a consequence, large voids resulting from the death of annual bluegrass populations tend to repopulate with annual bluegrass, largely from seed germination and subsequent seedling growth. Combating this requires successfully establishing creeping bentgrass in these voids—a formidable challenge, given the relatively rapid germination of annual bluegrass from the seed reservoir already present in the soil. If the annual bluegrass repopulating the voids is predominantly the annual biotype, new seedlings will tend to quickly colonize the voids. Conversely, if it is the perennial biotype, seedling growth will be relatively slow. Therefore, the likelihood that creeping bentgrass can be successfully established from seed would depend upon the severity of the competition from annual bluegrass seedlings, as influenced by the predominant biotype. In fairways, individual creeping bentgrass plants are larger and their capacity to fill voids is correspondingly greater. Therefore, creeping bentgrass can fill larger voids from strictly vegetative growth. For this reason, ethofumesate is generally more effectively employed for controlling annual bluegrass on fairways than on greens.

Solution: Successful control of annual bluegrass in creeping bentgrass greens will require an integrated program involving highly competitive bentgrass cultivars, adequate soil aeration and drainage, and an array of cultural interventions that consistently favor creeping bentgrass over annual bluegrass, including—but not limited to—the use of herbicides. In this scenario, ethofumesate applications, coupled with spring overseeding with creeping bentgrass, might significantly alter the relative proportions of creeping bentgrass and annual bluegrass in the greens, depending upon several factors: the creeping bentgrass cultivar used and the timing of overseeding, the annual bluegrass biotype present, and the specific kinds of cultural interventions selected and the manner in which they are employed. ■

▶ CASE STUDY 5.3

Scenario: Annual bluegrass (*Poa annua* L.) has invaded creeping bentgrass (*Agrostis stolonifera* L.) greens in many temperate zone golf courses. Can anything be done to prevent this from happening and remove what is there?

Analysis: While successful measures for enhancing the health and vigor of a creeping bentgrass population simultaneously enhance its resistance to annual bluegrass, there are circumstances in which annual bluegrass might have a temporary competitive advantage. For example, compared with creeping bentgrass, annual bluegrass usually initiates shoot growth earlier in the spring and maintains it later in the fall. Also, high rates of nitrogen fertilization may favor annual bluegrass in summer, when, at lower rates, creeping bentgrass would normally be at a competitive advantage. Annual bluegrass would also be at a distinct disadvantage during midspring, when most of the photoassimilates produced are directed at supporting seed head development in place of vegetative growth.

Solution: Prevention of annual bluegrass infestation of creeping bentgrass greens is often attempted with a late-summer application of bensulide (Bensumac, Pre-San) to control the emergence of new seedlings from fall germination; however, control is often unsatisfactory in greens in which annual bluegrass is a well-established component of the turfgrass community. This may reflect the predominance of perennial biotypes of annual bluegrass that are less dependent on seed germination for sustaining their presence in greens. Of additional concern is the fact that the residual activity of preemergence herbicides could conflict with overseeding practices that may be required where winter injury has occurred.

To the extent that small clumps of annual bluegrass develop in a new stand of creeping bentgrass, they can be physically removed with a knife or chemically removed by spot treatment with glufosinate ammonium (Finale) applied with a blotter pen. If necessary, recovery can be accelerated with the use of a ball-mark repair tool; however, small voids are often quickly filled by vegetative growth from adjacent bentgrass plants.

Selective chemical control may be possible with the use of a new herbicide called *bispyrobac-sodium* (Velocity) when labeled for greens; however, extreme care must be exercised to avoid unacceptable damage to the bentgrass. Also, since some creeping bentgrass cultivars are more sensitive than others to this herbicide, some small-area testing should be done before initiating a general application program. Where large patches of annual bluegrass are killed chemically, some replanting is often needed to restore the green to acceptable quality.

Finally, while selective suppression of annual bluegrass may be possible with one of the Class-B PGRs (e.g., paclobutrazol [Trimmit, Turf Enhancer]), results have been variable, presumably due to the biotype of annual bluegrass present (i.e., some perennial biotypes respond much like creeping bentgrass, with suppressed vertical shoot growth but stimulated lateral shoot growth, enhancing their competitive capacity) or the reduced capacity of creeping bentgrass to fully exploit its competitive advantage under the close mowing heights employed for greens. ■

▶ CASE STUDY 5.4

Scenario: A golf course in central Ohio with fairways composed of 70% annual bluegrass (*Poa annua* L.) and 30% creeping bentgrass (*Agrostis stolonifera* L.) has initiated a program of lightweight mowing, picking up clippings, and reducing irrigation frequency in order to increase the proportion of creeping bentgrass. The superintendent was exploring various chemical alternatives to accelerate the transition to predominantly creeping bentgrass, including PGRs, preemergence and postemergence herbicides, and glyphosate-tolerant bentgrass. Which of these programs offer the best prospect for achieving satisfactory results?

Analysis: The competitive capacity of creeping bentgrass in mixed communities with annual bluegrass has been dramatically enhanced with the use of lightweight mowers and the adoption of clipping-removal practices with each mowing. Although the scientific basis for this is not fully understood, clipping removal does reduce the canopy temperature, inoculum from infected leaves, nutrients from clipping decomposition, and the accumulation of annual bluegrass seed available for subsequent germination. Additionally, the reduced traffic intensity from

the use of lightweight mowers would be expected to yield corresponding reductions in turfgrass wear and soil compaction, along with the
associated infestations of annual bluegrass that are frequently observed
where the tires consistently travel.

As with greens, the chemicals that might be used to control annual
bluegrass infestations in creeping bentgrass fairways include herbicides
and PGRs (see Case Study 5.3); however, the number of alternatives for
fairways is greater.

Solution: With respect to preemergence herbicides, two applications
are required to provide season-long control of annual bluegrass; these
usually include a full-rate application in mid- to late August and a
half-rate application in late April or early May. Dithiopyr (Dimension),
oxadiazon (Ronstar), and several dinitroaniline herbicides, including
benefin and trifluralin (Team), pendimethalin (Pre-M, Pendulum), and
prodiamine (Barricade), are used for controlling annual bluegrass as
well as summer annual grasses. With season-long control from preemergence herbicides, however, opportunities to introduce creeping
bentgrass from seed are precluded. Also, the efficacy of preemergence
herbicides is limited to annual bluegrass emerging from seed germination. Established populations are largely unaffected, except perhaps for
some enhanced reduction of turf quality during summer stress periods.
Any disruption of the turf from divots or other causes also breaks the
chemical barrier, allowing annual bluegrass seed to germinate despite
the presence of preemergence herbicide residues nearby.

Ethofumesate (Progress) can be used to achieve partial control of
established populations of annual bluegrass—principally the annual
biotypes—in creeping bentgrass fairways. Because creeping bentgrass
is not as tolerant of this herbicide as is perennial ryegrass (*Lolium
perenne* L.), lower rates (i.e., not more than 0.75 lb a.i. per acre or
0.84 kg a.i. per ha) must be used; as a consequence, its efficacy is less
than in areas where higher rates can be used. Two to three applications 21 days apart are typically made in the fall. This reflects the role
that cold temperatures play in the control achieved with ethofumesate;
where mild temperatures follow ethofumesate applications, little control may be evident, while very good control has often resulted where
severe winter temperatures have occurred. Creeping bentgrass is often
discolored by applications of ethofumesate. This is most evident in

poorly rooted, shaded, waterlogged, heavily trafficked, or diseased turfs. Discoloration can be reduced by undertaking measures to correct these problems and by co-applying chelated iron or light rates of soluble nitrogen with ethofumesate. Different creeping bentgrass cultivars vary in their sensitivity; Pennlinks and Penneagle are less tolerant than Penncross. Other bentgrass species, including colonial bentgrass (*Agrostis capillaris* L.) and velvet bentgrass (*A. canina* L.), are intolerant and should not be treated with this herbicide. And since treated turfs should not be overseeded for at least 3 weeks following the last ethofumesate application, fall applications may require delaying seeding until the following spring. Where large expanses of annual bluegrass occur, effective control with ethofumesate has a disastrous effect on turf quality, requiring extensive overseeding to reestablish turfgrass cover. Ethofumesate is best used where annual bluegrass populations are small and recovery from the growth of adjacent creeping bentgrass populations can be achieved fairly rapidly. To the extent that spring overseeding might be necessary, one should consider the use of clear plastic covers to accelerate turfgrass germination and seedling development.

As discussed in Case Study 5.3, bispyrobac-sodium (Velocity) can be used for selectively controlling annual bluegrass in mixed stands with creeping bentgrass; however, because of limited experience with this herbicide, it should be used experimentally on small areas before broadening its use. Cultivars of Kentucky bluegrass (*Poa pratensis* L.) vary in their sensitivity to this herbicide; therefore, some localized testing should be done to establish the specific sensitivity level.

With respect to PGRs, certain gibberellic acid inhibitors have shown the greatest utility for selectively suppressing the growth of annual bluegrass in mixed stands with creeping bentgrass (Plate 10; see color insert). The Class-B PGR, paclobutrazol (Trimmit, Turf Enhancer), inhibits cell elongation by interfering with gibberellic acid biosynthesis; as a consequence, vertical shoot growth of turfgrasses, and thus their mowing requirements, are reduced. Where the annual bluegrass population is made up of primarily annual biotypes, paclobutrazol can suppress its growth while simultaneously stimulating lateral shoot (i.e., stolon) growth of adjacent creeping bentgrass plants (Plate 11; see color insert). Paclobutrazol can be applied two or three times in spring, but most importantly just after annual bluegrass seed shatter, and two or three times in late summer and early fall to suppress the growth of newly germinated annual bluegrass plants. As the turfgrass response can vary with soil type, climatic conditions, moisture levels, application timing, and other factors, careful experimentation should be done to establish how this material can best be used as part of an annual bluegrass control program.

Where it is desirable to convert a predominantly annual bluegrass fairway to creeping bentgrass through a complete renovation or reestablishment procedure, dazomet (Basamid Granular) may be used to kill the annual bluegrass seed reservoir in the soil. To ensure efficacy, treated sites must be sealed to prevent the methylisothiocyanate (MITC) gas released from the formulation from escaping into the atmosphere. This can be accomplished by covering the soil with a tarp for 5 to 7 days following application; it can also be attempted by employing irrigation to seal the surface for 4 to 5 days following application. Seeding can take place after the MITC gas has degraded to nitrates (NO_3^-), sulfates (SO_4^{2-}), bicarbonates (HCO_3^-), and other simple ions.

Finally, glyphosate- and glufosinate-tolerant creeping bentgrasses are under development. When they are commercially available, they will allow the selective removal of annual bluegrass from newly established or overseeded fairways. While these promise to be powerful new tools for controlling annual bluegrass, one can't help but wonder how soon glyphosate- and glufosinate-tolerant annual bluegrasses will evolve. ■

► CASE STUDY 5.5

Scenario: Dense fine fescue (slender creeping red fescue, *Festuca rubra* L. ssp. *litoralis* [Meyer] Auquier, and chewings fescue, *F. rubra* L. ssp. *comutata* [Thuill.] Nyman) greens were established on native dune sand for a new golf course located along the eastern coast of Scotland. Browntop bentgrass (*Agrostis capillaris* L.) was also included in the seed mixture (30%) used for planting greens, but very little of this species survived. Because of the high potential for annual bluegrass (*Poa annua* L.) invasion, the superintendent limited the amount of nitrogen and potassium fertilizer used to 1 and 2 lb, respectively, per 1000 ft² (0.5 kg N and 1.0 kg K per 100 m²) during the grow-in year and provided no phosphorus. The native sand contained 0.6% organic matter, the CEC was 1.5 to 2.0 meq/100 g, and the pH was above 8.0. What should the superintendent do in subsequent years to discourage annual bluegrass from invading his greens?

Analysis: While the climate of eastern coastal Scotland is cool temperate-oceanic (Dob), with 26.2 in. (66.6 cm) of evenly distributed annual rainfall and an average annual temperature of 47.3°F (8.5°C), there are only 4 months each year in which the average temperature exceeds 50°F (10°C). If only 3 months had average temperatures exceeding this threshold, the climate would be considered subarctic (E). Therefore, while this is a mild climate, it is so cool that turfgrass growth tends to be relatively slow throughout most of the year. As the native dune sand is a coarse, infertile medium, the limited amounts of moisture and nutrients would also constitute restraints on turfgrass growth unless abundant quantities of these inputs were provided through the cultural program. The turfgrasses best adapted to these conditions are the fine fescues; however, browntop bentgrass and annual bluegrass may also persist and be competitive, depending on irrigation and fertilization practices.

Solution: The greens should be mowed as high as possible, consistent with sustaining acceptable putting quality. For fine fescues under these conditions, a ¼-in. (6.4-mm) height is satisfactory. Based on tissue tests, sufficient nitrogen, phosphorus, and potassium, as well as other nutrients, should be provided to maintain minimum sufficiency levels for healthy plants. Light applications of iron and possibly sulfur should be made for color and enhanced growth of the fescue. Irrigation should be withheld as much as possible to minimize the potential for annual bluegrass invasion. To the extent that small clumps of annual bluegrass do invade, they should be physically removed as quickly as possible.   ■

► Case Study 5.6

Scenario: The quality of the turf at a 20-acre (8.1-ha) Little League baseball complex in New York had deteriorated due to inadequate fertility, frayed leaves from mowing with a dull rotary mower, and extensive weed populations, including crabgrass (*Digitaria* spp.) and an array of broadleaf weeds. Given its composition of Kentucky bluegrass (*Poa pratensis* L.) and tall and fine fescues (*Festuca* spp.), what can be done to improve the quality of the turf at the complex?

Analysis: A sufficient level of turfgrass growth is needed to resist weed invasion and to compensate for the deterioration of turfgrass tissues from natural senescence, as well as mechanical injury, disease, and other adversities. And sufficient growth requires adequate soil aeration, moisture, and fertility. It is also important to have turfgrass cultivars that are well adapted to prevailing conditions. Finally, the turf should be mowed at the proper height and frequency with sharp, properly adjusted mowers. Where any of these factors is lacking, the quality will inevitably decline.

Where turf quality is unacceptable, a comprehensive site assessment is needed, involving visual inspection, soil testing and probing, and equipment evaluation. A visual inspection is performed to determine the composition and condition of the plant community. For example, specific weed populations may indicate soil acidity (red sorrel, *Rumex acetosella* L.), low fertility (plantains, *Plantago* spp.; yarrow, *Archillea millefolium* L.), soil compaction (knotweed, *Polygonum aviculare* L.; goosegrass, *Eleusine indica* [L.] Gaertn.), and poor drainage (chickweed, *Stellaria media* [L.] Vill.; curled dock, *Rumex crispus* L.), and, thus, may suggest some of the corrective actions that should be taken. The turfgrasses should also be inspected for the presence of disease, injury from insects or large-animal pests, and mower damage, as these also suggest some of the corrective actions that should be taken.

Soil testing is needed to determine the fertility status of the soil. Representative samples of the top 2 to 4 in. (5–10 cm) of soil should be taken and submitted to a reputable soil-testing laboratory. In reviewing the soil-test report, deficiencies and excesses should be noted. For example, if the pH is too low, lime applications should be included in the cultural program. If there are indications that phosphorus, potassium, and other nutrients are deficient, they should also be applied as part of the cultural program. Soil probing is done to assess the physical condition of the soil. This may be done with a soil probe or a knife. If there is substantial resistance to penetration with the probe or knife, this may indicate severe compaction, or the presence of hardpans or other obstacles in the soil. Visual inspection of the soil extracted with the probe or knife may reveal the presence of different textural layers that may impede water movement through the soil profile, or the presence of a blue-colored "gley" layer, indicating severely reduced conditions from waterlogged soil. Peculiar odors emanating from the soil, reflecting the presence of sulfides or other gases, indicate unfavorable conditions for turfgrass growth. And the depth and condition of the roots may reflect some physical, chemical, or biological properties of the soil.

The presence and condition of specific types of equipment are reflections of the on-site capacity to implement a sound cultural program. The size and type—reel versus rotary—of mowing equipment would be indicative of the capacity for efficient and proper mowing. Dull or improperly adjusted cutting edges would account for the frayed leaves noted in this scenario's description. The presence of cultivation equipment would be indicative of the capacity for controlling thatch and soil compaction. And the presence and type of sprayers and spreaders would indicate the capacity for proper application of fertilizers, pesticides, and other materials.

Solution: Perform the site assessment as outlined above. Sharpen and adjust mowers to improve cutting quality, mowing at least twice each week. Initiate a fertilization program with 1 lb nitrogen per 1000 ft^2, along with other nutrients, at rates based on soil test results; continue as needed to correct deficiencies and sustain aggressive growth. Spray weeds with appropriate herbicides for control, including combinations of 2,4-D, mecoprop, and dicamba for broadleaved weeds and quinclorac (Drive) for crabgrass. Irrigate as needed to stimulate recuperative growth. At the end of the playing season, hollow-tine cultivate the field several times and reincorporate soil cores. Precede this operation with vertical mowing if needed to remove excess thatch, and open the remainder of the thatch layer to facilitate soil reincorporation from hollow-tine cultivation. Overseed with a blend of superior cultivars of Kentucky bluegrass or a mixture of Kentucky bluegrass and perennial ryegrass (*Lolium perenne* L.); then promote germination and seeding growth with irrigation and other cultural operations. Apply a preemergence herbicide the following spring to prevent crabgrass emergence in the turf. Mow, fertilize, irrigate, cultivate, and apply pesticides as needed to sustain vigorous growth and control pests throughout the playing season. ■

▶ CASE STUDY 5.7

Scenario: Large, smooth crabgrass (*Digitaria ischaemum* [Schred.] Muhl.) and hairy crabgrass (*D. sanguinalis* [L.] Scop.) populations had developed in a 2-year-old sodded Kentucky bluegrass (*Poa pratensis* L.) lawn in a new condominium complex located just outside of Columbus, Ohio. The maintenance crew supervisor responsible for the property knew that the planting bed had not been properly prepared prior to the installation of the sod. As a consequence, the turf was highly susceptible to crabgrass invasion and other pest problems. What should he do to control the crabgrass populations and reduce the likelihood of future infestations?

Analysis: Smooth and hairy crabgrasses are plants with bunch-type growth habits and short decumbent stems that root at the nodes. Seed heads appear as several finger-like projections at the terminals of seed stalks. The principal difference between these two species is the abundance of hairs along the leaf sheaths of hairy crabgrass and their absence in smooth crabgrass. Both are summer annuals that germinate in late spring or summer on warm, moist sites with moderate to full sunlight. The rapid tillering of these species during warm periods favorable to their growth tends to crowd out Kentucky bluegrass, especially weak stands that are not growing vigorously. Crabgrass growth slows considerably during cool weather in late summer and early fall, and plants are usually killed with the first hard frost, leaving unsightly brown patches in the turf.

Solution: As unfavorable growing conditions—including poor drainage and low soil fertility—reduce the vigor of Kentucky bluegrass and thus its resistance to crabgrass invasion, measures taken to correct these problems are important components of a crabgrass prevention program. However, locations where crabgrass pressure is severe usually require the use of herbicides to prevent populations from emerging in the turf or to control populations that have already emerged. Postemergence applications of fenoxyprop p-ethyl (Acclaim Extra) may be used to control newly germinated stands of crabgrass; however, its efficacy declines as crabgrass plants mature and produce more tillers. Efficacy is also reduced under droughty conditions or when fenoxyprop *p*-ethyl is mixed with 2,4-D and related phenoxycarboxylic acid herbicides. Well-established crabgrass (i.e., more than four tillers) is more easily controlled with postemergence applications of quinclorac (Drive). In addition to postemergence herbicides, some preemergence herbicides may be used, including dithiopyr (Dimension), pendimethalin (Pendulum, Pre-M), and a combination of benefin and trifluralin (Team). Dithiopyr is unique among the preemergence herbicides in that it also provides some early postemergence activity; where it is applied to untillered crabgrass, or to crabgrass with no more than two tillers, satisfactory control can be achieved. A possible alternative to conventional preemergence herbicides for crabgrass control is corn gluten meal (CGM), a by-product of corn wet milling containing a series of dipeptides that inhibit mitosis in root tips. ■

▶ CASE STUDY 5.8

Scenario: The creeping bentgrass-annual bluegrass (*Agrostis stolonifera* L., *Poa annua* L.) tees on a golf course in central New Jersey were seriously infested with goosegrass (*Eleusine indica* [L.] Gaertn.). Despite several applications of quinclorac (Drive), goosegrass populations persisted. What can be done to control this weed?

Analysis: Goosegrass is similar to crabgrass (*Digitaria* spp.) in appearance but is usually darker green in color (Figure 5.1). Because the center of the plant is a silvery color, it is also called *silver crabgrass*. Its seed heads are zipper-like in appearance. Goosegrass is a summer annual that begins germinating 2 to 3 weeks after crabgrass. It is usually found in compacted or poorly drained soils in warm temperate and warmer climates. Once germination begins, it often continues until frost occurs, whereas crabgrass rarely germinates after mid-July.

Solution: While quinclorac (Drive) can control crabgrass and a variety of broadleaved weeds, it is not effective against goosegrass. Fenoxyprop *p*-ethyl (Acclaim Extra) can be effective if applied at low rates every 2 weeks to control young populations of goosegrass germinating

Figure 5.1 Severe infestation of goosegrass in heavily trafficked turf sustained at tee height.

throughout the summer. These applications can be made in combination with fungicides where disease control is needed. Dithiopyr (Dimension), pendimethalin (Pendulum, Pre-M), and oxadiazon (Ronstar) are preemergence herbicides that are effective against goosegrass; however, their use may interfere with germination and seedling growth of over-seeded turfgrasses on tees. ■

▶ CASE STUDY 5.9

Scenario: Moss infestations were causing a noticeable effect on the quality of selected greens on a golf course in Mt. Laurel, New Jersey. The 7-year-old greens were built to USGA specifications and received adequate sunlight and air circulation for favorable growth; however, internal drainage was less than expected from sand-based greens. An examination of the soil profile revealed alternate layers of sand and dense organic matter near the surface of the greens. What should be done to address this problem?

Analysis: Mosses encompass many species of thread-like, branched, primitive plants that spread by spores. They do not produce true roots;

instead, filamentous structures called *rhizoids* absorb water from the soil but do not provide anchorage. Mosses are most likely to occur on moist, shaded sites; however, they can quickly populate both shaded and sunny sites where thinning of the stand provides infestation windows into the turf. With continued growth, dense mats form, crowding out all turfgrass plants. The increased incidence and severity of moss problems in greens probably reflect the closer mowing heights being used today, lower nitrogen fertilization rates, and the loss of mercury fungicides that were effective against not only selected diseases but moss populations as well.

Solution: Conditions associated with the deterioration of a turf and subsequent moss infestation should be corrected. Excessive surface moisture can be reduced by improving air circulation, light exposure, and drainage and by reducing irrigation. Spiking, vertical mowing, and topdressing can be performed to break up and remove moss mats.

Chemical control is erratic, especially if conditions favoring moss infestations are not corrected. Some success has been reported with multiple applications of various materials, including ferrous ($FeSO_4$) and ferric ($Fe_2[SO_4]_3$) sulfates, copper hydroxide ($Cu[OH]_2$,) alone (Kocide) and with mancozeb (Junction), and sodium carbonates, including sodium bicarbonate (baking soda, $NaHCO_3$) and sodium carbonate peroxyhydrate ($2Na_2CO_3 \cdot 3H_2O_2$, commercially available as Terracyte). In some tests, the best control has been achieved with carfentrazone-ethyl (Quick Silver); however, it is not currently labeled for moss control. Since many of these materials can be especially injurious to the turf during warm summer weather, careful experimentation should be done to determine specifically how these materials should be used under local conditions. ■

▶ CASE STUDY 5.10

Scenario: On a golf course in southern France (in the vicinity of Marseille), where golf is played 12 months of the year, the fairways were established with perennial ryegrass (*Lolium perenne* L.) because it remains green during the winter months. However, since bermudagrass (*Cynodon dactylon* [L.] Pers. var. *dactylon*) is so well adapted to summers in this region, it is constantly invading the perennial ryegrass fairways.

Analysis: Marseille has a warm subtropical dry-summer (Csa) climate, where the average monthly temperature ranges from 43.5°F to 72.9°F (6.4°C to 22.7°C) and annual precipitation averages 22.9 in. (58.2 cm). In such a climate, where winter and summer temperatures are relatively mild, both cool- and warm-season turfgrasses flourish and, as a consequence, tend to compete with each other seasonally. In the wetter and cooler winter months, perennial ryegrass grows vigorously, while bermudagrass is dormant; in the dryer and warmer summer months, bermudagrass is very competitive with perennial ryegrass. While bermudagrass may be a desirable alternative to perennial ryegrass in this climate, it would require overseeding with perennial ryegrass in the fall for winter color and growth. If one wished to avoid this expense and maintain perennial ryegrass throughout the year, specific operations would be required to control the bermudagrass.

Solution: Fenoxyprop p-ethyl (Acclaim Extra) can be used to selectively remove much of the bermudagrass from the perennial ryegrass fairways during the early and middle portions of the growing season. Later in the season, just before the bermudagrass goes dormant, ethofumesate (Progress) can be applied to kill it. ■

DISEASES

▶ CASE STUDY 5.11

Scenario: The curative application rate of chlorothalonil (Daconil Ultrex, Concorde, Manicure, Echo) was used in an attempt to control a severe outbreak of dollar spot disease; however, infected plants continued to decline and eventually died. Does this suggest that resistance to the fungicide has developed?

Analysis: Dollar spot disease is caused by *Rutstroemia flocossum* Powell & Vargas (formerly *Sclerotinia homeocarpa* F.T. Bennett). It appears as round, bleached-out spots ranging in size from a quarter to a silver dollar (Plate 12; see color insert). The name *dollar spot* reflects the silvery cast associated with the spots. The spots occur as sunken areas in the turf. Individual spots may coalesce, giving large areas of turf a silvery cast. In the early morning hours while the grass is still wet from dew, grayish white fluffy mycelium of the pathogen may be present. Dollar spot symptoms on individual leaves appear as bleached-out lesions that usually extend across the entire width of the blade. The characteristic reddish-brown bands present at the outer edges of the leaf lesions in most turf-grasses are absent in annual bluegrass (*Poa annua* L.). Dollar spot occurs at temperatures between 60°F and 90°F (16°C and 32°C). Over 20 vegetatively compatible groups of the pathogen have been identified. These have been shown to occur at different times during the growing season, depending on the temperature. High humidity and the presence of guttation fluid are important in the development of the disease.

As chlorothalonil is a contact or foliar-protectant fungicide, it can prevent the disease from spreading to noninfected plants; however, it does not affect the pathogen that has already infected a plant. Only systemic fungicides, which penetrate the epidermis and move within the plant, can kill a pathogen within an infected plant. No resistance to chlorothalonil is currently known to exist in turfgrasses.

Solution: Apply a systemic fungicide to kill the pathogen in infected plants. Systemic fungicides for controlling dollar spot disease are (1) benzimidazoles: thiophenate-methyl (Cleary's 3336, Fungo 50); (2) carboximides: boscalid (Emerald); (3) dicarboximides: iprodione (Chipco 26GT, Iprodione Pro) and vinclozolin (Curalan, Vorlan, Touche); and (4) demethylation inhibitors (DMIs), including the triazoles: propiconazol (Banner MAXX, Propiconazol Pro), triadimefon (Bayleton, Accost), and myclobutanil (Eagle), and the pyrimidines: fenarimol (Rubigan). ■

► CASE STUDY 5.12

Scenario: Given the growing concern over the loss of efficacy of benzimidazole, dicarboximide, and DMI fungicides, how can one forestall the development of resistant strains of *Rutstroemia flocossum,* the organism causing dollar spot disease?

Analysis: Given the natural variation that exists within *Rutstroemia flocossum* (as well as other fungal populations), the potential exists for the development of strains resistant to the fungicides used for controlling dollar spot disease (Figure 5.2). This potential is especially high for systemic fungicides, as they tend to block only one enzyme in the metabolism of the fungus, while contact fungicides typically inhibit several enzyme systems. There are two opposing philosophies for managing fungicide resistance: alternation and reservation. The historically popular *alternation* philosophy proposes that one should alternate the use of systemic fungicide chemical classes (i.e., benzimidazoles, carboximides, dicarboximides, DMIs)—usually in rotation with chorothalonil (Daconil Ultrex, Concorde, Manicure, Echo)—in order to prolong the life of each. It assumes that the development of resistance will be accelerated if a particular systemic fungicide chemical class is used exclusively. The *reservation* philosophy proposes just the opposite: only one chemical class of systemic fungicide should be used in rotation with chlorothalonil until *R. flocossum* develops resistance, reserving the other systemic fungicide chemical classes for use afterward. This is based on the assumption that alternating systemic fungicide chemical classes will impose selection pressures on *R. flocossum* so that strains with resistance to all chemical classes will survive. As a consequence, the collective lives of all systemic fungicide chemical classes may be shorter with alternation than with reservation.

Solution: The contact fungicide chlorothalonil should be an important component of the fungicide rotation system, as the development

Figure 5.2 Ineffective control of dollar spot caused by a strain of *Rutstroemia floccosum* with resistance to the triadimefon (Bayleton) fungicide.

of resistance to it is less likely than with systemic fungicides. This is especially important during periods of intense disease pressure, when resistance development is most likely. If you choose the reservation philosophy, use only one of the fungicide chemical classes in rotation with chlorothalonil until the development of resistance is evident (usually from reduced longevity of control); then switch to one of the other chemical classes. If there is resistance to all systemic fungicide chemical classes, they should be restricted to curative treatment of infected plants, as their use in preventive control programs—given their short period of control—would not be cost effective. Be sure to keep detailed records of the chemical used and when resistance development became evident. ■

▶ CASE STUDY 5.13

Scenario: Benzimidazole, dicarboximide, and DMI fungicides were applied in rotation to control dollar spot disease and prevent resistance. Eventually, the benzimidazoles were no longer effective on dollar spot (Figure 5.3), the dicarboximides provided only 3 to 5 days of control, and the DMIs provided only 7 days of control. What has happened to reduce the efficacy of these fungicides so dramatically?

Analysis: Alternating systemic fungicide chemical classes will not prevent dollar spot resistance from occurring, as the pathogen can develop resistance to more than one chemical class. Where *Rutstroemia flocossum* develops resistance to the dicarboximides, however, there is a "fitness penalty" in that the resistant strains are typically weak pathogens. This is evidenced by the occurrence of very small areas of blighted turf in place of the larger quarter- or dollar-size areas typically occurring with this disease. Simply avoiding the use of dicarboximides for a few years should cause this pathogenic strain to fade out, after which fungicides from this chemical class can be used again.

Solution: The contact fungicide chlorothalonil (Daconil Ultrex, Concorde, Manicure, Echo) should be used for preventive control of dollar spot, with one of the benzimidazole or DMI fungicides used only as needed for curative control. After a few years, try using one of the dicarboximide fungicides; if it is effective, fungicides from this chemical class can be used until evidence of resistance appears again. Whenever a new

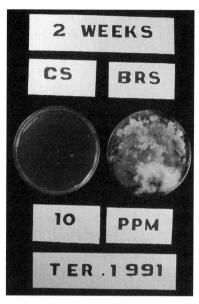

Figure 5.3 Growth of a benzimidazole-resistant strain of *Rutstroemia floccosum* (right) compared with the nonresistant control strain (left).

systemic fungicide chemical class becomes available for dollar spot disease, it should be evaluated and, if effective, incorporated into the disease management program. ■

▶ CASE STUDY 5.14

Scenario: DMI fungicides have been used to manage dollar spot disease for many years; however, the duration of control has been getting shorter at a golf course in southern Michigan for the past 2 years. Does this indicate that the dollar spot pathogen is becoming more aggressive?

Analysis: This is actually indicative of a resistance problem. Unlike resistance to the benzimidazoles—which is evidenced by complete lack of control—resistance to the DMI fungicides is expressed as a shortening of the duration of control, requiring more frequent applications.

Solution: Because of resistance to the DMI fungicides, their use should be discontinued. Rotations with chlorothalonil (Daconil Ul-trex, Concorde, Manicure, Echo), a contact fungicide, and one of the other systemic fungicide chemical classes, including the benzimida-zoles: thiophanate-methyl (Cleary's 3336, Fungo 50); carboximides: boscalid (Emerald); or dicarboximides: iprodione (Chipco 26GT, Ipro-dione Pro) and vinclozolin (Curalan, Vorlan, Touche) should be used instead.   ■

▶ CASE STUDY 5.15

Scenario: Large patches of deteriorating turf measuring several feet across appeared during a hot July afternoon in one of the fairways on a golf course in central Ohio (Plate 13; see color insert). Because of severe traffic and wear, the fairways were being irrigated daily and had been fertilized recently with soluble nitrogen to promote recuperative growth. The affected areas occurred in depressions in the fairway where water tended to collect during heavy rainfall. There was no evidence of insect activity or damage from large animals. Within the patches, leaf blades ranged from light to dark brown. Along the margins of affected areas, whole leaves could be easily extracted from turfgrass shoots. What is the cause of the deterioration, and how can it be controlled?

Analysis: This is actually brown patch disease, caused by *Rhizoctonia solani* Kuhn. The disease occurs as circular patches ranging from a few inches to several feet in diameter. The infected leaves first appear water-soaked and dark, eventually turning dark brown. When the humidity is high, a "smoke ring" consisting of the fungal mycelium is sometimes observed surrounding the outer margins of the diseased area, especially in the early morning hours. This typically disappears by midmorning as the foliage dries. *R. solani* survives adverse periods as sclerotia or as mycelium in plant debris. It can also survive as a saprophyte in the thatch. When the soil temperature rises above 60°F (16°C) in spring, the sclerotia begin to germinate and the fungus grows saprophytically. *R. solani* is basically a weak parasite that causes only mild damage until daytime temperatures reach approximately 86°F (30°C), with high humidity and nighttime temperatures exceeding 70°F (21°C). At low temperatures, *R. solani* grows as a saprophyte or causes minute infections

147

that do not seriously damage healthy grass plants; however, with heat stress or high-temperature growth stoppage of annual bluegrass, fungal infection is favored and serious disease incidences can occur. As with most fungi, growth occurs in a circular pattern. Under highly favorable conditions, large infected patches of annual bluegrass appear to develop overnight; however, these are the result of saprophytic fungal growth in the soil or thatch for many days prior to pathogenic infection.

Solution: Where drainage is poor and air movement severely restricted, corrective measures should be taken. A shift from nighttime to early morning irrigation could also help to minimize the persistently wet conditions that favor disease development. Finally, selected contact and systemic fungicides labeled for brown patch should be used in rotation for control, with the systemics restricted to a single chemical class for as long as it is effective. The contacts include chlorothalonil [Daconil Ultrex, Concorde, Manicure, Echo] and mancozeb (Fore). The systemics include the QoI fungicides: azoxystobin (Heritage), trifloxystrobin (Compass), and pyraclostrobin (Insignia); carboximides: flutolanil (Prostar); and dicarboximides: iprodione (Chipco 26GT, Iprodione Pro) and vinclozolin (Curalan, Vorlan, Touche).   ■

▶ CASE STUDY 5.16

Scenario: Crown rotting anthracnose has become a problem on all annual bluegrass (*Poa annua* L.) greens, despite a biweekly program of azoxystrobin (Heritage) fungicide application. The greens receive weekly soluble nitrogen applications of 0.1 lb N per 1000 ft^2. There is concern that the causal organism has become resistant to this fungicide.

Analysis: In contrast with foliar anthracnose (Plate 14; see color insert), which occurs in warm weather (i.e., daytime temperatures above 86°F [30°C] for at least 3 consecutive days, nighttime temperatures above 68°F [20°C], and continuous leaf wetness for at least 8 hours), crown-rotting anthracnose is a disease that occurs over a wide temperature range, presumably caused by different strains of *Colletotrichum graminicola* (Ces) Wils. It usually occurs in turf in which the soil is persistently wet due to poor internal drainage and intense rainfall or irrigation. Symptoms first appear as bronze- to yellow-colored spots in the turf about the size of a dime, reflecting infection of the crowns of individual plants. As the disease spreads to adjacent plants, the spots become larger. Entire annual bluegrass greens can be destroyed in a short period of time (Plate 15; see color insert). If the *C. graminicola* strain present only infects annual bluegrass, patches of healthy creeping bentgrass (*Agrostis stolonifera* L.) will be interspersed within an otherwise severely diseased turf. Elongated crowns of infected plants appear black under a hand lens. Under a dissecting microscope, the acervuli and setae of the pathogen are clearly visible on the lower leaf sheaths (Figure 5.4); with foliar anthracnose, the acervuli and setae appear on the leaf blades. (Figure 5.5).

Solution: As the severity of crown-rotting anthracnose can be reduced by optimum levels of nitrogen fertility, the fertilization rate should be increased from 0.1 lb N per 1000 ft^2 to 0.125 lb N per 1000 ft^2 every other week. As with many diseases, it is not the fungicide alone but the combination of fungicide and nitrogen fertility that provides control. Also, as crown-rotting anthracnose occurs in persistently wet soils, improving drainage through cultivation and topdressing, as well as other methods, can reduce the incidence of this disease. Finally, while crown-rotting anthracnose can be controlled with fungicides, specific guidelines must be followed for satisfactory results. The benzimidazole fungicides,

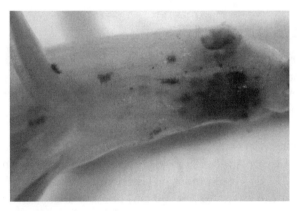

Figure 5.4 Close-up photograph of acervuli and setae on the lower leaf sheath of annual bluegrass from crown-rotting anthracnose.

Figure 5.5   Close-up photograph of acervuli and setae on the leaf blade of annual bluegrass from foliar anthracnose.

such as thiophanate-methyl (Cleary's 3336, Fungo 50), must be applied at relatively high rates and drenched in to be effective. The DMI fungicides, including the triazoles: propiconazol (Banner MAXX, Propiconazol Pro), triadimefon (Bayleton, Accost), and myclobutanil (Eagle), and the pyrimidines: fenarimol (Rubigan), must be applied with at least 5 gal of water per 1000 ft^2 (20 L per 100 m^2) to be effective, whereas the quinone outside inhibitor (QoI) fungicides, such as azoxystrobin (Heritage), can be applied at lower spray volumes and do not need to be drenched in to be effective.   ■

▶ CASE STUDY 5.17

Scenario: On a newly established golf course, circular disease patches developed on the creeping bentgrass (*Agrostis stolonifera* L.) greens, tees, and fairways. Laboratory diagnosis revealed that the disease was take-all patch. What are the options for controlling this disease?

Analysis: Take-all patch, caused by the fungus *Gaeumannomyces graminis* (Sacc.) Arx & Oliv. var. *avenae* (E.M. Turner) Dennis, is first observed as depressed more or less circular patches of blighted turfgrass that can extend to 2 ft (60 cm) or more in diameter. The centers of the patches are frequently invaded by other resistant grasses or weeds, thus creating a frog-eye appearance (Plate 16; see color insert).

The pathogen overwinters as dormant mycelia in living and dead plant tissues. The fungus forms dark brown to black ectotrophic runner hyphae on roots and stems of host plants. Infections result where the fungus penetrates subterranean plant tissues and spreads to adjacent plants by growing along roots and lateral shoots. The disease is most active during cool, wet periods, but symptoms become most noticeable during drier conditions in early summer to midsummer. It tends to be restricted to newly established turfs of creeping bentgrass; however, colonial bentgrass (*Agrostis capillaris* L.) is also susceptible to this disease. Sometimes confused with summer patch (Plate 17; see color insert), take-all is specific to bentgrasses, while summer patch is specific to bluegrasses.

Solution: For the greens to maintain desired green speed, fungicides are probably the best solution in combination with increasing nitrogen fertility. Systemic fungicides that provide control of take-all patch are the benzimidazoles: thiophenate-methyl (Cleary's 3336, Fungo 50); the DMIs, including the triazoles: propiconazol (Banner MAXX, Propiconazol Pro), triadimefon (Bayleton, Accost), myclobutanil (Eagle), and the pyrimidines: fenarimol (Rubigan); and the QoI fungicide, azoxystrobin (Heritage). For tees and fairways, nitrogen fertilization, possibly in combination with applications of magnesium, might be the best solution. ■

▶ CASE STUDY 5.18

Scenario: On new creeping bentgrass (*Agrostis stolonifera* L.) greens established in accordance with USGA specifications, turfgrass growth was slow, with less than a bucket of clippings removed with each mowing. A total of 10 lb of soluble N per 1000 ft^2 (5 kg N per 100 m^2) from a 22-0-22 fertilizer product was applied during the growing season; phosphorus was excluded in order to reduce the potential for annual bluegrass (*Poa annua* L.) invasion. Examination of the roots revealed mild infection from the fungus that causes take-all patch; however, infections were not severe enough to cause the patches characteristic of this disease.

Analysis: Phosphorus has been shown to be important in controlling take-all patch. While the exclusion of phosphorus from fertilization programs on pushup greens is sometimes acceptable, this practice on sand-based greens often results in phosphorus deficiencies and poor growth.

Solution: If careful monitoring of the condition of the turf—along with periodic soil and tissue testing—reveals phosphorus deficiencies, sufficient phosphorus should be incorporated into the fertilization program. Where phosphorus deficiencies are evident, foliar applications of a soluble phosphorus source, such as monoammonium phosphate ($NH_4H_2PO_4$) or diammonium phosphate ($[NH_4]_2HPO_4$), can be effective in addressing them. ■

▶ CASE STUDY 5.19

Scenario: After many years of providing high-quality turf, several Toronto (C-15) creeping bentgrass (*Agrostis stolonifera* L. 'Toronto') greens began wilting and severely thinning under moderate temperatures despite a preventive fungicide program that was effective in controlling diseases on the golf course's other Penncross greens. An analysis of samples from the affected greens did not reveal the presence of a fungal organism that could cause the observed symptoms. The major cultural change that had recently occurred was the introduction of sand topdressing. What caused the deterioration of the Toronto greens, and how should this problem be addressed?

Analysis: Since the fungicide program was not effective in controlling the problem, other factors—including other pathogenic organisms—should be investigated. Vegetatively propagated creeping bentgrasses, such as Toronto, are more genetically uniform than the cross-bred Penncross and other seeded types. As a consequence, they are generally more susceptible to single races of a particular pathogen. However, since no fungal organism could be identified in turf samples submitted to the disease diagnostic laboratory, nonconventional methods would be needed for an accurate diagnosis. In this case, scanning electron microscopic (SEM) examination of plant tissues revealed the presence of *Xanthomonas campestris* (Pammel) Dowson, the organism causing bacterial wilt. Death results from clogging of the vascular system of the

Figure 5.6   Sand topdressing.

plants, preventing the movement of water and nutrients from the roots to upper portions of the plants. Bacteria need wounds through which to enter the plant, along with an essentially sterile environment such as that provided within the sand layer formed from topdressing (Figure 5.6). Therefore, sand topdressing transformed a minor disease of Toronto creeping bentgrass into a major one. Bacterial wilt is also a disease of annual bluegrass (Plate 18; see color insert).

Solution: While some bactericides, such as oxytetracycline (Myco-shield), can be effective in controlling this disease, none are registered for turf. Therefore, the only effective method of control is to replace Toronto with one of the seeded cultivars of creeping bentgrass.   ■

▶ CASE STUDY 5.20

Scenario: On a particular golf course, there are two fairways that get *Pythium* blight disease every year, while the remaining fairways get this disease only once every several years. Is there anything that can be done to reduce the incidence of this disease? Also, when this disease occurs, should a contact or systemic fungicide be used for control?

Analysis: *Pythium* blight is caused by *Pythium aphanidermatum* (Edson) Fitzpatrick. Symptoms first appear as circular reddish-brown spots in the turf ranging in diameter from 1 to 3 in. (2.5 to 7.5 cm) (Plate 19; see color insert). Infected leaf blades appear water-soaked and dark, and may feel slimy when first observed in the morning. The blades shrivel and turn reddish-brown as they dry. Active purplish-gray mycelium can be seen in the outer margins of the spots as long as the foliage remains wet (Plate 20; see color insert). The infected grass plants collapse quickly. If the temperature and humidity remain high, the spots may coalesce, and large areas of turf can be affected. As *P. aphanidermatum* is a water mold, it can be spread by surface water movement and mower traffic on wet turf. The pattern of disease symptoms often reflects the pathogen's movement across the turf. Like *Rhizoctonia* and *Colletotrichum*, *Pythium* is a good saprophyte. It is usually present in the thatch, soil, or both, and simply requires favorable environmental conditions to become pathogenic. Since it can survive as a saprophyte in the soil for many years without becoming pathogenic, it can cause disease in marginal areas where environmental conditions for *Pythium* blight occur only once every 4 or 5 years.

Solution: As *Pythium* blight outbreaks preferentially occur on those portions of a golf course with drainage problems, it is more economical to improve drainage in these areas than to apply fungicides. Nighttime irrigation should be avoided in these areas; irrigation should be restricted to midday periods when there is sufficient time for the turf to dry before nightfall. Excessive rates of nitrogen fertilization should be avoided, as this results in lush growth that favors the incidence of this disease. With respect to chemical control, contact fungicides such as etridiazole (Koban) can be used for short-term preventive control. Systemic fungicides, including mefenoxam (Subdue), propamocarb (Banol), and fosetyl-aluminum (Signature), are needed for both preventive and curative control of this disease. This reflects the fact that, while a contact fungicide may prevent any new tissue from being invaded, it will do nothing to stop the advance of the fungus in infected tissue. In contrast, a systemic fungicide will enter the plant and prevent the fungus from doing any further damage. Active mycelium may be observed on dead tissue the morning after a systemic fungicide is used, but the healthy turf will be protected from any further damage. ■

▶ CASE STUDY 5.21

Scenario: Initially healthy stands of rough bluegrass (*Poa trivialis* L.) that developed from overseeding bermudagrass (*Cynodon dactylon* [L.] Pers. var. *dactylon* × *C. transvaalensis* Burtt-Davy) greens have died, despite the use of normally effective *Pythium* blight control program using fosetyl-aluminum (Signature). Could some other disease have killed it?

Analysis: While there is always the possibility that another disease could have been involved in the loss of the rough bluegrass population, fosetyl-aluminum has been shown to be phototoxic to this turfgrass under some conditions. Unfortunately, these conditions have not been well defined.

Solution: To avoid phytotoxicity from fosetyl-aluminum in the future, other *Pythium* blight fungicides, such as mefenoxam (Subdue) or propamocarb (Banol), should be used where rough bluegrass is the overseeded turfgrass.   ∎

▶ CASE STUDY 5.22

Scenario: Copper-colored spots developed on annual bluegrass (*Poa annua* L.) greens in late spring when daytime temperatures reached no higher than 63°F (17°C). Is this copper spot disease, and, regardless of the diagnosis, how should it be controlled?

Analysis: Copper spot disease is first evident as small reddish spots (lesions) on the leaves. As the lesions enlarge and coalesce, entire leaves become blighted and small salmon pink- to copper-colored patches 1 to 3 in. (2.5 to 7.5 cm) in diameter appear in the turf. The pathogen (*Gloeocercospora sorghi* Bain & Edgerton) overwinters as small black sclerotia that germinate in spring. The disease can spread rapidly during warm (optimum, 65°–80°F or 18°–27°C), moist weather as large numbers of asexual spores (conidia) are produced and infect other plants. The spores are spread by splashing or flowing water and by equipment. The disease evident in these annual bluegrass greens is not copper spot, which occurs at higher temperatures. Copper spot is primarily a disease of velvet bentgrass (*Agrostis canina* L.). The disease occurring here is

Microdochium patch (formerly, *Fusarium* patch; also called *pink snow mold*), which develops at lower temperatures, especially during rainy weather. *Microdochium* patch is caused by *M. nivale* [Fr.] Samuels & I.C. Hallett, which can survive as mycelium and spores in the thatch and will actively grow on the grass residue. Infection can take place when temperatures are below 60°F (16°C), but the disease develops most rapidly at temperatures between 60°F and 70°F (16°C and 21°C). *Microdochium* patch appears as reddish-brown spots in annual bluegrass turf. The spots normally range in diameter from less than 1 in. (2.5 cm) to about 8 in. (20 cm) (Plate 21; see color insert). Heavy rains or mowing equipment can transport fungal spores across the turf, causing streak-shaped disease symptoms similar to those occurring with *Pythium* blight; thus, it is often confused with *Pythium* blight despite the fact that these two diseases occur under entirely different sets of environmental conditions. When *Microdochium* patch occurs under snow cover, the circular spots usually range from 2 in. (5.0 cm) to 2 ft (60 cm) in diameter and are tan to pinkish gray in color. Shortly after the snow has melted, the pink mycelium of the fungus may be seen at the advancing edge of the spot, hence the common name *pink snow mold;* however, *Microdochium* patch can also develop without snow cover.

Solution: *Microdochium* patch can be controlled with preventive applications of the dicarboximides: iprodione (Chipco 26GT, Iprodione Pro) and vinclozolin (Curalan, Vorlan, Touche); DMI fungicides, including the triazoles: myclobutanil (Eagle), propiconazol (Banner MAXX, Propiconazol Pro), and triadimefon (Bayleton, Accost), and the pyrimidines: fenarimol (Rubigan); and QoI fungicides: azoxystrobin (Heritage), trifloxystrobin (Compass), and pyraclostrobin (Insignia). ■

▶ CASE STUDY 5.23

Scenario: Pink-colored tiny fungal spikes emerged ¼ to ½ in. (6.4–12.7 mm) above the turf in the fall on greens and fairways (Figure 5.7). Many of them were organized in distinct patches. What are they, and do they indicate an increased potential for disease development?

Analysis: These spikes are the fruiting bodies of the *Typhula* fungi that arose from sclerotia that were produced the previous spring. The

Figure 5.7 Pink-colored fruiting bodies of the fungus that causes *Typhula* blight.

sclerotia shrink in the spring to a very small size. They oversummer in the turf until the cool weather of the fall returns. They then germinate to produce the pink fruiting bodies called *basidocarps,* on which hundreds of basidiospores are produced and carried by the wind throughout the course. When they land in a turf, they can survive there until the snow cover occurs and then infect the plants. They tend to occur in patches because that is where the disease was located following snowmelt in the spring. Gray snow mold or *Typhula* blight is caused by *Typhula incarnata* Lasch ex Fr. and *T. ishikariensis* Imai. While *Typhula* blight can occur simultaneously with *Microdochium* patch, its range does not extend as far south (in the Northern Hemisphere) as that of *Microdochium* patch. Unlike *Microdochium* patch, which occurs with or without snow cover, *Typhula* blight does require some type of cover, usually by snow, but also by leaves, straw mulch, or desiccation blankets, to develop. At temperatures between 30°F and 55°F (−1°C to 13°C), the *Typhula* fungus grows and infects. As the snow melts, circular grayish or straw-colored to dark brown infection centers appear in the turf. The spots range from 3 to 24 in. (8–60 cm) in diameter, but most are between 6 and 12 in. (15–30 cm) across (Figure 5.8). Immediately after the snow melts, the grayish-white fungal mycelium can be seen, especially at the outer margins of the spots. The disease gets its common name, *gray snow mold,* from the color of the mycelium. *Typhula* blight is worse in winters when the snow falls on unfrozen turf or on turf that has not

Figure 5.8   Severe incidence of *Typhula* blight in a control plot.

been hardened off by frost. When snow falls on frozen ground, the disease often develops in the spring after the snow begins to melt. The two *Typhula* species can be easily separated when viewed shortly after snowmelt. *T. incarnata* produces large rust-colored sclerotia in infected turf, whereas *T. ishikariensis* produces small black sclerotia, which create the appearance that the turf has been sprinkled with pepper. The *Typhula* fungi oversummer as sclerotia in the thatch and soil, where they survive unfavorable conditions. Fungicides that may be part of a summer disease control program have no effect on these resting structures. Under cool, wet fall conditions and in the presence of ultraviolet light, the sclerotia swell and germinate, producing pink club-shaped sphorophores from which basidia and basidiospores arise. The basidiospores are carried by the wind to other locations, including areas where the disease was eradicated the previous season. The spores germinate and infect the grass plants under snow or other suitable cover. The sclerotia may germinate, form mycelium, and cause infection.

Solution: *Typhula* blight can be controlled by several aromatic hydrocarbon contact fungicides, including chloroneb (Teremec) and

PCNB (Terraclor), as well as combinations of PCNB at half rate with several systemic fungicides, including triadimefon + trifloxystrobin, fosetyl-aluminum + iprodione, and propiconizol + fludioxonil, or with combinations of the contact fungicide, chlorothalonil, and one of the systemic fungicides, iprodione or thiophanate-methyl. ■

▶ CASE STUDY 5.24

Scenario: Control of snow mold with PCNB fungicide has varied from year to year. What can be done to achieve acceptable control every year?

Analysis: As seen in Case Studies 5.22 and 5.23, snow molds include several diseases caused by different pathogens, including *Microdochium nivale, Typhula incarnata,* and *T. ishikariensis.* In addition, there are three different biotypes that make up *T. ishikariensis,* which have different sensitivities to various fungicides. The success achieved with PCNB in any given season will depend on the specific makeup of the pathogens present.

Solution: Where different snow molds are likely to occur simultaneously, they should be controlled using selected fungicide combinations from the lists provided in the solutions to Case Studies 5.22 and 5.23. ■

▶ CASE STUDY 5.25

Scenario: New ultradwarf bermudagrass (*Cynodon dactylon* [L.] Pers. var. *dactylon* × *C. transvaalensis* Burtt-Davy) greens developed brown spots 2 to 3 in. (5.0 to 7.5 cm) in diameter in late summer and early fall. What happened, and how can this problem be controlled?

Analysis: Because this disease was first discovered on creeping bentgrass (*Agrostis stolonifera* L.), it is called *bentgrass dead spot;* however, it has since been found on the ultradwarf bermudagrasses as well. The causal organism is *Ophiospaerella agrostis.* It is a turfgrass root pathogen similar to those involved in spring dead spot and necrotic ring spot diseases. It can be problematic on greens and, to a lesser extent, on tees and collars. Disease symptoms initially appear as small reddish-brown or copper-colored spots that can grow up to 3 in. (7.5 cm) in diameter. Symptoms are similar to those of dollar spot and copper spot; however, the leaves at the periphery of active patches are reddish brown. Disease activity may initially occur during warm, dry periods in late spring and persist until the first hard frost in the fall. The pathogen is believed to attach the leaves first and then move into the stems and roots. Numerous black flask-shaped fruiting bodies called *pseudothecia* may be found embedded in necrotic leaf tissues during the winter months. The pseudothecia contain numerous needle-shaped ascospores that, when released, can infect plants the following spring.

Solution: The disease can be controlled chemically with benzimi-dazoles: thiophanate-methyl (3336, Fungo); dicarboximides: iprodi-one (Chipco 26GT, Iprodione Pro) and vinclozolin (Curalan, Vorlan, Touche); QoI fungicides: azoxystrobin (Heritage), trifloxystrobin (Compass), and pyraclostrobin (Insignia); and the contact fungicide: chlorothalonil (Daconil Ultrex, Concorde, Manicure, Echo); however, these fungicides may suppress the disease for only 7 to 10 days, after which disease development may resume. Nitrogen fertilizer should be applied along with fungicides to stimulate recuperative growth. This disease is usually limited to new greens, eventually disappearing after 3 to 6 years.   ■

▶ CASE STUDY 5.26

Scenario: With several weeks of hot, humid weather, the perennial ryegrass fairways at a golf course in eastern Pennsylvania appeared wilted, with some reduction in shoot density and loss of turf in some areas. Some of the blades were severely twisted (Plate 22; see color insert). Close examination of these leaves revealed dark spots with gray centers and yellow halos surrounding them (Plate 23; see color insert). What is the problem, and how can it be solved?

Analysis: The disease is gray leaf spot, caused by the fungus *Pyricularia grisea* (Cke.) Sacc. It first appears as brown to gray dots on the leaves and stems that enlarge to form round to elongated spots with gray centers, reddish-brown to purple margins, and outer rings of chlorotic tissue.

Numerous lesions can develop on a single leaf, resulting in a scorched appearance of the grass. The pathogen overwinters as dormant mycelia and free spores (conidia) in older infected leaves and debris; new infections occur during warm, moist weather in spring and continue into the summer and fall months. Disease activity is favored by excessive nitrogen fertilization, prolonged periods of high moisture, and temperatures between 70°F and 85°F (21°C and 29°C).

Solution: The diseased turf should be treated with azoxystrobin (Heritage) to kill the fungus in infected plants and to prevent further disease development. In future years, several fungicides can be used on a preventive basis to control this disease, including thiophanate-methyl (Cleary's 3336, Fungo 50), propiconazol (Banner MAXX), chlorothalonil (Daconil Ultrex, Concorde, Manicure, Echo), and trifloxystrobin (Compass). ■

▶ CASE STUDY 5.27

Scenario: Large patches of annual bluegrass (*Poa annua* L.) have been dying in the greens on a golf course in southern California. There is no evidence of crown-rotting anthracnose, summer patch, or bacterial wilt. It is late summer, and there has been little rain since spring. The disease first appears as patches of water-soaked turf, slightly sunken and darker than healthy turf. The affected turf eventually becomes yellow and dies. Small patches can enlarge rapidly, eventually coalescing to form large areas of dead turf. Could the use of saline irrigation water have anything to do with this problem?

Analysis: There is a disease called *rapid blight* that is caused by *Labyrinthula* spp. It occurs only where saline water high in sodium is used for irrigation. In mixed stands with creeping bentgrass (*Agrostis stolonifera* L.), differential loss of annual bluegrass reflects the substantial difference in salinity tolerance of these two turfgrasses: creeping bentgrass is moderately salt tolerant ($EC_e = 3.7$ dS/m), while annual bluegrass is highly sensitive ($EC_e < 1.5$). This disease has also been observed on temporary winter turfs of rough bluegrass (*Poa trivialis* L.) that have been subjected to salt-induced stress.

Solution: While this disease can be controlled chemically with mancozeb (Fore), trifloxystrobin (Compass), and pyraclostrobin (Insignia), steps should be taken to improve the quality of the irrigation water and to flush the salts from the turfgrass rootzone. ■

▶ CASE STUDY 5.28

Scenario: A serious infestation of blue-green algae developed on a poorly drained browntop bentgrass (*Agrostis capillaris* L.) practice green located in close proximity to a dense planting of trees and the pro shop on a golf course in the Netherlands (Figure 5.9). Why did this problem develop, and what can be done to control it?

Analysis: Blue-green algae (also called *cyanobacteria*) are plant-like organisms that lack leaves, stems, and roots. They are composed of long single-celled filaments that reproduce by fission, eventually forming an algal mat covering the soil or thatch. Blue-green algae secrete a gelatinous substance called *mucilage,* which protects the filaments by conserving moisture. When allowed to dry, the algal mat forms a hard crust that limits water infiltration into the soil and evaporation of water from the soil. The presence of blue-green algae usually indicates one or more of the following: poor drainage, excessive irrigation, poor air

Figure 5.9   Blue-green algae infestation on poorly drained browntop (colonial) bentgrass green.

circulation, and shade. Active growth is especially favored by extended periods of rainy, overcast conditions during summer months.

Solution: Blue-green algae cannot be satisfactorily controlled unless the conditions that favor their growth are corrected. Persistently wet soil conditions should be alleviated by improving drainage and air circulation, and shade should be reduced to improve turfgrass growth. Cultivation methods should be employed to break the algal crust. And mancozeb (Fore) or chlorothalonil (Daconil Ultrex, Concorde, Manicure, Echo) should be applied to control the algae for as long as the problem persists.   ■

NEMATODES

▶ **CASE STUDY 5.29**

Scenario: A golf course in Miami Beach, Florida, had recently undergone a renovation involving the substitution of ultradwarf Tifeagle bermudagrass (*Cynodon dactylon* [L.] Pers. var. *dactylon* × *C. transvaalensis* Burtt-Davy 'Tifeagle') for Tifdwarf. After a successful transformation, with the new greens ready for play by mid-fall, the condition of the greens declined dramatically during the winter months. Following extensive tests, a large population (200/100-cc soil sample) of sting nematodes (*Belonolaimus* spp.) was discovered, despite the fact that the greens had been fumigated prior to planting. What can be done to improve the quality of these greens?

Analysis: Nematodes are microscopic roundworms that constitute one of the most abundant forms of animal life on earth. Most species that occur in soil feed on fungi, bacteria, and small invertebrate animals, but some are parasites of higher plants, including turfgrasses. Plant parasitic nematodes feed on turfgrass roots by puncturing the cells with a hollow needle-like structure called a *stylet*. Digestive enzymes are injected into the cells, and the liquefied contents are withdrawn through the stylet. Nematodes seldom kill plants directly, but they are capable of greatly curtailing their growth. Affected plants may be stunted or chlorotic or show symptoms of wilt under environmental stress. Endoparasitic nematodes invade roots and feed from within the host, while ectoparasitic nematodes feed mostly on the surface of young roots while their bodies remain in the surrounding soil.

The ectoparasitic sting nematodes (*Belonolaimus longicaudatus*)—the largest of the nematodes that feed on turfgrasses, averaging more than 3 mm in length—are considered the most important pests of turfgrasses in Florida. On greens and other turfs, damage is usually expressed as irregular patches of wilted, stunted, nutrient-deficient, or dead turf. Sting nematodes reproduce sexually. After mating, the female lays eggs in pairs in the soil and will continue to lay eggs as long as food is available. Once the eggs hatch, the young nematodes must find a root and begin feeding to survive. The juveniles undergo three molts before becoming adults. The total life cycle from egg to reproducing adult is 18 to 24 days. Damage from sting nematodes is likely when the population density exceeds a threshold of 10/100-cc soil sample. At lower population densities, the turf is often able to persist with no visible damage; however, at 200/100-cc soil sample, the population is well above the damage threshold.

Solution: Given the loss of roots from nematode feeding, frequent irrigation is necessary to ensure that the moisture requirements of the turfgrass are satisfied. Also, frequent foliar feeding may be needed to satisfy turfgrass nutritional requirements. To the extent that soil oxygen may be deficient, cultivation and topdressing practices should be implemented to improve soil aeration. Finally, nematicides may be used to control nematode populations. The most widely known nematicide is fenamiphos (Nemacur), an organophosphate with both contact and systemic activity. The efficacy of this material varies, depending in part on the speed with which it is degraded by soil microorganisms. Because fenamiphos has been so widely used, microbial populations that can utilize it as a food source have built up on some golf courses in Florida to levels that degrade it before it can kill the nematodes. Two soil fumigants—1,3 dichloropropene (Curfew) and metam sodium (Turf-cure 376)—are now being used to manage nematodes on established golf turf. They are injected 6 in. (15 cm) into the soil using a tractor-mounted slit injector. The liquid formulations turn into a gas after injection, permeating the soil and killing nematodes on contact. Because of

the high toxicity of these materials, they should be applied only by professional applicators under carefully controlled conditions, with strict
adherence to reentry and buffer-zone restrictions. ■

INSECTS

▶ CASE STUDY 5.30

Scenario: The annual bluegrass (*Poa annua* L.) greens and fairways
at a golf course in central Ohio exhibited severe wilting symptoms in
late June, despite a program of daily irrigation. Close examination of
the foliage did not reveal any characteristic symptoms of common diseases. What could be causing this problem, and what can be done to
control it?

Analysis: Some insects can cause damage that first appears as wilting in irregularly shaped patches. If root-feeding insects, called *grubs,*
are responsible for the damage, they can be detected by cutting into the
affected turf and pulling back sections of sod. If present, they should be
easily observed at the turf–soil interface, where most of the feeding is
occurring. Most grubs have annual life cycles, overwintering as larvae,
pupating in spring, emerging as adults and mating in early summer,
and releasing eggs to initiate the next cycle. Damage from these grubs—
including Japanese beetles (*Popillia japonica* Newman), masked chafers
(*Cyclocephala borealis* Arrow and *C. lurida* Bland), and European chafers
(*Rhizotrogus majalis* Razoumowsky)—usually does not begin until late
summer, when the larvae reach a size that can consume large masses of
turfgrass roots, seriously limiting the plants' capacity to absorb water.
But the seasonal life cycle of the black turfgrass *ataenius* (*Ataenius spretulus* Haldeman) grubs differs from that of other root-feeding scarabs in
that there are usually two generations per year, with damage appearing
in June and August, coinciding with the first and second annual broods.
Even where there is only one generation, as in the northernmost regions
where this species occurs, damage typically appears in July and early
August—much earlier than that from other grubs. The first symptoms
are patches of wilting turf; with continued root loss, turfgrass dies in

irregular patches that gradually expand and coalesce, forming extensive areas of dead turf. Heavily infested turf can be pulled up like a loose carpet, revealing large numbers of small grubs, pupae, and/or black adults. Huge populations of these grubs, measuring 200–300/ft² (22–33/dm²), are not uncommon. And large animal pests, including birds, skunks, and moles, may cause extensive damage to infested turfs while foraging for the adult beetles. The adults are small, shiny black beetles, about ⅛ in. (3.2 mm) in length and about half as wide. Newly emerging adults are reddish brown but turn black in a few days. Newly hatched grubs are about 0.1 in. (2.5 mm) long, second instars measure about ⅛ in. (5 mm), and mature third instars are about ⅜ in. (10 mm) long. The adults overwinter along the edges of wooded areas under leaves or grass clippings or in the upper 2 in. (5 cm) of soil. They return to annual bluegrass fairways and greens following a few warm days in late winter or early spring and begin laying eggs. *Aphodius* grubs (*A. granarius* L. or *A. paradalis* Le Conte) are almost indistinguishable from black turfgrass *ataenius* and can similarly damage annual bluegrass turf (Figure 5.10). Symptoms of initial damage from these insects are usually observed 2 to 3 weeks earlier than from black turfgrass *ataenius;* otherwise, the symptoms are the same. With respect to the locations where two generations of black turfgrass *ataenius* are said to occur, some believe that the first generation is actually the *Aphodius* grubs and is followed by a single generation of black turfgrass *ataenius.*

Figure 5.10　Close-up of tiny *Aphodius* grubs in annual bluegrass turf.

Solution: The turf should be examined for the presence of black turf-grass *ataenius* or *Aphodius* grubs to ensure that they are causing the observed damage. If present, insecticides should be applied as soon as possible to stop their activity and minimize the damage. Short-residual insecticides—such as bifenthrin (Talstar), chlorpyrifos (Dursban), cyfluth-erin (Tempo), ethoprop (Mocap), lambda-cyhalothrin (Battle, Scimitar) permithrin (Astro), and trichlorfon (Dylox)—should be washed into the thatch or soil for best results. Other insecticides with longer residual activity—such as imidacloprid (Merit) and halfenozide (Mach 2)—can be applied in the late spring and early summer, respectively, to provide season-long control. ■

► CASE STUDY 5.31

Scenario: The annual bluegrass (*Poa annua* L.) aprons first affected on a golf course in Connecticut were those surrounding the greens in close proximity to densely wooded areas. Beginning in late May, a gradual yellowing of the turf was evident, despite highly favorable growing conditions. This was followed by the appearance of irregular dead patches that increased in size with each passing day (Plate 24; see color insert). By mid-June, the damage had become quite severe. Some of the green shoots at the edges of dead patches of turf were easily pulled from their crowns. Examination of the crowns with a hand lens revealed that they had been hollowed out and filled with sawdust-like frass; some contained tiny white larvae. What caused this damage, and how can it be corrected? ■

Analysis: The damage was caused by annual bluegrass weevils (*Listronotus maculicollis* Dietz), formerly called the *Hyperoides* weevil, a serious pest on intensively cultured annual bluegrass turf in the northeastern United States. While the adults cause some damage by chewing on leaves, it is the larvae that pose the greatest threat to annual bluegrass. Young larvae feed inside the crowns, causing leaves to turn yellow and die. Older larvae feed externally on crowns, often separating shoots from roots. Larval densities may exceed 450/ft^2 (50/dm^2), causing severe damage to the turf. The annual bluegrass weevil has two generations per year throughout most of its range but only one generation in the northernmost portion. The adults are small, ranging from 0.13 to

0.16 in. (3.5–4.0 mm) in length. Initially, they are light reddish brown, but soon darken to charcoal gray and eventually to shiny black. Adults overwinter under leaf litter and other protected sites. They become active in midspring, feeding at night and hiding in the thatch during the day. Eggs are laid between leaf sheaths, with larvae hatching in 4 to 5 days. They burrow into the crowns to feed internally for the first few molts, packing the crown with frass. After larvae become too large to feed within the crowns, they burrow out and feed externally. Larvae are about 0.03 in. (1 mm) long when newly hatched and about 0.19 in. (5 mm) when fully grown. They are creamy white with brown heads. There are five instars, each lasting for 5 to 7 days. Most of the population reaches the fifth instar by late spring, when the most severe damage occurs. Then pupation occurs, and the second generation of adults emerges by early summer to mate and initiate the next cycle. Larvae of the second brood are nearly full size by midsummer, when damage extends farther into the centers of fairways, aprons, tees, and greens than that from the first generation. Where annual bluegrass weevil activity is suspected, a sample of the turf can be extracted with a cup cutter, broken up to examine for the presence of larvae, pupae, or adults, and placed in warm water to float out any remaining insects. A vigorously growing turf should tolerate larval populations of 30–50/ft^2 (3.3–5.5/dm^2); since a standard cup cutter measures 4 in. (10 cm) in diameter, this is equivalent to about 3 to 5 per cup cutter. Fewer larvae can cause damage if the annual bluegrass is stressed.

Solution: Chemical control is difficult once the eggs and larvae are sandwiched between leaf sheaths or the larvae are feeding within the crown. Where light traps are used to monitor adult activity in spring, short-residual insecticides—such as chlorpyrifos (Dursban), cyflutherin (Tempo), lambda-cyhalothrin (Battle, Scimitar), and trichlorfon (Dylox)—may be used during their spring migration from hibernation sites to the annual bluegrass turf. For turfs damaged by the first generation, applications of these insecticides in early July may be effective against emerging second-generation adults before they have laid their eggs. Long-residual, systemic insecticides—such as imidacloprid (Merit)—can be applied when the adults become active in the spring before eggs have hatched. The systemic action kills the young larvae within the crowns, and the extended residual activity provides season-long control of larvae that move into the soil. This preventive approach should be reserved for sites where annual bluegrass weevils constitute a perennial problem. ■

▶ CASE STUDY 5.32

Scenario: The creeping bentgrass (*Agrostis stolonifera* L.) greens were in fine shape as the weekend approached; on Sunday morning, however, numerous brown sunken spots destroyed their uniform appearance and playability. Close examination of the damage revealed small holes surrounded by the remains of shoots that had been chewed down to their bases (Plate 25; see color insert). What caused this damage, and how can this problem be controlled?

Analysis: The symptoms are characteristic of black cutworms (*Agrotis ipsilon* Hufnagel), a major pest of creeping bentgrass greens and tees. Black cutworm larvae dig a burrow in the turf or occupy coring holes, hibernating during the day and feeding at night by chewing down turf-grass shoots around the burrow. Damage may be compounded by foraging birds that create additional holes, pulling up turfgrass shoots with their beaks in search of the cutworms. In addition to the characteristic injury, diagnostic features of black cutworms include the presence of green frass—as well as the cutworms themselves—in the burrows and flocks of birds on greens and tees. In the United States, the number of broods varies from two to six, with the number increasing from north to south. As black cutworms generally do not survive subfreezing temperatures in winter, spring infestations on northern golf courses in the United States begin with migratory moths flying up from southern states. After mating, females lay hundreds of eggs, attaching them to turfgrass and other plant leaves. Larvae hatch and begin feeding on the leaves. They typically pass through seven molts, maturing in 20 to 40 days. Older larvae have voracious appetites, consuming large amounts of shoot tissue in a single night. They can also move more than 60 ft (20 m) during the night, sometimes reinfesting a green soon after treatment with short-residual insecticides. Pupation occurs within the larval burrow, and the adult moth emerges in about 2 weeks to start the next cycle.

Solution: Commercial pheromone traps containing a synthetic female sex attractant can be used to monitor black cutworm adult males. Sustained captures indicate that egg laying has begun. Initial damage on greens may be expected about 2 weeks later. The presence of black cutworm larvae on greens can be determined using a soap flushing solution made up of 1 fl oz (30 ml) of dishwashing detergent in 2 gal (7.6 L) of water. This should be applied to a 1-yd^2 (0.8-m^2) area and allowed to soak into the turf. Medium-sized to large cutworms (along with some other soil-inhabiting creatures) react within a few minutes by wriggling to the surface. This method can also be used to assess the efficacy of insecticide treatment. Chemical controls include an array of insecticides: bifenthrin (Talstar), carbaryl (Sevin), chlorpyrifos (Dursban), cyfluthrin (Tempo), ethoprop (Mocap), halofenozide (Mach 2), isofenphos (Oftanol), lambda-cyhalothrin (Battle, Scimitar), permithrin (Astro), spinosad (Conserve SC), and trichlorfon (Dylox). With properly timed applications, these can provide effective control, as long as certain guidelines are followed. Applications should be made in the late afternoon to minimize loss from photodecomposition and volatilization of the insecticides. Liquid formulations work better than granular materials, as they adhere to the foliage. They should not be watered in, and irrigation should be withheld until the day following application to ensure that the insecticide residues adhere to the foliage throughout the night when cutworms are feeding. Some biological controls, including entomopathogenic nematodes (e.g., *Steinernema carpocapsae*) and bacteria (e.g., *Bacillus thuringiensis*), as well as natural botanical insecticides (e.g., azadirachtin or neem), may work well for controlling young larvae but are less effective against larger cutworms. ■

▶ CASE STUDY 5.33

Scenario: The bermudagrass roughs at a country club located along the South Carolina coast were devastated by mole crickets during the summer months. At the end of the season, the superintendent was directed by the club's board of directors to develop an environmentally sensitive and cost-effective plan for controlling mole cricket populations during the next season. What should the components of this plan be, and how should they be implemented?

Analysis: Mole crickets (*Scapteriscus* spp.) are the most destructive insect pests in the southeastern United States. The two species most likely to occur in this region are the tawny mole cricket (*S. vicinus* Scudder), an herbivore that feeds on grasses and other plants (Figure 5.11), and the southern mole cricket (*S. borelli* Giglio-Tos), a carnivore that feeds on soil insects and earthworms. Because of its root-feeding habit, the tawny mole cricket is more damaging to turfgrass. Both the tawny and southern mole crickets also cause extensive damage by tunneling just below the soil surface, uprooting plants and causing desiccation. Extensive turfgrass loss is likely during late summer, when large nymphs are actively feeding and environmental stress is severe. Mole crickets have one generation each year. They spend most of their lives underground. They overwinter in deep burrows as large nymphs or adults. They may become active during warm periods in winter, producing short tunnels near the surface. By early spring, adults emerge to locate mates and egg-laying sites. Flights are typically heaviest on warm nights following a rain. They begin soon after dusk and last for 60 to 90 minutes. Males locate a suitable site, dig a small chamber opening to the surface, and call for females. During mating, the adults often throw up mounds of soil around their burrows. After mating, the female selects a site nearby, and tunnels and feeds for about 2 weeks before egg laying. She then digs a small chamber in which she lays a clutch of 26 to 60 eggs.

Figure 5.11   Mole cricket.

171

This process may be repeated several times before the adults die off. Eggs require about 3 weeks to develop into nymphs in warm soil. Nearly all of the nymphs will have emerged by early summer. After hatching, the nymphs tunnel to the surface to begin feeding. The most active burrowing and feeding occur just below the surface, especially on warm nights following rains or irrigation. The nymphs return to their permanent burrows during the day and may remain there for extended periods when conditions are dry.

Solution: According to Potter (1998), "Mole crickets are among the most difficult insects to control. It is important to know where damaging infestations are likely to occur, when the eggs hatch, and how hatching progresses to determine when the vulnerable young nymphs are present." One should begin in spring by scouting for tunneling and mound-making activities by the large nymphs and adults to determine where mole crickets are abundant and eggs are being laid. Infested areas should be mapped for treatment later in the season. While insecticide treatment at this time may be justified to reduce tunneling and other damage in intensively cultured turf, it will not eliminate the need for treatment later in the season, as the adults are not very susceptible to insecticides. Also, they tend to retreat underground during cold or dry weather, further reducing insecticide efficacy. The best time to control mole crickets with short-residual insecticides is midsummer, after most eggs have hatched and the crickets are still small (i.e., < ½ in. [1.25 cm] in length). This should control most of the annual brood, with sufficient insecticide residue remaining to kill most of the late-hatching stragglers. Waiting until damage from the new brood appears later in the summer will reduce control, as the crickets will be larger and more difficult to kill. Beginning in June, weekly soap flushes (see Case Study 5.32) can be used to monitor seasonal development of the mole cricket population. These should be applied following rains or irrigation, when nymphs are burrowing and feeding close to the surface. Insecticide applications are also most effective when nymphs are near the surface. Also, treat late in the day to minimize insecticide loss from photodecomposition and volatilization. Some biological materials, including entomopathogenic nematodes (e.g., *Steinernema riobravis* and *S. scapterisci*) and fungi (e.g., *Beauveria bassiana*), may be effective in reducing damage from adults in spring and fall, but they usually do not replace

172

the need for treating heavily infested sites in midsummer. A relatively new chemical called fipronil (Chipco Choice), a 0.1% granular formulation that must be professionally applied through slit openings in the turf, has provided excellent season-long control due to its long residual activity. ■

LARGE-ANIMAL PESTS

▶ **CASE STUDY 5.34**

Scenario: The appearance of long lines of raised turf on fairways and greens indicates the presence of moles. Would success in controlling grubs, the presumed source of food for the moles, solve the problem?

Analysis: Moles (*Scalopus aquaticus, S. townsendii,* and *S. latimanus*) belong to a group of mammals called *insectivores,* meaning "insect eaters." Fully grown moles are 5 to 8 in. (13–20 cm) long, with velvety fur, concealed eyes and ears, and sharp, pointed teeth. They feed mainly on earthworms, grubs, crickets, and invertebrates that live in the soil. Moles construct extensive underground tunnels; those close to the surface appear as raised ridges running through a turf. A single mole may dig up to 100 ft (30 m) of tunnels per day. Surface tunneling is greatest in spring and fall and after warm rains. Nest chambers are located 12 to 18 in. (30–46 cm) below the surface and connect to deep tunnels. Moles live alone except for a brief period in late winter when they mate. After a 6-week gestation period, a litter of three to five young is born in the nest chamber. They leave the nest and fend for themselves at about 6 weeks of age. Unless they are eaten by predators, their typical life span is 3 to 4 years in the wild.

Solution: Insecticides that successfully control grubs—but not earthworms or other soil invertebrates on which moles feed—may not eliminate the moles. When chlorinated hydrocarbon insecticides such as chlordane were used, they controlled a broader spectrum of organisms, including earthworms, and thus were more effective in eliminating moles; however, eliminating earthworms encourages problems with thatch buildup and soil compaction, requiring additional practices for sustaining healthy turf. With the exception of trapping, most other methods for controlling moles—including poison gas, poison baits, and chewing gum—are ineffective, inefficient, or too dangerous to be practical. Trapping is the most effective method for controlling moles, especially in early spring, when pregnant females can be eliminated, reducing the likelihood of having to confront the next generation of moles at a later date. To trap effectively, first locate the active main tunnel—the one that follows a straight course for some distance, usually running parallel to man-made boundaries (e.g., sidewalks, fences). To determine where traps should be placed, tramp down small sections of the tunnel and observe what happens over the next several days; moles will quickly repair the damage to an active tunnel. Once the active tunnels are located, place traps (3–5 per acre or 7–12 per ha) for killing or capturing the mole or moles causing damage to the area. Several types of traps are available, including the above-ground harpoon type and the below-ground scissor-arm type. The harpoon-type mole trap uses sharp spikes to skewer the mole as it passes underneath a constricted portion of the tunnel, while the scissor-arm type is set into the tunnel to capture the mole. ■

► CASE STUDY 5.35

Scenario: One of the crew members at a local minor league baseball park was the first to notice the large hole just inside the fence separating the outfield from a grass bank where fans sit and picnic during games. Further investigation revealed numerous holes connected by a system of below-ground channels just outside the fence. Because of the possibility of injury from stepping into one of the holes or from sinking into the loose ground above the channels, the park superintendent concluded that he needed to address this problem. What caused the problem, and how should it be addressed?

Analysis: Groundhogs (*Marmota monax*), also known as *woodchucks* or *whistle pigs,* are responsible for this problem. These are relatively large, furry animals that can grow up to 26 in. (66 cm) long and weigh as much as 11 lb (5 kg). They usually emerge from hibernation in early spring, mate, and, after a 32-day gestation period, produce a litter of up to nine young (usually three to five). At 5 weeks, the new ground-hogs are fully active. Their life span is about 5 years. Groundhogs are herbivores, feeding mostly on vegetative plant parts and consuming up to 1.5 lb (0.7 kg) per day. Groundhogs can move over 700 lb (318 kg) of soil digging a den, which is a nest chamber and a series of tunnels—2 to 4 ft below the surface and extending 15 to 25 ft horizontally—connecting the chamber to the surface, with as many as five entrances. Occupied dens can be identified by the mound of freshly excavated soil at the entrance. Groundhogs can burrow so extensively that adjacent building foundations may be destroyed.

Solution: Groundhogs can be controlled by several methods, includ-ing trapping, fumigation, repellents, natural predators (principally dogs in urban settings), and shooting. Trapping is the most humane and safest method. It is done with wire-mesh box traps situated immediately in front of the main entrance to the den and baited with apple slices, car-rots, or lettuce. Stones or logs placed around the entrance can aid in funneling the animal into the trap.   ■

▶ CASE STUDY 5.36

Scenario: Canada geese are beautiful birds. They would have been a welcome addition to the golf course were it not for the terrible messes left in their wake. Whole greens, as well as large sections of aprons and fairways, were virtually covered by white fecal matter, presenting a haz-ard to golfers, disrupting play, and impeding maintenance operations. There were even reports that a variety of human diseases could be transmitted by the birds. Clearly, something had to be done but, because of the Migratory Bird Act, control measures could not include killing or harming the birds. What can the superintendent do to solve this problem?

Analysis: Canada geese (*Branta canadensis* L.) are large migratory birds that establish nesting territories around ponds and lakes on golf courses (and elsewhere), damaging turfgrasses and posing a major nuisance—and possibly health hazards—from their droppings. Adult Canada geese are 25 to 43 in. (64–109 cm) long and weigh 11 to 15 lb (5–7 kg). They take up residence in early spring after returning with their mates from southerly wintering areas. A pair will typically establish a territory and raise a brood by midsummer. Eggs hatch in about 4 weeks, and the young goslings begin foraging soon thereafter. They readily feed on grass surrounding ponds, causing significant damage. Their grazing also makes them susceptible to poisoning by some pesticides applied to turf.

Solution: As geese avoid nesting in areas from which they cannot easily walk into an adjacent pond, they can be deterred by steepening pond banks or installing large boulders or fencing (3 ft [90 cm] high) at the water's edge. Planting less palatable tall fescue (*Festuca arundinacea* Schreb.) in place of Kentucky bluegrass (*Poa pratensis* L.) and other, more palatable species along the water's edge can also discourage them from grazing. Bird repellents, such as methylanthranilate (ReJeX-iT), that are sprayed on the grass and the adjacent water may discourage the geese from remaining in the area. Visible repellents—including scarecrows, flags, and noise-making devices—may be effective in frightening the geese away from ponds and turfgrass sites. Flocks can be trapped and transported to another area; this works best in late June or early July, when the adults are molting and have lost their ability to fly and the goslings have not yet fledged. Federal and state permits are required before geese can be trapped, and a suitable release site must be approved by wildlife authorities. Finally, an increasingly popular and effective method of discouraging geese is through the use of trained border collies to chase them away. ■

SUMMARY OF PEST AND PESTICIDE PROBLEMS

Weed Problems

Most weeds are either monocots (grasses) or dicots (broadleaf species) and include winter and summer annuals, as well as biennials and perennials. Winter-annual grasses, such as annual bluegrass (*Poa annua*), typically germinate in the fall, produce seed in the spring, and die in the summer. Summer-annual grasses, such as crabgrasses (*Digitaria ischaemum* and *D. sanguinalis*) and goosegrass (*Eleusine indica*), germinate in spring or summer and typically die with the first hard-killing frost in the fall. Chemical control of annual grasses may be attempted with either preemergence herbicides applied prior to the emergence of the weeds or postemergence herbicides applied afterward. While an array of herbicides can be used for control, creating environmental and cultural conditions that favor the competitive growth of desirable turfgrasses is often the most important determinant of success in resisting invasion by these weeds. Annual bluegrass can be especially problematic in that it often occurs as large patches in greens and fairways. If these patches are killed by herbicides, voids result that may be too large for adjacent turfgrasses to occupy within a reasonable period of time. As a consequence, annual bluegrass may reoccupy the voids through germination of seeds produced by earlier generations of plants. If the patches are not killed, the annual bluegrass population may recover before any appreciable change in the botanical composition of the turf occurs. Furthermore, perennial biotypes of annual bluegrass, if present, may neither die during the summer nor succumb to herbicides as expected. Small patches of annual bluegrass may be mechanically removed or selectively killed by such postemergence herbicides as ethofumisate and bispyribac-sodium under certain conditions. Also, certain PGRs, such as paclobutrazol and flurprimidol, can be used to selectively suppress the growth of annual bluegrass, allowing creeping bentgrass and other turfgrasses to expand their populations.

Summer-annual grasses can be controlled with applications of selected preemergence herbicides (e.g., benefin, bensulide, dithiopyr, oxadiazon, pendimethalin, and prodiamine) in spring or with applications of postemergence herbicides (e.g., fenoxyprop *p*-ethyl and quinclorac) after they are first evident in the turf. Perennial grasses that occur as weeds in turfgrass communities are usually controlled with nonselective herbicides (e.g., glufosinate-ammonium, glyphosate) applied as spot treatments. Most broadleaf weeds can be controlled with combinations of selected postemergence herbicides, including clopyralid, 2,4-D, dicamba, dichloroprop, mecoprop, and triclopyr.

Moss infestations in greens have increased as mowing heights have been lowered, especially where internal drainage is restricted. While several chemicals may be used to achieve some level of control, environmental conditions that favor moss growth and survival must be modified, including: improving air circulation, light exposure, pH, and drainage; raising the mowing height; and optimizing fertilization and irrigation practices.

Disease Problems

While many of the same measures for maximizing a turfgrass community's resistance to weed infestation can also be effective in minimizing disease incidence and severity, disease management on greens and other intensively cultured turfs often requires the use of fungicides. Contact (also called *foliar-protectant*) fungicides, such as chlorothalonil and mancozeb, must be applied on a preventive basis, as they are ineffective in killing fungi within the plant after infection had occurred. The period of control with these fungicides is short, usually lasting no more than 10 to 14 days, as mowing and precipitation remove fungicide residues from plant leaf surfaces. The development of resistance by fungi to contact fungicides is relatively rare, as these fungicides typically inhibit several of their enzyme systems simultaneously. Systemic fungicides can be used for both preventive and curative disease control, as they are absorbed by leaves and roots and can often kill fungi that have already infected the plant. Systemic fungicides include compounds from several chemical classes, including the benzimidazoles, carboximides, dicarboximides, DMIs, and QoIs. The likelihood that fungi will develop resistance to systemic fungicides is relatively high, as these fungicides typically inhibit only one enzyme system. Resistance of *Rutstroemia flocossum*—the organism causing dollar spot disease—to several classes of systemic fungicides has been documented, reducing the number of fungicides that can be used for control. Dollar spot is one of the most destructive diseases of intensively cultured turf, especially creeping bentgrass. With respect to strategies for delaying the development of resistance, there are two opposing philosophies: alternation and reservation. The alternation philosophy proposes using fungicides from different chemical classes on an alternating basis—usually in rotation with chlorothalonil—in order to prolong the life of each. The reservation philosophy proposes just the opposite: using only one chemical class of systemic fungicide in rotation with chlorothalonil until resistance is evident, reserving the other chemical classes for use afterward. Regardless of the philosophy selected, once resistance to a particular chemical class is observed, fungicides of that class should be used only for short-term curative disease control, as normal use would not be cost effective. After avoiding the use of a particular chemical class for several years, especially the dicarboximides, its efficacy may return as resistant fungal strains fade out. The severity of dollar spot disease may be lessened by adequate nitrogen fertilization, removing dew in the early morning hours, and periodic rolling.

Brown patch disease is caused by *Rhizoctonia solani,* a facultative parasite that lives primarily as a saprophyte but can infect living plants when conditions are favorable. The disease is likely to be active during hot days (86°F [30°C] or higher) and warm nights (70°F [21°C] or higher), especially where the humidity is high and drainage is poor. Cultural controls include removing dew, switching from nighttime to early morning irrigation, and improving drainage and air circulation. Chemical control can be obtained by rotating contact (chlorothalonil and mancozeb) and systemic fungicides (QoIs, carboximides, and dicarboximides).

Anthracnose disease is caused by *Colletotrichum graminicola,* another facultative parasite. There are two types of anthracnose: foliar and crown rotting. Like brown patch, foliar anthracnose is likely to be active during hot days (86°F [30°C] or higher) and warm nights (68°F [20°C] or higher), especially on wet turf. Crown-rotting anthracnose occurs over a wider temperature range, often in nitrogen-deficient annual bluegrass growing on wet or poorly drained soils. Because this disease is usually specific to annual bluegrass, adjacent creeping bentgrass populations may be healthy and vigorously growing. Cultural controls include providing adequate nitrogen fertilization, improving drainage, and avoiding excessive irrigation. Chemical control can be obtained with benzimidazole, DMI, and QoI fungicides; the benzimidazoles and DMIs must be applied at high spray volumes (~5 gal per 1000 ft^2, 20 L per 100 m^2) to be effective against this disease.

Take-all patch disease, caused by *Gaeumannomyces graminis,* is largely restricted to newly established stands of creeping and colonial bentgrasses. It is active during cool, wet weather in spring, but disease symptoms typically appear during the summer. Cultural controls include providing adequate nitrogen and phosphorus fertility and ensuring that magnesium is not limiting. Chemical control can be obtained with benzimidazole, DMI, and QoI fungicides. Because the symptoms of summer patch disease, caused by *Magnoporthe poae,* are similar to those of take-all patch disease, the two diseases are sometimes confused; however, summer patch is a disease of only bluegrasses, while only bentgrasses are susceptible to take-all patch. Cultural controls for summer patch include frequent irrigation of diseased turf and adequate nitrogen fertilization. Chemical control can be obtained with DMI and QoI fungicides.

Bacterial wilt, caused by *Xanthomonas campestris,* is responsible for the disease of Toronto (C-15) creeping bentgrass known as *C-15 decline.* The bacteria enter turfgrass plants through wounds, including those caused by working sand particles into the turf after topdressing. Death results where bacteria clog the vascular system, preventing the movement of water and nutrients from the roots to upper portions of the plant. Another species that is also susceptible to bacterial wilt is annual bluegrass. While the disease can be controlled with selected bactericides, none are currently registered for use in turf.

Pythium blight is caused by *Pythium aphanidermatum,* a facultative parasite that is spread by surface water movement and mower traffic on wet turf. The streaking pattern of disease symptoms reflects the pathogen's movement across the turf. It functions mostly as a saprophyte, infecting turfgrass only when conditions favor disease development. *Pythium* blight incidence is favored by daytime temperatures exceeding 86°F (30°C), nighttime temperatures exceeding 68°F (20°C), and relative humidity exceeding 90% for at least 9 continuous hours. Cultural controls include reducing nitrogen fertilization, avoiding nighttime irrigation where possible, and improving drainage and air circulation. Chemical control is obtainable on a strictly preventive basis with etridiazole, a contact fungicide. Both preventive and curative control are obtainable for longer periods with selected systemic fungicides, such as mefenoxam, propamocarb, and fosetyl-aluminum; however, fosetyl-aluminum should not be used where rough bluegrass was established for temporary winter cover on dormant bermudagrass turf, as it is phytotoxic to this bluegrass species.

Copper spot, caused by *Gloeocercospora sorghi,* is primarily a disease of velvet bentgrass. Annual bluegrass is not susceptible to this disease; however, initial disease symptoms similar to those of copper spot on annual bluegrass indicate the presence of *Microdochium* patch, caused by *Microdochium nivale.* Furthermore, copper spot typically occurs during warmer weather (65–80°F, 18–27°C), than *Microdochium* patch (60–70°F, 16–21°C). *Microdochium* patch appears as reddish-brown spots ranging in diameter from 1 to 8 in. (2.5–20 cm). Because heavy rains and mowing equipment can transport the fungal spores across the turf, streak-shaped disease symptoms similar to those of *Pythium* blight may appear. Another name for *Microdochium* patch is *pink snow mold,* reflecting the fact that when this disease occurs under snow cover, the pink mycelium of the fungus may be evident in the advancing edge of the spots. Cultural controls include avoiding levels of nitrogen fertilization that produce lush growth in the early fall. Chemical control is obtainable with preventive applications of dicarboximide, DMI, and QoI fungicides.

Typhula blight is caused by *T. incarnata* and *T. ishikariensis,* facultative saprophytes that oversummer as sclerotia and germinate in the fall. They produce pink-colored fungal spikes, called *basidiocarps,* that release basidiospores that are dispersed by wind and survive in the turf until snow cover develops. Infection occurs under at temperatures between 30°F and 55°F (–1°C–13°C). Another name for *Typhula* blight is *gray snow mold,* reflecting the presence of grayish-white mycelium at the outer margins of spots measuring 3 to 24 in. (8–60 cm) in diameter. Cultural controls include avoiding levels of nitrogen fertilization that produce lush growth in the early fall. Chemical control is obtainable with preventive applications of the contact fungicides chloroneb or quintozene, and with combinations of quintozene at half rate and various systemic fungicides, as well as with combinations of the contact fungicide chlorothalonil and one of several systemic fungicides. Because of the different fungal species and subspecific biotypes that can cause *Typhula* blight, consistent control is more likely from fungicide combinations than from individual fungicides.

Bentgrass dead spot is caused by *Ophiospaerella agrostis,* a root pathogen that can infect creeping bentgrasses and hybrid bermudagrasses. Disease symptoms are similar to those of dollar spot or copper spot; however, leaves at the margins of active patches are reddish-brown. The disease is active from late spring until the first hard frost in fall. It is generally limited to new greens. Short-term chemical control is obtainable with benzimidizole, dicarboximide, and QoI fungicides, as well as the contact fungicide chlorothalonil.

Gray leaf spot is caused by *Pyricularia grisea*. In perennial ryegrass, affected leaf blades may appear wilted and severely twisted. Leaf lesions have gray centers and are often surrounded by a yellow halo. Disease activity is favored by excessive nitrogen fertilization, persistently wet conditions, and temperatures between 70°F and 85°F (21°C–29°C). Chemical control is obtainable with both preventive and curative applications of benzimidizole, DMI, and QoI fungicides, as well as preventive applications of the contact fungicide chlorothalonil.

Rapid blight is a disease of annual bluegrass and rough bluegrass caused by *Labyrinthula* species. Initial symptoms are dark, water-soaked patches of turf that eventually become yellow and die. The disease occurs only where the salinity of the soil solution is high in response to the use of saline irrigation water. While chemical control is obtainable with mancozeb and some QoI fungicides, the best results occur where accumulated salts are flushed from the turfgrass rootzone.

Blue-green algae can form a dense mat covering the soil or thatch on poorly drained greens. These organisms secrete a gelatinous substance (mucilage) that protects the algal filaments from desiccation; however, when the mats dry, they form a hard crust that limits water movement into and out of the soil. Cultural controls include improving drainage and air movement, reducing shade intensity and excessive irrigation, and breaking through the surface crust by various cultivation methods. Chemical control is obtainable with the contact fungicides mancozeb and chlorothalonil.

Nematode Problems

Destructive nematodes are microscopic roundworms that feed on turfgrass roots, resulting in stunted growth, chlorosis, and wilting under environmental stress. The ectoparasitic sting nematode (*Belonolaimus longicaudatus*) is a serious pest of bermudagrass and other turfgrasses in Florida. Because of severe root loss, frequent irrigation and foliar feeding may be necessary on affected turfs to ensure that they have sufficient moisture and nutrients to survive. Cultivation can be helpful in improving soil aeration where soil oxygen levels are low. Chemical control is sometimes obtainable with the nematicide fenamiphos (Nemacur), as well as with the soil fumigants 1,3-dichloropropene (Curfew) and metam sodium (Turfcure 376) applied through slit injection by professional applicators.

Insect Problems

Grubs are the larvae of root-feeding scarab insects. Large grub species include Japanese beetles (*Popillia japonica*), masked chafers (*Cyclocephala borealis* and *C. lurida*), and European chafers (*Rhizotrogus majalis*). Damage is usually evident in late summer after the grubs reach a size sufficient to consume large masses of roots. Small grub species include the black turfgrass *ataenius* (*A. spretulus*) and *Aphodius* (*A. granaries* and *A. paradalis*). Initial damage may occur on annual bluegrass greens and fairways in early summer from very large populations of these insects. Chemical control is obtainable from short-residual insecticides washed into the thatch or soil; these include bifenthrin (Talstar), chlorpyrifos (Dursban), cyflutherin (Tempo), ethoprop (Mocap), lambda-cyhalothrin (Battle, Scimitar), permithrin (Astro), and trichlorfon (Dylox). Long-residual insecticides, such as imidacloprid (Merit) and halfenozide (Mach 2), can be applied in the late spring and early summer, respectively, to provide season-long control.

Annual bluegrass weevils (*Listronotus maculicollis*) are serious pests of intensively cultured annual bluegrass. Larvae feed on turfgrass crowns, causing the death of affected plants. Large populations of these small nocturnal-feeding insects can cause extensive damage by late spring from the first generation and additional damage in midsummer from the second generation. Chemical control is obtainable with short-residual insecticides, including chlorpyrifos (Dursban), cyflutherin (Tempo), lambda-cyhalothrin (Battle, Scimitar), and trichlorfon (Dylox), during the spring migration of first-generation adults from hibernation sites or in early July against second-generation adults before egg laying. Long-residual, systemic insecticides, such as imidacloprid (Merit), can be applied against adults emerging from hibernation for season-long control where annual bluegrass weevil is a perennial problem.

Black cutworms (*Agrotis ipsilon*) are a major pest of creeping bentgrass greens and tees. They feed at night from burrows in the turf, chewing down shoots adjacent to the burrows. Additional damage is likely from birds in search of these insects as a food source. Chemical control is obtainable from late afternoon applications of bifenthrin (Talstar), carbaryl (Sevin), chlorpyrifos (Dursban), cyfluth-erin (Tempo), ethoprop (Mocap), halofenozide (Mach 2), isofenphos (Oftanol), lambda-cyhalothrin (Battle, Scimitar), permithrin (Astro), spinosad (Conserve SC), and trichlorfon (Dylox). Biological control of young populations of black cutworms is possible with entomo-pathogenic nematodes (e.g., *Steinernema carpocapsae*), bacteria (e.g., *Bacillus thuringiensis*), and natural botanical insecticides (e.g., aza-dirachtin or neem).

Mole crickets, including the southern mole cricket (*Scapteriscus borelli*) and especially the tawny mole cricket (*S. vicinus*), can cause ex-tensive damage to susceptible turfgrasses through their tunneling and feeding activities. Chemical control is obtainable with late afternoon applications of short-residual insecticides in midsummer after most eggs have hatched and the cricket nymphs are small. Some biological materials, including entomopathogenic nematodes (e.g., *Steinernema riobravis* and *S. scapterisci*) and fungi (e.g., *Beauveria bassiana*), may be effective in reducing damage from adults in spring and fall.

Large-Animal Pest Problems

Moles (*Scalopus* spp.) feed on earthworms, grubs, crickets, and other animals living in the soil. Their damage is from extensive under-ground tunneling that raises large ridges in the turf. They are best controlled by placing traps in active tunnels during early spring to kill or capture them.

Groundhogs (*Marmota monax*) are large animals that feed vora-ciously on vegetation and produce an extensive system of tunnels along with large mounds of soil at their entrances, posing a hazard to people walking in their vicinity. They are best controlled by placing baited traps immediately in front of the main entrance to their den.

Canada geese (*Branta canadensis*) are large migratory birds that can damage turfgrass and pose a major nuisance to golfers and others from their droppings. While various methods of control may be effective, the most popular one is the use of trained border collies to chase them away.

CHAPTER

6

People Problems

Of all the problems a turfgrass manager faces in the performance of his duties, none is likely to be more challenging than those involving people. One must answer to superiors, work with peers, and supervise subordinates, often during the same day. All of these communications and the relationships they support are important. Each should be accomplished with patience, skill, respect, and, perhaps most importantly, integrity. Since superiors control the resources needed to accomplish tasks and achieve goals, they deserve everything they need to make informed decisions and perform their duties. Likewise, peers with whom you are engaged in interdependent activities deserve your best effort to work with them in a harmonious and mutually beneficial fashion. And your subordinates deserve all that they need to be successful and appropriately rewarded for their efforts.

SUPERIORS

▶ **Case Study 6.1**

Scenario: The superintendent of a golf course in the New York Metropolitan Area was asked by the chairman of his Green Committee

187

to reduce the mowing height of his predominantly annual bluegrass (*Poa annua* L. f. *reptans* [Hauskins] T. Koyama) greens from 0.156 in. (4.0 mm) to 0.118 in. (3.0 mm) and to reduce irrigation in order to significantly increase their putting speed. The superintendent responded that the lower mowing height coupled with dryer conditions would result in a significant loss of turf during periods of heat stress and initially refused to do so. The chairman returned time and time again to this subject, stating that other golf courses in the area were being managed this way without adverse affects on the health and persistence of their greens. Finally, the superintendent relented and gradually reduced the mowing height and irrigation intensity as instructed; however, during a period of severe high-temperature stress, he withheld syringing and allowed the greens to die in order to support his contention that the 0.118-in. (3.0-mm) height jeopardized the health of the turfgrass.

Analysis: Failing to pursue every reasonable course of action to sustain turfgrass during periods of high-temperature stress is inimical to the professional standards and status of golf course superintendents everywhere. But intentionally allowing greens to die in order to make a statement of protest is grossly unprofessional and irresponsible. While a superintendent is certainly justified in pointing out the downside of consistently mowing at heights that he believes are below the mowing tolerance limits of a particular turfgrass, ultimately it is the country club members (or golf course owners) who decide what they want and it is the superintendent's responsibility to provide it, if at all possible. And he must accept the fact that standards of turf quality—including green speed—change and that he has a professional obligation to accept and adopt those changes wherever and whenever feasible.

Solution: The superintendent should initially respond by expressing his concerns and attempting to answer all questions posed by the green chairman and other members. The superintendent might attempt to persuade the members to experiment on a specific green to determine if what they want is, in fact, feasible under the conditions at that particular golf course. But even if they agree, he is professionally obligated to conduct a legitimate investigation by making every reasonable attempt to sustain the turfgrass during stress periods. If, in the final analysis, he feels that he cannot do what is requested of him and he is unable to convince the members to pursue an alternate course of action, he should resign. Under no circumstances is it justified to intentionally allow turfgrass to die in order to support his position. ∎

▶ CASE STUDY 6.2

Scenario: A young superintendent at a private country club in Las Vegas, Nevada, was hailed by his Green Committee chairman while inspecting the golf course and asked about the status of a particular renovation project. Based on the tone of the conversation, it was obvious that the chairman was annoyed that the project had not even been initiated, despite his requests since the beginning of the golfing season several months earlier. When the superintendent responded that the project would be initiated the following Monday, the chairman nodded, returned to his fellow players, and grumbled, "I'm not sure this fellow is going to work out."

Analysis: Golf turf management involves many things, including being responsive to the requests of others, especially the green chairman. If this person is within your chain of command (i.e., the person to whom you report), an important part of your job is to develop and maintain effective communication with him (or her) on matters relating to the condition of the golf course and the resources required to conduct routine—as well as nonroutine—operations. As in many relationships between seniors and subordinates, the subordinate (in this case, the superintendent) is often more knowledgeable about the technical aspects of the job, while the senior is better able to reflect the wishes and demands of the Green Committee, the Board of Directors, and the membership. Therefore, their relationship is a mutually dependent one; the chairman needs from the superintendent information and understanding about golf turf operations, including what can be done and the time and resources required to do it, while the superintendent needs from the chairman information and understanding about what the membership wants and the time and resources they are willing and able to allocate to get it. Qualities that are important in this relationship are patience, trust, integrity, and respect.

Solution: The superintendent should request regular meetings with the chairman to review routine operations and assess progress on specific projects. Such meetings tend to be better environments for establishing effective communication than chance meetings on the golf course when each person is involved in other pursuits. The superintendent should prepare properly for these meetings to ensure that all important items are covered in an adequate but succinct fashion. The preparation of handouts sent before the meeting can reduce the meeting time and provide the chairman with the information needed to make timely decisions and respond to members' questions and concerns. Always remember that an important role of subordinates is to educate their superiors on the things they need to perform their functions properly. This should be planned and conducted in a purposeful way to enhance mutual understanding, build trust, and develop the kind of relationship that best serves the membership. ■

▶ CASE STUDY 6.3

Scenario: A superintendent of a private golf course with several severely shaded greens attempted to convince the members of the Green Committee of the essential importance of selectively removing some trees and pruning the others to allow sufficient sunlight in to sustain healthy turfgrass growth. Some committee members accepted the importance of direct sunlight, but they believed that the superintendent was underestimating how much sunlight the green actually received and would not approve his proposal. Others emphasized that the stately trees were an important feature of the golf course and should not be removed. How can the superintendent convince the Green Committee to address this problem satisfactorily?

Analysis: Despite how much a superintendent knows about turfgrass science and management and how little Green Committee members know, he can expect to have his proposals—as well as some of his decisions—challenged by them from time to time. This does not necessarily indicate a lack of confidence in the superintendent; rather, it is a reflection of the desire of Green Committee members to be involved in making nonroutine decisions, especially those dealing with matters of great interest. That is probably why they agreed to serve on this committee. And there is hardly an issue of greater interest than the impact of tall, stately trees on the aesthetics and playability of a golf course. The prospect of removing even one tree can be offensive, generating intensely emotional responses, sometimes from the least vocal members. Therefore, it may be wise to involve the entire membership, perhaps with the Green Committee functioning as intermediaries and facilitators of this decision-making process. This will involve a technical analysis of the problem: tree management is just as important as turfgrass management, and the two are, in fact, intertwined. As trees get larger, their effects on the adjacent turf also grow. Small trees begin to compete with turfgrasses in their immediate vicinity for water and nutrients. As they grow, this competition increases, as does the turf area affected. At the same time, shade becomes a factor of increasing importance (see Case Study 3.1). The combination of reduced photosynthetically active radiation (PAR) and altered light quality on turfgrass growth results in thinner, longer leaves with a more upright growth orientation; lower shoot density due to reduced tillering; substantially reduced rooting; and lower levels of carbohydrates reserves, which are needed to support growth at night, when there is no photosynthetic activity, and for recuperative growth when a turf has been damaged or diseased. Thus, a shaded turf is often of lower quality and more susceptible to damage from traffic and other environmental stresses. And because of the dynamic relationship between trees and turf quality, an acceptable situation this year may become unacceptable sometime in the next year or two as this relationship evolves. The problem will also involve an economic analysis in which the costs of a particular course of action, or perhaps several alternative courses of action, are detailed, along with the impacts of these corrective actions on the quality of play for a specified period of time.

Solution: The superintendent's objective should be to obtain from the membership, through—or in cooperation with—the Green Committee, an informed decision on an appropriate course of action for dealing with the problem on these greens. To achieve this objective, he should begin by documenting the amount of sunlight (specifically PAR, i.e., red and blue light) received throughout the day on both shaded and full-sun greens. These results should be illustrated in a written report with a graph or table and an explanation provided on how shade has reduced the quality of selected greens. Photographs taken at various times of the day to show shading patterns and specific effects on turf quality should be included. The report should conclude with options, such as (1) accept the prospect of decreasing turf quality on these greens over time, (2) selectively remove some of the trees (expressed as a number or percentage) and prune branches on others to increase light penetration by a designated amount, or (3) move the green to a less light-restricted location. An alternative would be to hire a consultant or a USGA Green Section agronomist to prepare such a report. With the submission of the report, a decision from the Green Committee—or from the membership through the Green Committee—on the specific option to be implemented should be requested.   ■

▶ CASE STUDY 6.4

Scenario: The superintendent of a municipal golf course located just north of Chicago was called to the office of the city manager in mid-March—2½ months into the fiscal year—and informed that, because of a fiscal crisis facing the city, his budget for the year was being reduced by nearly 13%. A substantial portion of his crew consisted of seasonal workers from Mexico, all of whom were either en route or preparing to travel north for the new golfing season. While several capital-improvement projects and capital-equipment purchases were planned for the current year that, if deferred, could just about cover the shortfall in funding, the superintendent wondered if that would be the best way to deal with his budget problem. Under these difficult circumstances, what should he do?

Analysis: The key questions at the outset are: is this reduction temporary or permanent, and, if permanent, will it be followed by further reductions in future years? If the superintendent can be assured that it is temporary and nonrecurring, the problem can be addressed by simply postponing capital-improvement projects and capital-equipment purchases until next year; however, if there is any likelihood that the reduction will be permanent and perhaps followed by further reductions in succeeding years, an entirely different approach will be needed. Since turf-grass management is a resource-dependent enterprise, the level of turf quality is determined by the financial resources available; therefore, a significant reduction in the resources allocated for turfgrass management must be accompanied by corresponding reductions in turf quality. This might involve reductions that include all turfs or reductions specifically targeted at some turfs (e.g., fairways and roughs) but not others (e.g., greens and tees). The reductions would usually involve shifts to higher mowing heights and lower mowing frequencies; however, they could also involve a suspension of mowing operations on some roughs and other previously mowed turfs. Additionally, irrigation might be reduced or suspended, as well as some fertilization, cultivation, and pest-management operations. The savings would obviously be in labor costs but would also include some consumptive costs (e.g., fuel, electricity, water, fertilizers, and pesticides), as well as equipment-related costs, including equipment replacement, repair, and maintenance.

With respect to labor savings, the choices would be to hire fewer personnel, provide less overtime, or both. If the decision is made to hire fewer seasonal personnel, this may be complicated by the commitments made to these workers and the fact that at least some of them have already departed Mexico, anticipating that a job will be waiting for them when they arrive. Alternatively, a decision to reduce overtime could be a major disappointment to employees with specific seasonal earnings expectations. In either case, employee morale could be aversely affected.

With respect to budgeted capital-equipment purchases, delaying these could increase repair and maintenance costs and reduce reliability and operational efficiency, with corresponding increases in labor costs. Similarly, depending on the nature of the capital-improvement projects budgeted, delaying them could lead to associated increases in other costs.

Solution: If a continuation of reduced funding is anticipated in future years, significant and continuing reductions in several expenditure categories must be made. Since labor costs usually make up at least half of the total budget, they should be reduced to provide a substantial portion—perhaps most—of the funding shortfall. As this would require hiring fewer seasonal laborers, those not hired, but for whom commitments were made, should be assisted in finding alternate employment. Overtime should be reduced, but not much more than the proportionate reduction in personnel, so that the earnings expectations of the other employees are largely realized; otherwise, employee morale could be seriously eroded. To the extent that planned capital expenses over the next several years can be reduced without adversely affecting operational efficiency, some should be delayed and others rethought, with the possibility of eliminating them. Most importantly, the likely impact of these proposed reductions should be communicated to all stakeholders and, where feasible, opportunities should be provided for their input into the decision-making process. This should certainly include the city manager and other city officials, as they will have to bear the brunt of any criticisms directed at the city for the obvious changes in the golf course. ■

PEERS

▶ CASE STUDY 6.5

Scenario: With the construction of a new elementary school across the street from his business site, the owner of a lawn-care operation in eastern Pennsylvania was asked by the school board to address concerns raised by the children's parents about the safety hazards posed by the storage and use of concentrated pesticides in such close proximity to the school. As the date of the school board meeting approached, the owner learned that the attendance was expected to be large and would likely include representatives from various antipesticide groups who were planning to use this event to advance their respective agendas. How should the owner prepare for the meeting, and what should he say (or not say) in his interaction with the audience?

Analysis: If parents perceive that their children are exposed to hazards from concentrated pesticides in close proximity to their school, many will do whatever they feel is necessary to reduce or eliminate those hazards. Where actual hazards exist, measures should be taken to deal effectively with them, and parents should be properly informed of these measures so that they can be assured that their children are safe, despite the presence of stored pesticides. A lawn-care operator placed in the position described in this scenario faces a formidable task, given the general concerns over pesticides and the likelihood that anti-pesticide groups will capitalize on this opportunity to promote their agendas. The lawn-care operator's objectives at the meeting should be to introduce himself and his business to the audience, to address the concerns raised regarding the actual hazards posed by the concentrated chemicals to the school children, to set a professional and empathetic tone for the meeting, and to establish a favorable baseline against which other behaviors will be compared.

Solution: The lawn-care operator should prepare a presentation for the school board meeting that clearly explains the steps taken—including describing the pesticides used and the hazards posed by them to people, animals, and the environment, the design and construction of pesticide storage and handling facilities, and applicator training and licensing programs—to ensure the safety of company employees, customers, and neighboring personnel. Rules should be established with the school board president regarding the conduct of the meeting to ensure that things don't get out of hand. These might include the following: don't allow speeches and long diatribes by audience members; insist that participants behave in a respectful and courteous manner; require attendees to raise their hands and wait to be recognized before speaking; allow only one person to speak at a time; allow reporters to attend but not to videotape the meeting, as this might encourage grandstanding by some attendees, especially those with an agenda; stick to the issues in the discussion; and avoid personal attacks. Some of the things the lawn-care operator *should not do* are to assess blame, get angry, yell, talk down to the participants, make wisecracks, get too technical, downplay concerns or the importance of the meeting, give long answers, raise new issues, fake an answer, and be argumentative or defensive. Some things he *should do* are to be patient, demonstrate a caring attitude, establish common ground with the audience, listen, establish credibility, and communicate using appropriate analogies. If confronted by a person with an antipesticide agenda, he could respond to his or her statements as follows: "With respect to your position on pesticides, obviously I don't agree with you. If you have specific evidence to support your claims or allegations, I'd appreciate your sharing these with me so that I can review them and draw my own conclusions. I can tell you this: I believe that the materials I am currently using are safe;

however, if you can convince me that some of them are not, I will stop using them. Finally, I would be happy to meet with you and members of your group to address any specific concerns that you may have." If confronted by a *petrochemical-sensitive* person (i.e., determined by a physician to suffer from exposure to the odors sometimes associated with pesticide formulations), he could respond by stating: "We use a registry of people who are verifiably petrochemical-sensitive to inform them prior to making applications in their area." If confronted by an "antilawn" person, he could respond with the statement: "You are entitled to your opinion, and I respect that. Others, including my customers, have different opinions, and they are the basis for my business." It is also possible that he might be confronted by a person expressing a belief that any pesticide should be available for use, regardless of the environmental consequences. To that person, he might respond: "Some of the pesticides used in the past—such as DDT, dieldrin, chlordane, inorganic arsenicals—did pose a hazard to people and/or the environment; we don't use them anymore, and that's a good thing."   ■

▶ CASE STUDY 6.6

Scenario: The new superintendent had his first run-in with the head golf professional only 2 days after beginning his employment at the club. The pro angrily complained about having to wait several minutes while a green was being syringed during an especially hot summer day. This was clearly witnessed by all of the members with whom the pro was playing. The superintendent soon learned that such displays of anger were commonly directed by the pro at anyone whom he considered inferior, including all other club employees. Because of the unpleasantness of these encounters and their devastating effect on employee morale, the superintendent concluded that he had to do something. What should he do?

Analysis: Bullying and offensive behavior are never acceptable and should not be tolerated. Thus, the issue is not whether to tolerate the pro's behavior, but how to attempt to change it. Often, offensive behavior is symptomatic of an individual's insecurity; the individual attempts to secure his or her own standing by demeaning others, especially when convinced that the victim of the assault is in no position to fight back or pose a significant threat. However, when that individual realizes that his or her standing may be jeopardized by a continuation of this behavior, it is very likely to change.

Solution: Generally, the best approach is to meet with the individual and calmly—but firmly—explain that his behavior is unacceptable and will not be tolerated. Selected authorities—including the Green Chairman, club president, or owner—should be quietly apprised of the situation in order to obtain their support if and when needed. As in Case Study 6.5, a professional attitude should be consistently demonstrated. Finally, if the situation does not improve, despite all reasonable attempts to correct it, seek employment elsewhere. Of course, a preventive approach would be to carefully research the environment surrounding a new position to ensure that the people with whom you will be associating will be worthy colleagues. If that is not the case, look elsewhere.   ■

▶ CASE STUDY 6.7

Scenario: The superintendent would never have anticipated that water could be such a controversial subject. Given the age and unsatisfactory condition of his irrigation system, the approval he received from the club's Board of Directors to initiate planning on a new system would have been an entirely positive experience, were it not for the response of the local community. In Colorado, water is a precious natural resource. With annual rainfall averaging only 15 in. (38 cm), water must be used wisely by all sectors of the community. It should never be wasted. When an article appeared in the local newspaper stating that a new irrigation system with many more sprinklers was being considered for the golf course, the response was immediate and intensely negative. When he received a request from a local TV reporter for an interview, the superintendent began anticipating the questions he would be asked and how he should respond.

Analysis: Water is a precious natural resource that must be used sensibly to ensure its sustained availability for all legitimate purposes. Where limited, water must be allocated wisely for domestic, agricultural, and industrial uses. While a convincing case can be made that golf course irrigation is a legitimate and important use of water, it is also essential to ensure that irrigation water is used properly and efficiently, even where it is in abundant supply. When water use is restricted

197

during periods of limited availability, however, it should also be allocated and used in accordance with the priorities and limitations established within a particular community or region. This may require some temporary limitations on golf course irrigation, with the range of alternatives extending from prohibiting irrigation of roughs to restricting irrigation to greens. Efficient and/or prioritized use of irrigation water requires a distribution system that specifically provides for uniform, precise, and targeted application. Without uniform application, some turfs must be overwatered in order to provide adequate water for other turfs within the sprinkler distribution pattern. Irrigation can be timed during periods of lowest wind velocity to minimize displacement and evaporative losses. If the precipitation rate from the nozzles is higher than the infiltration capacity of the turf, runoff is likely, resulting in inadequate irrigation of sloping sites and excessive accumulation of water in depressions located downslope. There is some capacity to compensate for inadequate infiltration through a procedure called *multiple cycling*, by which specific sprinklers or sets of sprinklers are operated intermittently over an extended period (e.g., three 10-minute sets 20 minutes apart) to effectively reduce the precipitation rate. Therefore, proper installation of a well-designed, modern irrigation system can provide greater control over the distribution of water, often resulting in substantial savings in water use and superior turf quality.

Solution: The reporter should be invited to the golf course and shown the plans for the new irrigation system. He or she should be shown how the features of the new system will substantially improve water-use efficiency and turf quality. In other words, the new irrigation system will use less—not more—water. Furthermore, if the reporter does not understand how turfgrass sites, especially golf courses, contribute to the community through the provision of expansive green space, economic development, employment opportunities, and environmental quality, take the time to provide some education. Even if you don't convince the reporter, he or she is likely to be impressed with your dedication and enthusiasm. ■

► CASE STUDY 6.8

Scenario: Over the years, the long-serving superintendent at a golf course in northern Illinois gradually lost interest in his work. He no longer looked forward to greeting the crew each morning at the maintenance building, at least not the way he once did. Somewhere along the way, his enthusiasm for turfgrass science and technology had waned. He rarely read the trade magazines or attempted to keep up with the changes going on around him. He seldom attended conferences and seminars on golf turf management; when he did, he spent his time in the hallways or in bars. While retirement was still a long way off, he was, for all practical purposes, retired as well as bored.

Analysis: Golf course superintendents are in a position to create and sustain the beauty of a living landscape and to provide pleasure and recreation for many people. They have opportunities each day to derive considerable satisfaction from the work they do and the results they achieve. Each growing season presents new and different challenges—as well as opportunities—for generating renewed interest and excitement. And with the rapid changes taking place in turfgrass science and technology, taking advantage of continuing educational opportunities provides them with additional tools with which to expand their capabilities. For many, this is sufficient to sustain them throughout their careers.

Solution: Work to develop and maintain a professional attitude toward your industry and your role in it. Ask yourself the hard questions about why certain things happen, and be persistent in your quest for good answers. Make the effort to learn new things every week through critical observation, reading, and frequent participation in educational events. Appreciate the people in your employ as valuable resources through whom you can create beauty and achieve important goals. And always regard the glass as half full, never as half empty. ∎

SUBORDINATES

▶ CASE STUDY 6.9

Scenario: A new branch manager with a national lawn-service company, who had performed well as a lawn specialist and later as a service coordinator, had difficulty adjusting to his new management responsibilities. In attempting to copy the gruff style of his predecessor, he so alienated his employees that their overall performance declined dramatically. This was reflected in all of the indices used for assessing the branch's performance, including substantial declines in productivity and profits and corresponding increases in customer cancellations, credits issued, accounts payable, and service calls. What should his supervisor, the regional manager, do to address this problem?

Analysis: A manager is responsible for everything his branch or region does or fails to do. In this case, the failure of the branch manager to perform satisfactorily is the responsibility of the regional manager. If he assumed that the new branch manager had been adequately trained by the previous branch manager, his assumption was obviously incorrect. Perhaps he should have been more involved in the new branch manager's training to ensure that the new branch manager would be better prepared for his new role. And perhaps he should have monitored the new branch manager's behavior more closely and been of greater assistance to him in his first few months on the job. Regardless of what he should have done earlier, he now must identify the reasons for the new manager's poor performance and address them; otherwise, his own position could be in jeopardy.

Management has been defined as *"the skill of attaining predetermined objectives with and through the voluntary cooperation and effort of others"* (Brown, W. S. 1985. *13 Fatal Errors Managers Make and How You Can Avoid Them*. Berkley Books, New York. 200 p.). Mismanagement is often the result of one or more "fatal errors" that managers make in the performance of their duties, including:

Refuse to accept personal accountability. Harry Truman had a sign on his desk stating "The buck stops here." Through this statement, he indicated his acceptance of personal accountability for the results of his actions. Thus, the most important questions an effective manager must ask when things go wrong are: "What did I do wrong?" "What should I do to rectify this situation?" and "What can I learn from this?" A manager must focus on performance, not excuses for why something failed. Those who make excuses are attempting to escape the responsibility for their own failure. Those who project an image of being *all-knowing* are reflecting their emotional immaturity and will eventually lose credibility and their ability to lead.

Fail to develop people. One of management's major purposes is to provide for the continuation of operations despite personnel changes and absences. Managers must therefore build the independence of their subordinates to enable them to function with little or no supervision for reasonable periods of time. Managers who build dependency often do so out of personal insecurity. Denying a subordinate the experience of solving routine problems denies him or her the opportunity for growth. When confronted with a problem by a subordinate, look at the person and listen with your eyes as well as your ears so that you can understand not only the problem but also your employee's reaction to it in the form of anger, fear, irritation, or eagerness; then provide advice and counsel. Teach employees to approach major challenges one step at a time. If each step is handled properly, the entire project can get done. In promoting people to management positions, be sure to do it in a manner that enables them to retain a reasonable level of confidence. While sending the new manager to a training course is often a good first step, it is rarely adequate. The organization must also provide the intermediary steps to ensure that a potentially effective manager doesn't fail. The manager-designate should be given new responsibilities by degrees so that there is a progressive delegation of responsibilities and associated authority. This is often the essence of an assistant manager position. If the discovery is made that the person has no real aptitude for the position, he or she should be eased back into the one where he functions best. This should be done in a way that does not destroy the person's self-esteem; otherwise, the organization may lose not only a manager, but a productive employee as well.

Try to control results instead of influencing thinking. The first question people ask themselves when confronted with a challenge is: "Can I succeed?" If they believe that a particular task is beyond their capability, they are not inclined to attempt it. Even if they do, they are not likely to be successful. Consider the reaction of the tree cutter who is asked to fell twice as many trees per day as in the past using the same double-bladed ax. The likelihood that he will respond affirmatively is zero. But, if provided with a chain saw and the training in how to use it, his reaction will be quite different. A manager's responsibility is to provide the tools for increased productivity, along with the training in how to use those tools. This begins with attempts to change the employee's concept of his or her ability to accomplish specific tasks. The second question people ask themselves when confronted with a challenge is: "Where is the value to me?" If they perceive greater value in performing the task, they will perform it. If not, they will simply refuse to do so. The value, in this case, is not necessarily in the form of money; it is more likely to be in the form of self-esteem. People develop intense interest in an activity and take pride in higher levels of performance only if they can derive self-esteem from doing so. If, through your actions as a manager, you destroy the ability of an employee to derive self-esteem from a job, you risk losing an employee or, worse, you precipitate a work stoppage or slowdown.

Forget the importance of profit. No business or institution can long survive without generating a surplus over and above its costs of operation. Even nonprofit institutions must maintain this discipline. Therefore, investments should always be made with a time factor in mind. And if they do not show favorable results after a reasonable period, the manager should accept the losses, learn from the errors, and select another course of action.

Join the wrong crowd. This has to do with fostering the right attitude, not with organizational gamesmanship. One of the serious maladies that can infect an organization is the improper use of pronouns, which is the tendency of some employees to use *they* instead of *us,* especially when referring to higher levels of management. If a manager uses *they* when referring to his superiors, he obviously does not identify with them, he does not consider himself a part of the management team, and, either consciously or inadvertently, he drives a wedge between his group and the rest of the organization.

Manage everyone the same way. There are different approaches to management. Many are good; some are awful. For example, managers who "play the role" send a message to employees that they do not feel up to the task and, thus, need these trappings to seem capable of doing the job. Second is the "management by staff meeting" approach, primarily to avoid the stress associated with confronting problems—and the people associated with them—individually. Like it or not, management is largely a one-to-one proposition. By individual communication, you learn the root of problems and are provided with the opportunities to correct them.

Concentrate on problems rather than objectives. Ineffective managers spend 90% of their time dealing with problems that influence only 10% of their productivity. Creativity fails us when we become absorbed in problems and ignore the end results we wish to obtain. For example, if you throw a nonswimmer into the water, he thrashes about, exhausts his energy, and drowns. A swimmer, in contrast, will float or tread water, select a shoreline destination, and swim there at a reasonable pace while continually checking to ensure that she is heading in the right direction. From our educational experiences, we may be inclined to conclude that, for every problem, there is only one right answer. While this is true in math and perhaps in science, it is not true in the management of operations. The real danger in the one-right-answer approach is that it breeds intolerance of alternatives, and it leads to paralysis when the plan is obstructed en route. When faced with a roadblock to success, the failure-prone manager asks "What?" (as in "What will happen to me if I fail?"), while the creative manager asks "How?" (as in "How can I use this situation to my advantage?").

Be a buddy, not a boss. You are either a buddy or a boss; you can't or shouldn't be both. Successful hybrids do not exist. This doesn't mean that you can't relax and have fun in the presence of an employee (or a boss). It does mean, however, that the company of an employee is never entirely social; it is a business relationship. In a conversation with a former peer, you might say, "As your manager, I want to give you the support you need. In return, I want you to give me the performance I need." You can't be responsible for people; however, by necessity, you must be responsible to people. When managers become responsible for people, they overstep their bounds and adopt those individuals. Each individual is responsible for himself or herself. To manage, you cannot place the welfare of any individual above the welfare of the organization. This is a tough rule to live by; sometimes, it hurts.

Fail to set standards. The guidelines an organization establishes need not aim at forcing compliance with a list of regulations, but they should have the goal of building personal and organizational pride. If a manager fails to establish standards, the employees will, and the results may be less than pleasing. Standards may encompass such things as ethics and morality, safety, dress, and performance. With respect to performance, there are four categories: (1) quantity—the amount of product or service produced; (2) quality—the errors or mistakes made, the appearance or impressions given; (3) timeliness—meeting deadlines; and (4) cost—living within the budget with respect to personnel, money, and materials. Standards eliminate management pressures by removing personality from tough decisions. Guidelines established for stating what management should reasonably expect an employee to do as a minimum provide a basis for business-like decision making. Standards serve as a covenant between an employee and the company or institution based on understanding, good faith, and mutual commitment. Through this covenant, the company or institution guarantees the employee that, by upholding the standards, the employee will enjoy a certain quality of work environment and career opportunities. In turn, the employee will uphold the standards in order to enjoy the benefits those standards assure.

Fail to train your people. Management's job is to induce employees to consistently perform at PAR (i.e., performance at or above the minimum standards); thus, a manager's dual responsibility is to get people from entry level to PAR and maintain PAR once attained. PAR's three inseparables are (1) precedents (P)—guides for evaluating future behavior (e.g., job description, policies, objectives); (2) actions (A)—what employees do; and (3) results (R)—the consequences of the actions. If the hiring manager has not made a mistake in selection, only three reasons remain for failure to do the job: the individual does not know what the job is; the individual does not know how to do the job; someone or something interferes with his or her desire or ability to do the job. These three reasons for nonperformance constitute the manager's basic obligations to his or her employees. You have not begun to be responsible to them until you have assumed responsibility for establishing the basic precedents to successful behavior by making sure they know what the job is and how to do it. Nor have you begun to lead until you have strengthened their resolve so that they can handle the conditions and the people who interfere with their desire and ability.

Condone incompetence. Managers may condone a job inadequately done for several reasons: they feel the need to be loved and seek it on the job; they hope the problem will disappear if they ignore it; they lack the willingness or ability to confront others. While we all need to feel loved, managers must settle for respect in the workplace and seek love elsewhere. Management is not a popularity contest. When deviations in behavior necessary to maintain PAR performance may be seen as momentary lapses in concentration, they usually require intervention by the manager and should not be ignored. Confronting incompetence requires skill and timeliness. Each time a deviation from acceptable behavior is ignored, it tends to become greater. When it grows to the point of becoming a major irritant, you may become emotionally involved and respond with an angry confrontation. As a consequence, potentially productive communication is supplanted by a personal attack. Confrontation should be directed at correcting deviant behavior; it should never be done to punish. Principles of effective confrontation are: confront immediately, confront privately, be specific with respect to unwanted behavior, be clear with respect to how you feel by sharing your concerns and frustrations about the unwanted behavior, provide redirection, and follow up to reinforce the desired behavior. If you have done all in your power to deal with incompetence and the employee's performance does not come up to PAR, you have an obligation to the employee, yourself, and the organization to make a career adjustment. This means having the employee transferred to a more suitable job or terminating his or her employment.

Recognize only top performers. An important function of management is to create winners by encouraging employees to exceed PAR performance. If only top performers are recognized, however, those just below the top may feel unappreciated and unrewarded for their performance. When mediocre performers are compensated the same way as the most productive workers, incentives are cut off, self-esteem withers, and productivity declines. Management should ensure that everyone is recognized for accomplishment, and that doesn't necessarily mean a big raise or bonus. Management functions at its highest level when it helps people achieve their objectives. In order to reach goals, employees need to have reasonable yet challenging targets at which to aim. It is the manager's job to break down objectives by week or by month, provide a support system to help each person reach his or her objectives, and provide personal and timely recognition for the attainment of objectives.

Try to manipulate people. In attempting to influence the attitudes and performance of employees, managers must exercise care in the methods used. Good influences will add to self-esteem and productivity; bad ones will cause employees to feel manipulated, and productivity will decline. Traditional management motivational approaches include fear—the manipulative *stick* approach may be largely counterproductive in that it encourages sabotage and destroys employee loyalty and performance; rewards—to the extent that the manipulative *carrot* approach works to improve performance, its effect is usually temporary, as today's incentives quickly become tomorrow's entitlements; and belief building—a nonmanipulative approach based on the notion that lack of belief generates lack of performance. Productive people achieve much because of their inner strengths; therefore, productivity reflects the individual's belief in himself, the organization, and the products and services they render. Overuse of fear and rewards (i.e., manipulation) destroys these essential characteristics.

Solution: There are three possible solutions: (1) increase the level of supervision to improve the branch manager's performance, (2) move the individual to another branch in a subordinate role to provide additional training and experience under a competent manager, or (3) move him to a nonmanagement role in which he can perform at an acceptable level. By all means, do not lose the services of a worthy employee. If it becomes obvious that the individual cannot perform effectively in a management role, but did perform well as a lawn specialist or service coordinator, move him back to a role in which he can resume making a valuable contribution to the company. ■

▶ CASE STUDY 6.10

Scenario: When he decided to accept an intern from Penn State for the summer, the superintendent fully intended to provide the student with as many educational opportunities as time and circumstances would permit. But the summer was a busy one, and the times spent with the intern were far fewer than planned and always rushed. At the end of the summer, one of the full-time crew members related that the student left very dissatisfied with his experience, as he had worked much more but learned much less than anticipated. The superintendent felt bad and wondered if accepting the intern was such a good idea and if he would ever do it again.

Analysis: Interns have two roles. They are employees who should be expected to work as productive members of the crew. They are also students who are acquiring not only essential knowledge and skills, but also a professional perspective that will shape their careers and more clearly establish their future potential. Likewise, superintendents with interns under their supervision have two roles: they are supervisors of the work performed by the interns and teachers of future superintendents. Superintendents can teach by taking the time to demonstrate and explain specific operations, but they also teach by the example they set in the workplace and elsewhere. When working under the guidance of an experienced superintendent, interns will either attempt to emulate his or her behavior or they will be turned off by the experience and reject it. While it may be desirable for the superintendent to take the time to do some active teaching occasionally during the course of a summer internship, his or her most important role is to demonstrate how a professional does the job. If all the superintendent does in addition to being a role model is respond to the intern's questions regarding specific actions, he or she will have done the job; the rest is "icing on the cake." Sometimes student interns are turned off by the experience, regardless of the superintendent's performance. This may reflect a realization that the work is simply too demanding, especially during the summer months. In that case, it was a very productive experience, as they learned that this is not the profession for them. It is often said that you should *choose a career that you love; then you will never have to work a day in your life.* The long hours and hard work during the summer months only seem that way to outside observers; people who truly love their work don't really notice. On the other hand, student interns are not slaves and should not be exploited. Their internship should introduce them to the life of a superintendent, including most—if not all—of the pluses as well as the minuses. The superintendent should not oversell the profession. It is what it is; interns should decide for themselves if it is the life they want. But it's never all work. For those who love it, there is the joy of the early morning breeze and the dew springing into the air as they drive across the turf. There is the sheer beauty of dense carpets of green grass covering the landscape in all directions. There is the exhilaration of watching golfers enjoying themselves in an arena that the employee, his or her colleagues, and Mother Nature have cooperated in creating. And there is the satisfaction of a job well done at the end of the day, along with the realization that there's more to be done tomorrow to make things even better. There should also be some time for other things, including family and friends, good food, and relaxing, but not a lot, mind you, for it's summertime and there's much work—if you can call it that—to be done.

Solution: While a superintendent with interns teaches primarily by example, he or she should take a few minutes from time to time to explain why particular decisions were made. If time pressures preclude doing this when asked by the intern, be sure to do it as soon as possible. Even if the intern doesn't ask questions, set aside some time each week to pose questions to the intern about the technical and operational bases for doing things a certain way. This provides an opportunity not only to blend theory and practice, but also to review for yourself why you do things a certain way. Such reflection can stimulate fresh thinking and possibly lead to new and better ways of doing things. When a superintendent takes on interns, he or she forms a learning community within which the student–teacher relationship is sometimes reversed, in that the teacher also learns either from the student or by reflecting upon—and perhaps actively investigating—things that come up in their communication. To make the most of this experience, develop a plan and schedule activities to maximize the benefits for everyone involved. ■

▶ CASE STUDY 6.11

Scenario: For some members of the staff and crew, the firing of the long-time superintendent was the last straw. Despite their anger and frustration, they continued to work under the supervision of the assistant—now the interim superintendent—for the remainder of the season. In mid-September, the new superintendent was hired and assumed his duties, only to have the assistant, the mechanic, and three of six full-time crew members resign. Hearing rumors of possible sabotage, he decided that he needed to safeguard the course while filling essential positions. What should he do?

Analysis: Any superintendent faces a significant challenge when accepting a new position. Given the resentment of the staff and crew evident in this scenario, the challenge is especially formidable. The advantage the new superintendent has is that he was not directly responsible for firing his predecessor, nor was he a contributor to the conditions that led to his termination; however, this advantage can be quickly lost if he doesn't properly handle his initial communications with the staff and crew. His challenge is to earn the respect and loyalty of his personnel by patiently listening to their grievances and communicating his goals and vision for the future. Especially important in this process is instilling in the staff and crew the conviction that they will be treated in a fair, respectful, and considerate manner.

Solution: Before accepting his position, the new superintendent should have thoroughly investigated the circumstances leading to the firing of his predecessor. If the former superintendent was treated unfairly, there is reason to believe that his successor will eventually be subjected to the same treatment. Under these circumstances, the position should not be accepted. However, if the former superintendent was fired for justifiable reasons—perhaps due to unsatisfactory performance, failure to properly implement the wishes of his superiors, or poor communication skills—the new superintendent has a clear understanding of what he must do to be successful in his new position. After accepting the position, the superintendent should immediately assemble the members of his staff and crew to introduce himself and provide an opportunity for them to communicate their feelings about the organization and how the former superintendent was treated—or, in this case, mistreated. Whenever general statements are made about specific persons in authority, the superintendent should listen patiently and then ask questions about these individuals and their behavior. Since most of what the staff and crew believe about the situation was probably acquired from communication with the former superintendent, this exercise can be helpful in separating facts and beliefs. Where discrepancies exist, these should be accurately—but gently—pointed out. Most importantly, no attempt should be made to undermine the loyalty that existed between the former superintendent and his subordinates; rather, the objective should be to carefully transfer it to the new superintendent. Even if he wasn't the greatest golf course superintendent in the world, he obviously earned the respect and loyalty of his staff and crew. His successor must do the same; however, to minimize the loss of valuable employees and possible damage from sabotage, he must do it quickly. ■

▶ CASE STUDY 6.12

Scenario: When he discovered that one of his employees had been stealing gas from the pump at the maintenance shop for his personal use, the superintendent was fit to be tied. How could this individual—one of the most reliable members of the maintenance crew and a friend for many years—be so stupid? Since he learned of this from another crew member, others likely knew as well. With a major tournament coming soon and so many things to attend to, he didn't need this problem on top of everything else. But it was there, a very serious problem, and one that needed to be addressed now. How should this be handled?

Analysis: Regardless of the circumstances, stealing is illegal and unacceptable behavior. Those who steal from their employer have shown through their behavior that they cannot be trusted. The bonds of trust exist not only between employer and employee, but also among employees. Any person who steals receives compensation he or she has not earned and thus has acquired an unfair advantage over the other workers. If a thief is allowed to continue working, the message to the other employees is that stealing—while not condoned—will be tolerated. The likely consequences will either be more theft by the same person or other individuals, or a serious breakdown in morale throughout the organization.

Solution: As a general principle, those who steal should be fired and prosecuted for their crimes. If an exception is to be granted, the individual should be required to pay for all of the property he has stolen. Other punitive actions should include a public reprimand for his behavior and a reduction in pay. ■

SUMMARY OF PEOPLE PROBLEMS

Problems with Superiors

Your bosses may not always be right, but they are your bosses and have the last say on all matters relating to your employment. You can attempt to persuade them to change their minds when you feel they are wrong, but the final decision is theirs. The only time you, as a subordinate, have the last say is when you resign; otherwise, you are duty bound to follow orders to the best of your ability. If and when the time comes that you can't do so, you should resign. Under no circumstances is it acceptable to deliberately undermine their objectives by allowing turf to die when you had the capacity to prevent it. Effective communication with your boss is necessary to ensure that you are working together in a mutually beneficial fashion. When an expectation exists that something will be accomplished by a certain time, you should do everything possible to meet that expectation. If unforeseen circumstances prevent that from happening, you should inform your superior of the change and propose an alternate date for completion. Also, be sure to explain what is involved in performing a specific task so that the superior does not develop an unrealistic expectation of its accomplishment. Remember, an important part of your job is to educate your boss so that this person can do *his or her* job properly.

Some disagreements between superiors and subordinates may reflect differences in their respective value systems. A proposal to remove large trees that severely shade a green is one that is likely to dramatically bring these differences to light. In discussing such a sensitive issue, be sure to approach the subject calmly, rationally, accurately, and thoroughly. It might be best to prepare a written report in which the proposal is clearly stated and carefully justified so that all parties can acquire a thorough understanding of the issues and the alternatives. And, to the extent possible, try to avoid direct conflict by presenting the situation and the alternatives for dealing with it, and asking the parties involved to work with you in finding a satisfactory solution.

The allocation of resources to support the operation of a golf course or another turfgrass facility largely determines the level of turf quality obtainable from maintenance operations. Therefore, reductions in an operating budget require corresponding reductions in the frequency and intensity of operations that, in the aggregate, determine the level of turf quality. While one may be inclined to delay some important capital expenditures in order to sustain a specific quality level under these circumstances, this could be counterproductive; for example, attempting to operate with faulty equipment could result in higher expenditures from reduced reliability and higher equipment repair and maintenance costs.

Problems with Peers

Because turfgrass cultural operations sometimes require the use of pesticides for controlling weeds, diseases, insects, and other pests that threaten turfgrass health and turf quality, professionals in the turfgrass industry are susceptible to criticism from those who feel that the pesticides used in turfgrass pest management pose a significant hazard to human health. Clearly, turfgrass professionals must choose the pesticides they use wisely, and they should store, mix, apply, and dispose of these pesticides in a safe and effective manner. They also have a responsibility to address the concerns expressed by members of society over the presumed hazards posed by these pesticides. Whenever a meeting is arranged for this purpose, be sure to establish several rules governing the conduct of the meeting to ensure that things don't get out of hand, including the following: don't allow speeches and long diatribes by audience members; insist that participants behave in a respectful and courteous manner; require attendees to raise their hands and wait to be recognized before speaking; allow only one person to speak at a time; allow reporters to attend but not to videotape the meeting, as this might encourage grandstanding by some attendees, especially those with an agenda; the discussion should stick to the issues in the discussion; and avoid personal attacks. Don't assess blame, get angry, yell, talk down to the participants, make wisecracks, get too technical, downplay concerns or the importance of the meeting, use long answers, raise new issues, fake an answer, or be argumentative or defensive. Do be patient, demonstrate a caring attitude, establish common ground with the audience, listen, establish credibility, and communicate using appropriate analogies.

The general public may also indicate its concerns over a perceived misuse of water, perhaps our most important environmental resource. Where a new irrigation system is being installed or planned, the perception may be that this will result in more water use than with an older, less sophisticated system. In this instance, it's important to be patient and explain that among the advantages of the new system is greater control over the application of water and, therefore, less total water use in meeting the moisture requirements of the turf.

Where a peer engages in bullying and offensive behavior toward you or one of your employees, meet with the individual and calmly—but firmly—explain that his or her behavior is unacceptable and will not be tolerated. Selected authorities should be quietly apprised of the situation in order to obtain their support, if and when needed. Provide a good example of professional behavior by always behaving professionally yourself.

Professionalism also extends to your attitude toward your industry and your role in it. Develop a positive attitude and try to avoid looking at the negative side of events. There is much joy and satisfaction to be gained from your work, but you must adopt an attitude that recognizes and celebrates them.

Problems with Subordinates

Good managers value their employees and seeks to obtain the best results from their efforts. They do this by accepting personal accountability for the results of their actions, continually seeking to develop their people so that they can perform with minimal supervision, trying to influence employees' thinking by providing them with the tools and training they need to be successful and in helping them to understand the value of the things they are asked to do, remembering to be cost effective in the use of resources, fostering a proper attitude about the organization of which they and the employees are a part, recognizing the uniqueness of each employee and communicating with them individually, concentrating on objectives instead of problems, being a boss and not a buddy, setting realistic standards and training employees to perform in accordance with those standards, intervening when performance is not in accordance with established standards, appropriately recognizing satisfactory performance, and fostering a proper belief system encompassing the employee, the organization, and the services performed.

If you accept responsibility for interns in your operation, your interaction with them can be mutually beneficial. While interns may learn primarily by example, you should plan to spend some time with them discussing various aspects of the operation, as well as posing questions and responding to their questions. Specific questions may cause you to reflect on why you do things a certain way. With some interns, a learning community is established in which the teacher and learner roles can sometimes be reversed.

Before accepting a new position, be sure to investigate the circumstances leading to the former superintendent's departure. If he or she was dismissed because of unsatisfactory performance, this can contribute to your understanding of what you must do to be successful in this position. If his or her dismissal was for other reasons, consider them carefully in deciding whether to accept the position. After accepting a new position, assemble the members of your staff and crew for a meeting to present yourself and your goals for the golf course. Demonstrate your willingness to listen; respond to their questions, sometimes with follow-up questions directed at obtaining accurate information. And be sure to let them know how much you value their service and performance.

If confronted with the realization that a valued employee has stolen gas or other materials from the golf course, use careful judgment to determine the course of action that should be taken. As a general principle, those who steal should be fired and prosecuted for their crimes. If an exception is to be granted, the individual should be required to pay for all of the stolen property.

Finally, a word about honesty and integrity. An honest person "says what he does" and a person of integrity "does what he says." Integrity and honesty are two sides of the same coin. Both are indispensable qualities in dealing with superiors, peers, and subordinates. They are also the hallmarks of a true professional.

APPENDIX

1

List of Herbicides

Common Name	Trade Names	Class	Formulations	Manufacturer	Signal Word
atrazine	Atrazine 4L	s-triazines	4 L	UHS	caution
	Atrazine 90 WDG		90 WDG	UHS	caution
benefin	Balan 2.5G	dinitroanalines	2.5% G	UHS	caution
benefin & trifluralin	Team Pro 0.86%	dinitroanalines	0.86G fertilizer	Dow AgroSciences	caution
	Team Pro w fertilizer		0.86G fertilizer	LESCO	caution
	Team 2G		2% G	LESCO	caution
	Team 2G		2% G	UHC	caution
bensulide	Bensumec 4LF	phosphorodithioates	4 lb/gal LF	PBI/Gordon	caution
	Pre-San 12.5G		12.5% G	PBI/Gordon	warning
	Pre-San 17G		7% G	PBI/Gordon	warning
bentazon	Lescogran	benzothiadiazinones	4 lb/gal SC	LESCO	caution
	Basagran T/O		4 lb/gal SL	TopPro	caution
carfentrazone[1]	many	aryltriazolinone	many	PBI/Gordon	caution
chlorsulfuron	Corsair	sulfonylureas	75 WDG	Riverdale	caution
clopyralid[2]	Lontrel	pyridinecarboxylic acids	40.9% SC	Dow AgroSciences	caution
2,4-D[2]	many	phenoxycarboxylic acids	many	many	danger
dazomet	Basamid Granular	thiadiazine	99 G	BASF	warning
dicamba[2]	many	benzoic acids	many	many	caution
dichloroprop[2]	many	phenoxycarboxylic acids	many	many	caution
dithiopyr	Dimension 0.10% Plus Fertilizer	pyridines	0.10% G fertilizer	LESCO	caution
	Dimension 0.15% Plus 13-2-5		0.15% G fertilizer	LESCO	caution
	Dimension		1 lb/gal EC	Dow AgriSciences	caution
	Dimension Ultra WSP		40% WSP	Dow AgriSciences	caution
ethofumisate	Prograss EC	benzofuranes	1.5 lb/gal EC	Bayer	danger
fenoxyprop p-ethyl	Acclaim Extra	aryloxyphenoxypropionates	0.57 EC	Bayer	caution
foramsulfuron	Revolver	sulfonylurens	0.19 SC	Bayer	caution
glufosinate-ammonium	Finale	phosphinic acids	1 lb/gal SC	Bayer	warning

common name	product name	chemical family	formulation	manufacturer	signal word
glyphosate	GlyphoMate	glycines	4 lb/gal SC	PBI/Gordon	caution
	Prosecutor		4 lb/gal SC	LESCO	caution
	Roundup PRO		4 lb/gal SC	Monsanto	caution
	Razor		4 lb/gal SC	Riverdale	caution
halosulfuron	Manage	sulfonylureas	75 WDG	Monsanto	caution
imazaquin	Image 70DG	imidazolinones	70 DG	BASF	caution
mecoprop[2]	many	phenoxycarboxylic acids	many	many	caution
metolachlor	Pennant	chloroacetamides	8 lb/gal EC	Syngenta	caution
metribuzin	Sencor 75 Turf Herbicide	a-triazines	75 DF	Bayer	caution
oryzalin	Surflan A.S.	dinitroanalines	4 lb/gal EC	Dow AgroSciences	caution
oxadiazon	Ronstar 50WSP	oxidiazoles	50 WSP	Bayer	warning
	Ronstar 0.95% + 20-2-20 Fertilizer		0.95% G fertilizer	LESCO	warning
	Ronstar 0.95% + 5-10-15 Mini Fertilizer		0.95% G fertilizer	LESCO	warning
	Ronstar G		2 G	Bayer	warning
pendimethalin	Pendulum 2G	dinitroanalines	2 G	BASF	caution
	Pendulum 3.3EC		3.3 EC	BASF	caution
	Pendulum 75DF		60 WDG	BASF	caution
	Pre-M 0.86% Plus Fertilizer		0.86% G fertilizer	LESCO	caution
	Pre-M 3.3EC		3.3 lb/gal EC	LESCO	caution
prodiamine	Barricade 65WG	dinitroanalines	65% WG	Syngenta	caution
pronamide	Kerb WSP	benzamides	51% WSP	Dow AgriSciences	caution
quinclorac	Drive 75DF	quinolinecarboxylic acids	75 DF	BASF	caution
rimsulfuron	TranXit GTA	sulfonylureas	25 DF	Griffin	caution
siduron	Tupersan	ureas	50 WP	PBI/Gordon	caution
simazine	Princep	s-triazines	4 lb/gal F	Syngenta	caution
triclopyr[2]	Turflon Ester	pyridinecarboxylic acids	61.6 % EC	Dow AgroSciences	danger
triclopry & clopyralid	Confront	pyridinecarboxylic acids	EC 12.1% clopyralid & 33% triclopyr	Dow AgroSciences	danger

[1] A new herbicide that is included in combinations with 2,4-D, mecoprop, and dicamba for broad-spectrum control of broadleaf weeds.

[2] These herbicides are often included in two-way, three-way, and four-way combinations for broad-spectrum control of broadleaf weed species.

2

List of Fungicides

Common Name	Trade Names	Class	Formulations	Manufacturer	Signal Word
azoxystrobin	Heritage	methoxyacetylate (Qol)	50 WP	Syngenta	caution
chloroneb	Teremec	chlorophenyl	65 WP	PBI/Gordon	caution
chlorothalonil	Daconil 2787	nitrile	4.17 F	Bayer	warning
	Daconil Ultrex		82.5 WDG	Bayer	danger
	Daconil Weather Stik		6 F	Bayer	warning
	Manicure 6 Flowable		6 F	Lesco	warning
	Manicure Ultrex Turf Care		82.5 WDG	Lesco	danger
fenarimol	Patchwork	pyrimidine (DMI)	0.78 G	Riverdale	caution
	Rubigan A.S.		1 EC	Gowan	caution
flutolanil	Prostar 70 WP	benzamide	70 WP	Bayer	caution
etridiazole	Koban 1.3 G	triazol (DMI)	1.3 G	Andersons	caution
	Koban 30		30% liquid	Andersons	warning
	Terrazole		35 WP	Crompton	warning
fosetyl-al	Chipco Signature	phosphonates	80 WP	Bayer	caution
	Prodigy 80 DG		80 DG	Lesco	caution
iprodione	Chipco 26GT Flo	dicarboximide	2 F	Bayer	caution
mancozeb	Flowable Mancozeb 4	carbamate	4 F	Lesco	caution
	Fore		80 WP	Dow Chemical	caution
	Fore Flowable		4 F	Dow Chemical	caution
	Fore FloXL		4 F	Dow Chemical	caution
	Mancozeb DG		75 DG	Lesco	caution
	Protect T/O		80 WSB	Cleary	caution
mefenoxam	Subdue MAXX	acylalanine	21.3% F	Syngenta	caution
	Subdue GR		0.97% G	Syngenta	caution
myclobutanil	Eagle 40WP	triazol (DMI)	40 WP	Dow AgroSciences	warning
pentachloronitrobenzene (PCNB)	Defend 10G	chlorinated hydrocarbon	10 G	Cleary	caution
	Defend 4^F		4 F	Cleary	caution
	Engage 10G		10 G	UHS	caution
	PCNB 12.5% and fert		12.5 G	Lesco	caution
	Revere 4000 Flowable Fungicide		4 F	Lesco	caution

Active ingredient	Product	Class	Formulation	Manufacturer	Signal word
propiconazol	Revere WSP		75 WSP	Lesco	caution
	Terraclor		75 WP	Gowan	caution
	Terraclor 400		4 F	Gowan	caution
	Turfcide 10% Granular		10 G	Gowan	caution
	Banner GL	triazol (DMI)	41.8 WSP	Syngenta	warning
	Banner MAXX		14.3% EC	Syngenta	warning
	Propiconazol Pro				
propamacarb	Banol	carbamate	6 E	Bayer	caution
pyraclostrobin	Insignia	methoxycarbamate (Qol)	20 WDG	BASF	caution
thiophanate-M	3336 F	benzimidazole	4.5 F	Cleary	caution
	3336 G		2.08 G	Cleary	caution
	3336 WSP		50 WSP	Cleary	warning
	Cavalier 2G		2.08 G	Lesco	caution
	Cavalier 4.5F		4.5 F	Lesco	caution
	cavalier 50 WSB		50 WSB	Lesco	caution
	Fungo Flo		4.5 F	The Andersons	caution
	Fungo 50 WSB		50 WSB	The Andersons	caution
	Systemic Fungicide		2.3 G	The Andersons	caution
	Systec 1998 Flowable		4.5 F	Regal Chemical	caution
	Systec 1998 WDG		85 WDG	Regal Chemical	caution
triadimefon	Accost 1G	triazol (DMI)	1 G	UHS	caution
	Bayleton 25		25 WSP	Bayer	caution
	Bayleton 50		50 WSP	Bayer	caution
	Granular Turf Fungicide		1 G	Lesco	caution
	Strike 25 WDG		25 WDG	Olympic	caution
trifloxystrobin	Compass	oximinoacetate (Qol)	50 WDG	Bayer	caution
	Compass O		50 WDG	Olympic	caution
vinclozolin	Curalan	dicarboximide	4.17 F	BASF	caution
	Curalan DF		50 DF	BASF	caution
	Curalan EG		50 WDG	BASF	caution
	Vorlan DF		50 DF	Andersons	caution
	Touche Flowable		4.17 F	Lesco	caution
	Touche EG		50 WDG	Lesco	caution

3

List of Insecticides

Common Name	Trade Names	Class	Formulations	Manufacturer	Signal Word
acephate	Orthene Turf, Tree & Ornamental Spray	organophosphate	75 WP	Valent	caution
	Pinpoint		15 G	Valent	caution
azadirachtin	Azatin XL	insect growth regulator	0.265 lb/gal	Olympic	caution
bacillus thuringiensis kurstaki (Bt)	Biobit	bacteria	14.5 BIU/lb	Abbott	caution
	Dipel 2X		14.5 BIU/lb	Abbott	caution
	Dipel DF		14.5 BIU/lb	Abbott	caution
	Mattch		14.5 BIU/lb	Mycogen	caution
	MVP II		14.5 BIU/lb	Mycogen	caution
bendiocarb	Turcam	carbamate	76 WP	Bayer	warning
	Turcam 2.5 G		2.5 G	Bayer	warning
bifenthrin	Talstar Lawn & Tree Flowable	synthetic pyrethroid	0.66 lb/gal	FMC	caution
	Talstar GC Granular		0.2 G	FMC	caution
	Talstar GC Granular		0.66 lb/gal	FMC/Whitmire	caution
	Talstar Nursery Flowable		0.66 lb/gal	FMC	caution
carbaryl	8% Sevin Granular	carbamate	8 G	The Andersons	caution
	Carbaryl Insecticide Fertilizer with Sevin		6.2 G	The Andersons	caution
	Sevin 4% with fertilizer		4 G	Lesco	caution
	6.3% Sevin brand Granular Carbaryl Insecticide		6.3G	Lesco	caution
	Sevin brand SL		4 lb a.i./gal	Lesco	caution
	Chipco Sevin brand 80 WSP		80 WSP	Bayer	warning
	Chipco Sevin brand SL		4 lb a.i./gal	Bayer	caution
	Sevin 10 G		10 G	United Hort Supply	caution

Active ingredient	Chemical class	Product	Formulation/Rate	Manufacturer	Signal word
chlorpyrifos	organophosphate	2.32% Dursban	2.32 G	The Andersons	caution
		0.97% Dursban	0.97 G	The Andersons	caution
		0.5% Dursban	0.5 G	The Andersons	caution
		Fertilizer with Dursban (various)	0.92/0.65/0.57 G	The Andersons	caution
		Dursban 50 W WSP	50 WSP	Dow AgroSciences	warning
		Dursban Pro	2 lb a.i./gal	Dow AgroSciences	caution
		Professional Pest Control		Lesco	caution
		Dursban 0.5 G	0.5 G	Lesco	caution
		Dursban 0.74% & fertilizer	0.74 G	Lesco	caution
		Dursban 0.97% & fertilizer	0.97 G	Lesco	caution
		1% Dursban	1 G	The Andersons	caution
		2.32 Granular Insecticide	2.32 G	The Andersons	caution
		Insecticide III	1.34 G	United Hort Supply	caution
		Turf fertilizer plus Insecticide	0.65 G	United Hort Supply	caution
		Dursban 2 Coated Granules	2 G		warning
		Dursban TNP	4 lb a.i./gal		warning
cyfluthrin	synthetic pyrethroid	Tempo 20 WP	20 WP	Bayer	caution
		Tempo 20 WP	2 lb a.i./gal	Bayer	warning
		Tempo 20 WP (Golf Course WSP)	20 WP	Bayer	caution
		Tempo 20 WP (Power Pak)	20 WP	Bayer	caution
deltamethrin	synthetic pyrethroid	DeltaGard GC	5 SC	Bayer	caution
		DeltaGard T & O	0.1 G	Bayer	caution
		DeltaGard T & O 5 SC	5 SC	Bayer	caution
		DeltaGard GC Granular	0.1 g	Bayer	caution
diazinon	organophosphate	5% Diazinon	5 G	The Andersons	caution
		Fertilizer with 3.33 Diazinon	3.33 G	The Andersons	caution
		Diazinon	3.33 G	Lesco	caution
		Diazinon AG 600	4.67 lb a.i./gal	Lesco	caution
		Diazinon 4 E	4 lb a.i./gal	Terra	caution
		Diazinon	5 G	United Hort Supply	caution
ethoprop	organophosphate	Chipco Mocap brand 10G GC	10 G	Bayer	warning
fipronil	phenyl pyrazoles	Chipco Choice	0.1 G	Bayer	caution

Common Name	Trade Names	Class	Formulations	Manufacturer	Signal Word
halfenozide	Mach 2 Granbular	insect growth regulator	1.5 G	Rohmid	caution
	Mach 2 Liquid		2 lb a.i./gal	Rohmid	caution
imidacloprid	Fertilizer with Merit Insecticide	neonicotinold	0.2 G	The Andersons	caution
	Merit 0.5 G		0.5 G	Bayer	caution
	Merit 75 WP		75 WP	Bayer	caution
	Merit 75 WSP		75 WSP	Bayer	caution
	Lebanon Fertilizer with Merit 0.3% Insecticide		0.3 G	Lebanon	caution
	Merit 0.2 plus fertilizer		0.2 G	Lesco	caution
	Turf Fertilizer plus Merit Insecticide		0.2 G	The Andersons	caution
isofenphos	Oftanol 1.5%	organophosphate	1.5 G	The Andersons	caution
	Fertilizer with Oftanol		1.5 G	The Andersons	caution
	Oftanol 2		2 lb a.i./gal	Bayer	warning
	Oftanol 1/5% and fertilizer		1.5 g	Lesco	caution
	Oftanol 1.5%		1.5 g	Lesco	caution
lambda-cyhalothrin	battle CS	synthetic pyrethroid	0.88 lb a.i./gal	Lesco	caution
	Battle GC		0.88 lb a.i./gal	Lesco	caution
	Battle WP		10 WP	Lesco	warning
	Scimitar CS		0.88 lb a.i./gal	Syngenta	caution
	Scimitar GC		0.88 lb a.i./gal	Syngenta	caution
	Scimitar WP		10 WP	Syngenta	warning
permethrin	Astro	synthetic pyrethroid	3.2 lb a.i./gal	FMC	caution
soap	M-Pede	insecticidal soap	49% a.i.	Mycogen	warning
spinosad	Conserve SC	actinomycete-fermentation derived	1 lb a.i./gal	Dow AgroSciences	caution
trichlorfon	Dylox 6.2 G	organophosphate	6.2 G	The Andersons	caution
	Dylox 6.2 G		6.2 G	Bayer	caution
	Dylox 80 T&O		80 WP	Bayer	warning

4

List of Plant Growth Regulators (PGRs)

Common Name	Trade Names	Class[1]	Formulations	Manufacturer	Signal Word
ethephon	Proxy	E: Phytohormone	2 lb/gal SL	Aventis	danger
maleic hydrazide	Royal Slo-Gro	C: Cell-division inhibitor	1.5 lb/gal SC	Uniroyal Chemical	caution
mefluidide	Embark 2-S	C: Cell-division inhibitor	2 lb/gal SL	PBI/Gordon	caution
paclobutrazol	Turf Enhancer	B: Cell-elongation inhibitor-early*	2 lb/gal SC	The Andersons	caution
	Trimmit 2SC	B: Cell-elongation inhibitor-early*	2 lb/gal SC	Syngenta/Zeneca	caution
trinexapac-ethyl	Pimo MAXX	A: Cell-elongation inhibitor-late**	1 lb/gal EC	Syngenta/Novartis	caution
	Primo WSB	A: Cell-elongation inhibitor-late**	25% WSB	Syngenta/Novartis	caution

[1]PGR classes are A: Cell-elongated inhibitors late in the gibberellic-acid biosynthesis pathway; B: Cell-elongated inhibitors early in the gibberellic-acid biosynthesis pathway; C: Cell-division inhibitors; D: Herbicides with plant-growth inhibiting properties; and E: Phytohormone generators.

Bibliography

Bloom, B. S. (ed.). 1956. *Taxonomy of Educational Objectives: Handbook 1, The Cognitive Domain.* Longman, New York.

Brown, W. S. 1985. 13 *Fatal Errors Managers Make and How You Can Avoid Them.* Berkley Books, New York.

Dernoeden, P. H. 2000. *Creeping Bentgrass Management: Summer Stresses, Weeds, and Selected Maladies.* Ann Arbor Press, Chelsea, MI.

Kolb, D. A., I. M. Rubin, and J. M. McIntyre (1979). *Organizational Psychology: An Experiential Approach.* Prentice-Hall, Engelwood Cliffs, NJ.

Potter, D. A. 1998. *Destructive Turfgrass Insects: Biology, Diagnosis, and Control.* Ann Arbor Press, Chelsea, MI.

Turgeon, A. J. 1993. Application of systems thinking to turfgrass management. *International Turfgrass Society Research Journal* 7:930–936. R. N. Carrow, N. E. Christians, and R. C. Shearman (eds.). Intertec Publishing Corp., Overland Park, KS.

Turgeon, A. J. 2005. *Turfgrass Management,* 7th ed. Prentice Hall, Upper Saddle River, NJ.

Vargas, J. M. 2005. *Management of Turfgrass Diseases,* 3rd ed. John Wiley & Sons, Hoboken, NJ.

Vargas, J. M. and A. J. Turgeon. 2003. *Poa Annua: Physiology, Culture, and Control of Annual Bluegrass.* John Wiley & Sons, Hoboken, NJ.

Index